The Asymmetries of Globalization

The discourse on globalization has become polarized. Proponents consider globalization as the silver bullet for targeting growth in the world economy and for poor countries specifically, while opponents see it as the poisoned arrow of exploitation and impoverishment of the Third World.

The Asymmetries of Globalization deals with the "what" and "how," but primarily with "why" globalization has most often negative outcomes for developing countries. It breaks new ground in approaching globalization not only as trade in commodities, but also as trade in positional goods ("decommodified trade.")

The two novel and munificent forms of post-Ricardian decommodified trade, trade in services and trade in hard currency in the form of currency substitution, are sculpted in the introductory chapter as the foundation of the systematic asymmetries of globalization. Decommodified trade involves exports of developed countries that cater mostly to the elites of the developing world. The developing countries, in turn, procure the foreign exchange to pay for these imports by exporting commodities that trade on comparative advantage at the least cost of production. The analytical approach of introducing "positional goods" in the form of decommodified trade, in the discourse on globalization, is original. It is also timely in a situation where the tail of trade in "services" has grown enough to wag the traditional trade-in-commodities dog of globalization.

The balance of the chapters in this volume constitute a tapestry of case studies that elaborate and empirically investigate the causes of systematic asymmetries of globalization. The book's appeal transcends economics to make it also highly useful to students across the disciplines of sociology and political science, especially in the fields of international political economy and the politics of international trade. It will certainly enlighten all those working in the general areas of globalization, poverty and economic development.

Pan A. Yotopoulos is Distinguished Professor, University of Florence, Italy and Professor Emeritus, Stanford University, USA. **Donato Romano** is Professor, University of Florence, Italy.

Routledge studies in development economics

The Asymmetries of Globalization

Edited by **Pan A. Yotopoulos**
and **Donato Romano**

Routledge
Taylor & Francis Group

LONDON AND NEW YORK

First published 2007
by Routledge
2 Park Square, Milton Park, Abingdon, Oxon OX14 4RN

Simultaneously published in the USA and Canada
by Routledge

711 Third Avenue, New York, NY 10017

Routledge is an imprint of the Taylor & Francis Group, an informa business

First issued in paperback 2012

© 2007 Selection and editorial matter, Pan A. Yotopoulos and Donato Romano; individual chapters, the contributors

Typeset in Times by Wearset Ltd, Boldon, Tyne and Wear

British Library Cataloguing in Publication Data
A catalogue record for this book is available from the British Library

Library of Congress Cataloging in Publication Data
A catalog record for this book has been requested

ISBN13: 978-0-415-42048-8 hardback
ISBN13: 978-0-415-64599-7 paperback

Contents

Figures

Tables

Contributors

Marijke D'Haese is Assistant Professor at Wageningen University, the Netherlands.

Michel A.C. Fok is head of research team at Centre de Coopération Internationale en Recherche Agronomique pour le Développement (CIRAD) and research member of UMR Marchés, Organisations, Institutions et Stratégies d'Acteurs (MOISA), Montpellier, France.

Yujiro Hayami is Chairman at the Graduate Faculty of the Foundation for Advanced Studies on International Development (FASID), and Visiting Professor at the National Graduate Institute of Policy Studies (GRIPS), Tokyo, Japan.

Guido Van Huylenbroeck is Professor at Ghent University, Belgium.

Weili Liang is Professor at the Hebei Agricultural University, Baoding, People's Republic of China.

Bih Jane Liu is Professor at the National Taiwan University, Taipei, Taiwan.

Alan Yun Lu is Professor at the National Taiwan University, Taipei, Taiwan.

Rania S. Miniesy is Lecturer at the British University in Egypt, Cairo, Egypt.

Jeffrey B. Nugent is Professor at the University of Southern California, Los Angeles, USA.

Ugo Pagano is Professor at the University of Siena, Italy, and at the Central European University, Budapest, Hungary.

Kolleen J. Rask is Associate Professor at the College of the Holy Cross, Worcester, USA.

Norman Rask is Professor Emeritus at the Ohio State University, Columbus, USA.

Donato Romano is Professor at the University of Florence, Italy.

Yasuyuki Sawada is Associate Professor at the University of Tokyo, Japan.

An-Chi Tung is Associate Research Fellow at the Academia Sinica, Taipei, Taiwan.

Jan Vannoppen is head of the advocacy department at Vredeseilanden, Leuven, Belgium.

Pan A. Yotopoulos is Distinguished Professor at the University of Florence, Italy, and Professor Emeritus at Stanford University, USA.

Acknowledgments

Chapter 1: Asymmetric globalization: impact on the Third World

- Pages 7–8: quotation reprinted from p. 3 of Richard Baldwin and Philippe Martin (1999), "Two Waves of Globalization: Superficial Similarities and Fundamental Differences." In Horst Siebert, ed., *Globalization and Labour*. Tübingen: J.C.B. Mohr, for Kiel Institute of World Economics, pp. 3–59, with permission by the Kiel Institute of World Economics.

Chapter 5: Communities and markets for rural development under globalization: a perspective from villages in Asia

- Figure 5.1: reprinted from *Agricultural Economics*, Volume 20, Yujiro Hayami, Masao Kikuchi and Esther B. Marciano, "Middlemen and Peasants in Rice Marketing in the Philippines," pp. 79–93, copyright 1999, with permission from Elsevier.
- Table 5.1: Yujiro Hayami and Toshihiko Kawagoe, *The Agrarian Origins of Commerce and Industry: A Study of Peasant Marketing in Indonesia*, 1993, Macmillan, reproduced with permission of Palgrave Macmillan.

Chapter 8: Genetically modified seeds and decommodification: an analysis based on the Chinese cotton case

- Page 147: quotation reprinted from p. 191 of Michael Pollan (2001), *The Botany of Desire: A Plant's-Eye View of the World*. New York: Random House, with permission by Michel Pollan.
- Table 8.1: reprinted from Table 1 on p. 48 of Michel A.C. Fok, Weili Liang, Guiyan Wang and Yuhong Wu (2004), "I risultati positivi della diffusione del cotone Bt in Cina: limiti al trasferimento dell'esperienza cinese in altri paesi in via di sviluppo," *Nuovo Diritto Agrario*, 3/2004: 45–67, with permission by Nuovo Diritto Agrario.
- Table 8.2: reprinted from Table 8 on p. 52 of Michel A.C. Fok, Weili Liang, Guiyan Wang and Yuhong Wu (2004), "I risultati positivi della diffusione

del cotone Bt in Cina: limiti al trasferimento dell'esperienza cinese in altri paesi in via di sviluppo," *Nuovo Diritto Agrario*, 3/2004: 45–67, with permission by Nuovo Diritto Agrario.

- Table 8.3: reprinted from Table 14 on p. 58 of Michel A.C. Fok, Weili Liang, Guiyan Wang and Yuhong Wu (2004), "I risultati positivi della diffusione del cotone Bt in Cina: limiti al trasferimento dell'esperienza cinese in altri paesi in via di sviluppo," *Nuovo Diritto Agrario*, 3/2004: 45–67, with permission by Nuovo Diritto Agrario.
- Table 8.4: reprinted from Table 8 on p. 21 of Michel A.C. Fok, Weili Liang, Guiyan Wang and Yuhong Wu (2005), "Diffusion du coton génétiquement modifié en Chine: leçons sur les facteurs et limites d'un succès," *Economie Rurale*, 285: 5–32, with permission by the Société Française d'Economie Rurale (SFER).
- Table 8.5: reprinted from Table 15 on p. 63 of Michel A.C. Fok, Weili Liang, Guiyan Wang and Yuhong Wu (2004), "I risultati positivi della diffusione del cotone Bt in Cina: limiti al trasferimento dell'esperienza cinese in altri paesi in via di sviluppo," *Nuovo Diritto Agrario*, 3/2004: 45–67, with permission by Nuovo Diritto Agrario.

Chapter 9: Globalization and small-scale farmers: customizing "fair-trade coffee"

- Figure 9.1: reprinted from *World Development*, Volume 30, Stefano Ponte, "The 'Latte Revolution'? Regulation, Markets and Consumption in the Global Coffee Chain," pp. 1099–1122, copyright 2002, with permission by Elsevier.
- Figure 9.3: reprinted from the Figure on product and control flow of Max Havelaar (2002), "Max Havelaar: Het keurmerk voor eerlijke handel. Criteria, certificering en controle," September 2002, with permission by Max Havelaar Belgium. Online, available: www.maxhavelaar.be (accessed 31 March 2004).

Editors' introduction

Pan A. Yotopoulos and Donato Romano

It is beyond contention that globalization, in the form of trade openness, is an important driver for economic growth. Economic growth, in turn, is a precondition for development, especially in less developed countries. The seemingly inexorable increase in poverty among plenty is also beyond dispute. The solution predicated by the supporters of the strategy of trade openness resonates highly in this volume that is dedicated to the challenges of globalization for the Third World.

At the same time, it is widely recognized that globalization is not the silver bullet to achieving development. Even enthusiastic proponents of globalization acknowledge that there is a wide array of institutional, macroeconomic and microeconomic conditions to be met, along with a set of social policies to be instituted if globalization is to bear fruit, and especially so in developing countries. This type of elegiac ode to globalization usually comes from the side of economics. The kindred disciplines of sociology, political science and economic geography, to mention a few, appear much more vocal and certainly trendy in stressing the polar view that globalization is a poisonous arrow. There is, in fact, some consensus that certain operating aspects of globalization are punitive for developing countries, while the same are remunerative for the richer countries that participate in trade and openness. Both these types of critique of globalization, the benign and the vitriolic, rest on observing certain aspects of globalization and associating trade and openness with some negative outcomes in the developing and, most recently, also in the developed world. The characteristic of these critiques is that they observe the world and they describe the "what" and "how" of the positive or negative aspects of globalization in a specific environment.

The Asymmetries of Globalization is certainly a critique of globalization's impact on the Third World. Not unlike some other studies of globalization it is also pragmatic, based on observing globalization in action. However, in contrast to the critiques mentioned above, the chapters in this volume describe not only the "what" and "how," but primarily the "why" globalization has, most often, negative outcomes for developing countries. The volume highlights the *systematic* asymmetries of globalization that weigh down on the growth and development of the less developed countries. One set of systematic asymmetries has its origin in inherent characteristics of poverty. The outcomes of globalization are negative in poor countries because of the lack of modern infrastructure, whether it is physical in the form of transportation networks and market networks, educational infrastructure, as in good public schools, or social infrastructure as in the non-existence of safety nets. These infrastructural investments serve as lubricants to growth and as adjustment mechanisms in the case of abrupt transformational change; in their absence free trade may not be automatically also mutual advantage trade.

Any form of trade that systematically bestows disproportional benefits on the richer nations can be viewed as presumptively unfair trade. The origin of such unfair trade can be the nature of a trade agreement, the regulatory framework in which free trade is contracted, or some inherent characteristics in the nature of certain forms of trade. While the Ricardian comparative advantage trade in commodities delivers fair trade outcomes, the "decommodified trade" (including trade in services which exists at the other end of trade in commodities in the continuum of globalized trade) incorporates also economic rents. To the extent that these accrue disproportionately to developed countries, they can be the source of presumptively unfair trade. The analytical component for approaching this post-Ricardian form of trade is the role that reputation plays in a "flattened" globalized world. Within the ambit of "positional competition" reputation is a natural accoutrement of wealth and power and as such it is incorporated in decommodified trade, which represents the bulk of exports from the developed countries to the rest of the world. The returns to reputation, in turn, are captured in the form of economic rents, which also accrue to those who have wealth and power. This is a novel asymmetry of globalization that operates to deliver disproportional benefits of trade to the rich countries.

The two kinds of post-Ricardian trade launched in the introductory chapter, trade in services, including decommodified trade, and trade in currency, in the form of currency substitution, enter as imports to developing countries and cater mostly to the needs of the elites and the wealthy. It is the well-off in the Third World who can afford to buy the brand names of the developed world – from the iPods to the burgers of the Arches of McDonald's – and who have the liquid assets to protect by denominating them into dollars, whether the dollars are kept under the mattress or they are whisked to the safe-harbor of a bank deposit in the developed world. It is the rich in the Third World who have most to gain from reputation-intensive decommodified trade: they gain primarily the freedom to engage in First World consumption. But the poor are consumers, too. Would they not also benefit from the bargain prices at which commodities are purveyed by globalization? That would have also been correct for the poor, whether they are in developed or in developing countries, if it were not for the fact that the poor, unlike the rich, cannot afford to be consumers of the cornucopia of goods that globalization purveys without first being producers. When the poor of the poor countries have too little, as opposed to the rich, who have too much, the benefits of globalization are lost for the former while they are lavished on the latter. Similarly, the poor in some developed countries cannot afford to take

Editors' introduction 3

advantage of the consumer benefits of globalization because globalization has outsourced their jobs to yet poorer people elsewhere in the world. In either case, presumptive logic suggests that the divide between the poor and the rich within a country, developed or developing, must have been increasing under globalization.

Globalization and free trade certainly generate the gains that classical political economy identified. The current globalization, on the other hand, bestows its benefits asymmetrically, and largely to the rich countries, as this volume attempts to demonstrate. Within a country, whether rich or poor, the presumption is that the rich classes gain disproportionately as compared to the poor.

The main body of the volume, the nine chapters that follow the introductory chapter, weave a case-study tapestry around the theme "Asymmetric Globalization: Impact on the Third World" that the opening chapter outlined. On the question raised about the fairness of the distribution of the gains from globalization, the focus is mainly at the country level, while the socioeconomic class distinction is brought in only tangentially in some instances.

The germ of the idea that grew into this volume was conceived at the Florence Symposium on "Globalization: Asymmetric Processes and Differentiated Outcomes" of September 2004 that was sponsored by the University of Florence and the European Association of Agricultural Economists. This book started as a conference volume, which is the academic equivalent of a business conglomerate – "a little of this and a little of that." After various iterations over the period of two years, the editors discovered – and the authors accepted, initially grudgingly – that economic development is not like the Russian dolls, where the same basic mold is repeated in successively smaller sizes. Thus this volume acquired a central theme and the various chapters developed synergies around that theme – which is missing from many conglomerate business enterprises.

Part I

Decommodification

From trade in commodities to trade
in services

1 Asymmetric globalization

Impact on the Third World[1]

Pan A. Yotopoulos

Introduction

There has been abundant coverage of globalization and its implications both in professional and in popular media, spanning the entire range from extolling its benefits to damning it for all kinds of ills. There seems to be a widespread view that globalization is a new phenomenon, but there is substantially less agreement on what globalization means. A broad definition of globalization that covers a lot of the disputed ground highlights the increased connectivity and interdependence of the world's markets, businesses and even cultures. The outcomes of globalization have been pronounced, on balance, positive although this balance is strongly disputed by the detractors of globalization.

The operational formulation of the institutional setting of globalization rests on the universal adoption of a common set of "rules of the game"[2] for economic interactions in the form of "free-markets, free-trade, laissez-faire" (FM-FT-LF), which is also known as the "Washington Consensus." The same freedom of comportment is in principle extended to other aspects of life, be they educational, cultural, social or political, covering tastes, mores and forms of governance (participatory). The global connectivity of the phenomenon of globalization is enabled by the technological advances of the twentieth century and the ease of transportation, communication and transmission of information.

While the catchwords of globalization and Washington Consensus are certainly new, the phenomenon is not. The first wave of globalization transpired, roughly, from 1870 to 1914, while the current one started in the 1980s and is going strong today. Baldwin and Martin (1999), who have studied the two waves of globalization, find superficial similarities between the two, but also some important differences:

> The chief similarities lie in aggregate trade–to GDP and capital flows–to GDP ratios. These stand today approximately at the level they attained at the end of the 19th century. Moreover, both globalization waves were driven by radical reductions in technical and policy barriers to international transactions [...] which were reconstructed by protectionist barriers in between the two world wars. Taking a very high level of abstraction, [...]

we believe that one fundamental difference lies in the impact that these reductions had on trade in goods versus trade in ideas. While both waves saw reduction in both costs, the uniqueness of the recent globalization is heavily shaped by the dramatic reduction in communication costs, what is sometimes referred to as "the death of distance." A second fundamental difference lies in the initial conditions. At the beginning of the first wave, the world was fairly homogeneous, homogeneously poor and agrarian, that is. At the beginning of the second wave, the world was sharply divided between rich industrial nations and poor primary producers.

(Baldwin and Martin, 1999: 3)

In their analysis of production structures and of income levels in the two globalization waves, the authors find that the initial conditions at the beginning of the current globalization (twentieth century globalization) included a very large north–south income differential that has by now developed into the de-industrialization of the north, while the industrialization of (part of) the south is still in progress. The first globalization wave (nineteenth century globalization), on the contrary, industrialized the north and de-industrialized the south, primarily India and China, thus producing enormous income differences among nations that were not that far apart in the middle of the nineteenth century.

This volume, and more specifically the present chapter that sets its theme, takes a different tack. It does not challenge the benefits of globalization. Those are significant for the north and in some cases also for the south. The focus is on the costs of globalization that happen to be considerable. What is even more important, the positive and negative outcomes of globalization are not distributed randomly. The asymmetries of globalization are systematic and work against the developing countries (less developed countries, or LDCs).

This chapter formalizes the challenge of globalization as a development strategy for the LDCs. From this standpoint, the antecedent characteristic differences between the two waves of globalization lie in the two novel features of the twentieth century globalization, trade in services and free movements of financial capital, that were absent in the nineteenth century globalization. The task that lies ahead, therefore, is to build an analytical model of the asymmetric outcomes that are the signature of the twentieth century globalization by tracing their causal origin in the growing importance of trade in services (in the third section of this chapter) and also in the free market in foreign exchange (in the fourth section) which, coupled with free flows of financial (portfolio) capital, sends torrid amounts of hot money sloshing around the world. The concluding section extends the conceptual model beyond the between-countries asymmetries to cover also the increasing chasm between the rich and the poor within a country, whether developed or developing.

Asymmetries based on institutional infrastructure

In the current environment of globalization free markets are championed for dispensing optimal outcomes in the form of bountiful benefits to consumers as well as to the efficient producers – without regard to the endowments, the social class or the states of the world a trading individual/country finds itself in. Competition is the automatic, homeostatic mechanism that favors the least-cost producer (in the process of the Schumpeterian "creative capitalist destruction") and delivers the benefits of Ricardian *comparative* advantage trade to consumers. (And parenthetically it is occasionally mentioned that even if the benefits from trade are not *mutual* for producers and consumers, the gains of the winners are big enough to compensate the losers.)

On the other hand, if the free market and free trade, or globalization for short, delivered the majority of benefits *systematically*, say, to the developed countries, and the poor ones were for the most part the losers, then FM-FT-LF does not mete out mutual advantages in this specific configuration, and the question becomes "why?"

Adam Smith, the first and arguably the most enthusiastic advocate of free markets, made it abundantly clear that markets need all the help they can get in order to perform as intended. He properly emphasized the important role of the state in providing defense for its citizens with an army, security with a police force, justice with a court system, plus whatever we would currently call "good governance." He especially noted the need that the state provides the "institutions for facilitating the commerce of society," like roads, bridges and ports. He implicitly signaled a sequence of institutional requisites that lengthens as the market expands its reach, as the complexity of transactions increases and as the requirements of international commerce become more exigent. Today the most basic Smithian infrastructure would probably include, among others, a high-speed venue of telecommunications infrastructure, telematics technology, plus the requisite transport infrastructure for the movement of people, merchandise, documents and ideas. All this modern infrastructure is necessary for providing the appropriate setting for contingent markets to develop in order to span time, space and uncertainty, thus paving the way to an Arrow-Debreu world.

The Arrow-Debreu world is the world of benign competition – a competition without tears.[3] It bestows mutual benefits to (efficient) producers and to consumers. As long as markets exist and are ensconced in the basic (enhanced) Smithian infrastructure, FM-FT-LF can deliver the optimal outcomes that the Fundamental Theorems of Welfare Economics (FTWE) extol, *in most cases*. The "new" development economics, however, identifies an important area of the market economy where the homeostatic mechanisms of FM-FT-LF and of the FTWE do not operate. There is *need for intervention* where there is market failure, and especially in the case of incomplete markets that are characterized by asymmetric information and adverse selection of risk.[4] Intervention, in turn, requires an even heavier dose of *good governance* in terms of the reservoirs of competence and integrity that are needed in the public sector. This represents another tall order of institution building.

An important, and certainly not new, message of this chapter is that globalization is *institution laden* and its success is predicated on the presence of some key institutional parameters above and beyond the basic ones identified by Adam Smith. Institution building, however, becomes an expensive proposition that comes easier in the richer countries while most poor countries can ill afford it. One would expect, therefore, that globalization, in the form of FM-FT-LF, delivers benefits that flow mainly to the well-endowed countries, those with wealth and a reliable nexus of political, social and economic institutions – and by extension to the elites of the rest of the world. On the other hand, the costs of the failure of globalization afflict the masses of the population of the poorer countries that become the victims of rent-seeking activities culminating in kleptocratic regimes, in general anomy and in the eventual derailment of economic development (Stiglitz, 2003). To say the least, free trade and free markets, although they may often serve as drivers to growth, they are certainly not the silver bullet and the "up-by-the-bootstraps" cure-all for LDCs that the messengers of the Washington Consensus have marketed to the Third World. Here lies one type of *systematic asymmetries* of globalization.

Trade in commodities and trade in services: another asymmetry

In the nineteenth century globalization international trade consisted exclusively of transactions in commodities – agricultural primary commodities, semi-finished intermediate products and manufactures. Trade in commodities can be readily accommodated within the standard neoclassical theory and can be fitted into either version, the static or the dynamic, of the FTWE. In other words, free trade in commodities is the classical case of mutual advantage trade: it matches the supply of the least-cost producers with the demand of consumers who are able and willing to pay the marginal cost of production.

The paragraph above is a distilled summary of the stylized Ricardo (1817) and Mill (1844) version of comparative advantage trade. In simple words, comparative advantage trade is the case of the best lawyer in town who also happens to be the best typist in town. Notwithstanding, she still hires a typist who is mediocre, but he has a comparative advantage: a low opportunity cost of his time, and thus low wages, as compared to the absolute advantage that his boss enjoys in lawyering.

Comparative advantage trade in commodities is still an important part in the twentieth century globalization – after all, it is the "secret weapon of mass destruction" that China possesses. What is new in the contemporary scene is trade in services that first featured as a significant component of international trade in the 1980s and has by now become the tail that wags the international trade dog – at least as it relates to the asymmetries of mutual advantage trade. The share of services in international trade – from transportation and communications, to insurance and financial services, to royalties, license fees and copyrights – quadrupled in value in 16 years (1986–2002) accounting in 2002 for 20 percent of total World Trade Organization (WTO) international trade (Figure 1.1).

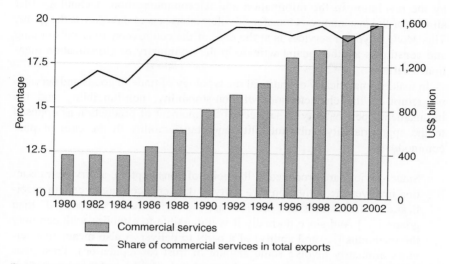

Figure 1.1 International trade in commercial services value and share in total exports, 1980–2002 (based on WTO, 2004).

Why is trade in services different from trade in commodities?

The economics literature highlights the germane characteristics of trade in services based on the distinction from trade in goods. Goods are appropriable, and therefore transferable between economic units; they can be stored, transported and accumulated. Services, on the other hand, are intangible, instantaneous (in that they perish in the very instant of production) and therefore involve the interaction of the consumer with the provider – which can take any form in a continuum from face-to-face to arm's length interaction (Fuchs, 1968; Hill, 1997).

Building on those characteristics the terminology of the WTO distinguishes four classifications ("*modes*") of international trade in services, based on the type of interaction between the consumer and the provider (Bhagwati *et al.*, 2004). In the case of providing medical care to foreign patients or education to foreign students, as well as in the case of international tourism, the consumer moves to the location of the provider (*Mode 2* services). *Mode 4* services cover the cases where doctors or teachers move to the location of the recipient, as well as the case of guest workers (*gastarbeiter* in Europe or Mexican migrant labor in the USA). *Mode 3* services require the move of the provider to another country in proximity to the consumer and that involves some direct foreign investment which often is miniscule so that the main element consists of the "right to establish" or to trade the *brand name*. Examples vary from shelving the Kellogg's box of cereals in the local supermarket, to establishing banking or insurance agencies, and exporting McDonald's franchises to another country. Finally in *Mode 1* services the supplier and the buyer remain in their home bases and their at-arm's-length interaction is made possible by snail mail, or more prominently by the revolution in the information and telecommunications technology that allows for the instantaneous transfer of voluminous sets of data across the globe. This *Mode 1* type of services is at the core of the controversy over outsourcing and constitutes another quaint wrinkle in the asymmetry of globalization mentioned earlier.

In making analytically operational the typology of trade in goods and services we return to the characteristics of non-storability, non-fungibility and the instantaneous perishability of services at the moment of production as opposed to the appropriability, substitutability and transferability in the case of pure commodities.

> Since services are produced at the point of consumption, a service transaction involves the obligation by a party to deliver according to certain specifications. This means that services are ordinarily more "customized" than goods. [. . .] And since normally it is impossible to establish with certainty the intentions [. . . and ability] of a party to deliver, it also means that services ordinarily involve some amount of trust (or reputation). Trust goes beyond a simple personal contact between the provider and the consumer. It can be viewed as the qualitative factor-augmenting face-to-face interaction that is needed for the production of services. Trust becomes an important element of cost in transactions involving uncertainty.
>
> (Yotopoulos, 1996: 105)

Trade in services is distinguished from trade in commodities by two characteristics that are interactive: customization and trust. Customization implies that something is distinct, for which the consumer is willing to pay a premium. Trust means that the producer of services will deliver according to specifications and therefore can claim a premium. Both are components of the more general "atmospheric" condition of reputation that yields the economic rents. Lest it becomes ephemeral in international trade, the customization component is often sheltered by patents, copyrights and intellectual property rights that generally enjoy legal protection and more recently have been endowed with WTO global recognition. Similarly, the trust is grounded on licensing for providing a service, on the certification of a certain process of production (e.g. organic agriculture) and on registration of brand names or of a recognized denomination of origin (e.g. Champagne). Customization and trust are registered in the market place in terms of reputation, which makes the specific market less contestable. Reputation is thus rewarded with economic rents that accrue to the producers.

The market of services is different from the market of commodities that operates on the basis of the least cost of production. But since customization and trust, in one word reputation, create profits, there is no reason that they be restricted to apply to services only. Trade in commodities also can be founded on reputation, to a certain extent, by "moving up the value-added chain" in order to deliver economic rents.[5] In effect customization starts where pure commodity trade ends, which probably ended with the trade in agricultural commodities, in raw materials and in semi-finished products of the nineteenth century globalization! And customization finishes with trade in pure services, say the personal valet – human, as opposed to the PDA, the personal digital assistant. In between those two extremes of pure commodities and pure services lies a huge band of "decommodified" trade that involves a lesser or greater degree of customization and trust. Examples of such decommodified trade are Lipton tea, Kona coffee, the Hilton Hotels or the business class airfare.[6] It must be noted that this entire sector of "decommodified" trade is missing from the WTO data of trade in services in Figure 1.1. In other words, the 20 percent share of "commercial services" in total exports in Figure 1.1 suffers a statistical undercounting if one considers also the missing component of decommodified trade.

Decommodification and positional goods

The kindred sociological literature deals with reputation, as well as with power and prestige, under the categorization of positional goods, and finds that they constitute "social limits to growth" (Hirsch, 1976; Frank and Cook, 1976; Frank, 1985; Pagano, 1999). As Pagano (Chapter 2) observes, the characteristic of positional goods is that a positive amount of the good (reputation) must be jointly consumed with a negative quantity of it because:

> It is impossible for somebody to consume prestige or "social superiority" if others do not consume some social "inferiority." [. . .] Positive and negative amounts of the positional good must be jointly consumed. No (European) soccer team in a tournament can consume three points of advantage if another team is not consuming three points of disadvantage.

The implication is that positional goods are ranked in an ordinal (reputational) ladder from first, or best, to last or worst.[7] This makes it possible for the team ranked third to improve its position either by winning or by a higher-ranked team losing to anybody else in the rank ordering.

Applying the typology of positional goods to decommodified trade we have a distinctly different category from the price-competition based trade. Within the continuum of customization a good is traded at a price that reflects its cost of production, a *cardinal* number, but includes also a component for the "reputation payoff" that consists of the monopoly returns and the economic rents that accrued in the process of creating reputation. Decommodified trade, therefore, and especially trade in services that incorporates to a considerable degree a "reputation payoff" becomes trade in positional goods. In this formulation reputation is a general term for the quality of the decommodified good and as such it enters the rank ordering that determines choice. In the final analysis, reputation is a matrix of various components that establish the ranking of a good in the positional scale. When a Fortune 500 multinational corporation sets shop in a developing country, it attracts its clientele not because it has a comparative advantage but primarily because of its reputation (which may or may not have been earned) of having been successful: being more reliable, being better capitalized, having better corporate governance, in other words for having a better "brand name."[8] Whatever the core component of trust is in this case, it is certainly enhanced by advertising, it is supplemented by a conforming culture, and all contribute to making a successful "branding" ("swashing"). Developed countries are better situated to engage in decommodified trade in general and to provide services in specific, and thus to capture the economic rents that accrue to reputation. The reason is that reputation in the international arena is most often an attribute of wealth and power and is nourished by visibility; all three characteristics are found more readily in the developed countries. It is easier for the developed countries to market the reputation that already exists than it is for poor countries that have first to create it from scratch!

Another factor that favors developed countries in producing decommodified exports and especially in exporting services, is the pre-existing domestic demand that is the result of their higher income levels. Miniesy and Nugent (Chapter 4), dealing with the effects of income inequality on trade incorporate the Linder (1961) hypothesis that the export of manufactures (and services) is predicated on the pre-existing local demand for their production in more developed countries. The advertising that created demand for more "sophisticated" goods, in Linder's terms, whether it addresses the middle-income classes and the elites in the developed countries or in LDCs, has the same effect of promoting these exports from the developed countries.[9] The reputation embedded in successful branding travels fast among socioeconomic classes in a globalized world. The middle-class mothers that appreciate the "convenience" of buying the box of Cornflakes in the supermarket of Caracas, as an example, have been exposed to the same media advertising by Kellogg that convinced the mother in New York that Cornflakes are better for her baby. The proliferation of McDonald's and of the United Colors of Benetton does not constitute the triumph of comparative advantage trade. It is, instead, the triumph of the globalization of pop culture. In the extreme case, the universal bulldozer of popular culture magnifies the reputation advantages of an international franchise and bestows on it ample reputation payoffs, while driving out of the market its local counterparts which, controlling for the quality of the good, lack the reputational advantage that accrues from trading in a global market. The globalization asymmetry in the case of services arises from the fact that the reputation component in that trade favors in general the developed countries at the expense of the poor.

The extreme case of the asymmetry in trade arises when *network effects* are bundled in the provision of a service, resulting in a winner-takes-all situation. This happens in a wide range of services, from telephony, to information technology, to banking and insurance. A typical example is the case of Microsoft Windows where reputation, enhanced by network effects, created a winner-takes-all environment. Controlling for the similarities and differences in the respective operating systems, it was the popularity contest that led to the demise of Apple in the 1980s since the users of the Mac operating system could not communicate with their (more numerous) Windows-using correspondents. Network effects create systematic winners in the developed countries to the detriment of a swath of service sectors in the developing world. It is not so much the cost advantage or the quality of service as it is the network effect that has Bank Megara Indonesia and Star Insurance Malaysia on the ropes when the Bank of America and Lloyds Insurance move in under the services liberalization protocol of the WTO.[10] It is all the more surprising that this huge systematic asymmetry in outcomes was signed away in 1996 in Singapore by the developing countries without any reciprocal concessions from the developed world. A generous gift indeed it was, given the vertiginous increase in recent years of trade in services (Figure 1.1).

Outsourcing and other trade in commodified services

Trade competition in services is a competition in which developing countries are bound to be the losers overall, as long as developed countries have the advantage that earns a reputation payoff in international trade. This is not to deny that some developing countries are important exporters of tourism and others export service-provider workers. More often than not, however, the mass tourism in developing countries becomes commodified, i.e. it is reduced to backpack tourism that, not unlike commodities, trades on the lowest common denominator of price competition. The munificent sector of luxury tourism is by and large controlled by multinational hotel chains which, based on the "right to establish," export well-paying brand-name services to the main tourist destinations around the globe, often with only a nominal contribution in direct foreign investment (*Mode 3* services). Similarly, the *Mode 4* exports of LDCs, the temporary movement of people to supply services that has become a major source of earning foreign exchange for many countries, is largely based on arbitrage in the minimum wage between developed countries and LDCs.[11] Finally there are some indications that the international tourism type of *Mode 2* services can be extended to cover elective surgery procedures which are imports of developed countries from certain LDCs that are gradually achieving credibility for compliance with international medical standards (such as India or Thailand). Despite the initial success of this type of service export, it still remains to be seen whether such provision of medical services will not elide to the luxury-tourism prototype to be captured by multinational health-care conglomerates.

One type of export of services that does not fit the mold I have been casting is the much celebrated (or notorious) outsourcing of services relating to information technology and back-office support that has been directed from the developed countries to India and China in recent years. This *Mode 1* type of service certainly represents profitable trade for the developing country and as such is an asymmetry which, as noted by Samuelson (2004), works against the developed world. Two idiosyncrasies of this type of service outsourcing should be noted, however, unless one rushes to the conclusion that the case vindicates the obligatory economists' complacencies about the overall benign effects of globalization for the developing world. First, the outsourced services have often been parsed to the extent that they are devoid of any element of trust or reputation, which is what claims the economic rents in the trade of services. The export of services in the case of outsourcing constitutes to a large extent commodified trade that is transacted in arbitraging the wage differential for technical support workers between, say, Silicon Valley in California and Bangalore in India.[12]

The other notable point is that the current wave of US outsourcing is not representative of the garden-variety service exports that could be easily accessible to developing countries. The public infrastructure that has made such export specialization possible usually comes at great cost to the countries involved. It requires excellent education in technical and language skills (including fluency in the English language), infrastructure in the form of technology and biotechnology parks, high speed fiber optics communication networks that make the instantaneous transmission of data possible, and especially an army of well trained engineers.[13] The happy accident for the developing countries that became the beneficiaries of the US services outsourcing was their timing. The bursting of the Silicon Valley technology bubble in 2001 and the ensuing American recession drastically decreased the cost of technological outfitting for new entrants in this market. Such propitious happenstances notwithstanding, we can conclude that, on balance, developing countries are bound to remain net importers of services in world trade. Moreover, the more unequal the distribution of income is within a country, the greater the imbalance in trade that the service component is likely to represent.[14]

There exist also two different scenarios with respect to outsourcing that feature a rainbow at the end of the day for the developing country. In the classical paradigm of free trade globalization, where a developed and a less developed country (country *1* and *2*) trade in two goods (good 1 and 2), with the former "developed country" having an absolute advantage in the production of good 1 (legal services) and the latter (developing country) only a relative advantage in the production of good 2 (back-office work for legal services), free trade benefits both countries. In the previous example of outsourcing from the US to India, an increase in the productivity of the outsourcee (the secretary of the lawyer acquires the skills that raise him from mediocre to good) will still hurt India's terms of trade. As Lewis, (1978: 18) had observed, India would benefit by improving its share in the mutual benefits of trade only if it increased productivity in the third common good that the two countries share (production of food in his case) that is a proxy for the standard of living in a country. In our earlier example of the lawyer/secretary, this would correspond to a broad-based increase in wages in the outsourcee country, India. There is some evidence that this process has started already in India, a country that has the advantage of established and globalization-fit infrastructure in the form of enough bandwidth to reach also big villages. As a result, the former outsourcee, (Satyam Computer Services of Bangalore) has started outsourcing some of its work that was previously done at headquarters to educated and eager villagers in the countryside who used to migrate to the cities in search of wages (Friedman, 2006). This is equivalent to increasing productivity in Lewis' home-good, in the form of increasing wages on a broader level.

While the logic of comparative advantage trade in the example of the lawyer and her secretary is unassailable for a single country, in its application to India with the back-office work, Samuelson (2004) casts, not unlike Lewis above, serious doubts on the simplified version of professional wisdom regarding the mutual benefits of fair free trade. He finds that outsourcing work from the US to India to be done at Indian wages, while definitely benefits the outsourcee, it can permanently hurt the outsourcing country by reducing its share in the combined gains of trade that are possible for the two countries. It is this form of *dynamic free trade* that has been overlooked in the classical argument in favor of free trade. This case of "immiserizing growth" constitutes another asymmetry of globalization which, however, in this instance hurts the developed country and benefits the poor. Although bad for the US, it is part of the rainbow of globalization for the developing countries.

Samuelson (2004: 143) considers this challenge that arises for free trade and he rejects the protectionist solution: "In 1900 free traders proclaimed, 'Tariffs are the Mother of trusts.' In the millennium a more pregnant truth may be: 'Tariffs are the breeder of economic arteriosclerosis'." Protectionism, however, is a multi-headed Lernaean Hydra arising in a different form each time it becomes decapitated. In the millennial environment the novel form of protectionism consists in setting the industry standards at the national/regional level and in legitimizing these standards internationally, e.g. in the Service Liberalization Protocols at the WTO level. As mentioned earlier (cf. end note 10) the developed countries within the framework of WTO exercise their control at that level by promoting a stream of IPR (intellectual property rights) regulations that consistently enhance the reputation content (and monopoly returns) of internationally traded services. The overall asymmetry of globalization arises because the developed countries' absolute advantage in providing these services is possibly stronger than their erstwhile absolute technological advantage that was lost to outsourcing to the Indias and Chinas of this world.[15]

The conclusion is that globalization of services (in the broader sense of decommodified trade) benefits the developed countries and the elites of the LDCs, but it is not the silver bullet for promoting development and decreasing poverty in the rest of the world. The question then arises: does it matter if the wealthy in the Third World spend their money in buying First World brand names to the detriment of the domestic production of (internationally) "non-traded" commodities? The cost of shrinking the indigenous service sector is not insignificant, especially when network effects are involved and create a winner-takes-all situation for the multinational service exporter. To this cost one should add the damage to poor countries' trade balances, the deficits of which must be covered by international borrowing, normally of dollars that slosh from country to country taking advantage of the interest rate differential that depreciating currencies provide relative to the reserve/hard currency. The scourge of systematically depreciating "soft" currencies is treated presently.

The commodification of soft currencies and currency substitution

The significant damage that asymmetric reputation in the provision of services does to trade and the balance of payments of the Third World is still a minor evil, compared to the financial wreckage that *asymmetric reputation in currencies* has meted to poor (and to some rich) countries in the last three decades. At the domestic level, a country's currency is used as a medium of exchange – in parallel with any consensual fiat money, like "trading stamps" or "frequent flier miles" that also can do service for transaction purposes. In settling international transactions, however, the reserve currency and a handful of other (hard) currencies are exclusively used as foreign exchange. When currency is held as an asset, the number of eligible currencies decreases further. On their capital account, central banks hold the reserve currency in their reserves, and individuals also hold the reserve currency and hard-currency denominated assets. This pecking order of currencies held as assets is an affirmation that not all currencies were created equal. As opposed to the use of currency for transaction purposes, the currency held as asset trades as a positional good based on *reputation*. In the ordinal reputational ranking of currencies for asset-holding purposes, from "best" to "worst," the reserve currency ranks at the top of the reputational ladder. The dollar, therefore, substitutes in agents' portfolios for a wide swath of less-preferred currencies because of its reputation. The reserve currency's reputation in turn, in a process of cumulative causation, earns the munificent seigniorage returns. Moreover, in continuing the same cumulative process, the reserve currency's reputation as the "best" currency is reinforced by the network effects that it generates by doing better service as a medium of exchange and as a store of value because it has a large transactional domain, i.e. it has greater *liquidity* than other currencies. The currency (dollar) that is used by 500 million people, in the USA and elsewhere, is 50 times more liquid than a currency that is money for ten million people (Mundell, 2000).[16] In the case of positional goods, and in the currency competition business, the network effects are even more important than they are in the case of cell phones or international banks that were mentioned earlier.

Currency substitution as a case of market incompleteness

The asymmetries in the reputation of currencies induce asymmetric demand for holding currencies as assets. Citizens of developing countries, for example, include in their portfolio the reserve/hard currency for asset-holding purposes. The motivation is buying insurance against a devaluation which is more likely to happen for their countries' soft currencies than for the substitute reserve currency. Citizens of hard-currency countries, on the other hand, have not a matching interest in holding soft currencies, those of developing countries. Controlling for the current account, this currency substitution of the reserve currency for the soft in the capital account of the central bank will lead to the devaluation of the soft currency. Thus currency substitution "commodifies" the soft currency (the "peso") and makes its devaluation a self-fulfilling prophecy.[17] This is on the demand side. On the supply side, the current (neo-liberal) system of international finance extends FM-FT-LF also to foreign exchange rates and to financial capital flows. Thus while monetary interventions intended to prevent this type of currency substitution-induced devaluation are proscribed, on the other hand, the freedom of speculative capital to empower this self-serving game and to participate in its spoils is countenanced.

The type of devaluation that occurs as a result of currency substitution is different from the benign devaluation featured in economics textbooks that improves the macro-fundamentals of an economy. In the conventional case of currency devaluation as a result of current account imbalances, its impact in the real world will restore equilibrium in the economy by increasing exports, that now earn more in local currency, and decreasing imports that correspondingly cost more. Post-devaluation the prices of tradables (in domestic currency) have increased relative to non-tradables, which contributes to restore the equilibrium in the allocation of resources. It is a process of *good competition* that remedies the macro-fundamentals of the economy along with the original current account imbalances.

The case of the currency substitution-induced devaluation, on the other hand, can be viewed as the result of *bad competition* and of a *race for the bottom* by extending the standard Stiglitz and Weiss (1981) model of incomplete markets to cover also the market defect of *asymmetric reputation* – as opposed to asymmetric *information* that is familiar in the literature. Controlling for the state of the current account and the reserves of the central banks, it is the developing (soft-currency) countries that bear an additional risk of devaluation of their currencies by the positional-good nature of reputational asymmetry. Replicating the implications of the standard incomplete markets model, the *asymmetric reputation*-induced devaluation of the peso is the result of the wrong incentives that are motivated from gaming the devaluation; and when the inevitable devaluation happens, it rewards those who caused the crisis by fleeing away from the local currency in favor of hoarding dollars. When coupled with free flows of capital, the spoils of devaluation go also to international speculators who move financial capital (hot money) across borders for the purpose of placing a (leveraged) one-way, "cannot-lose" bet against, in this example, the Mexican central bank (Yotopoulos, 1996; Yotopoulos and Sawada, 1999). This type of "bad" competition, in the limiting case, can lead to serial devaluations, thus provoking financial crises.[18]

As in the standard case of incomplete credit markets, the remedy for the market incompleteness of foreign exchange lies in rationing, i.e. making foreign exchange available at the prevailing free market rate for transaction purposes only, while holdings of foreign monetary assets by individuals are prohibited or otherwise penalized (for example delegated to the black market).[19] While in the standard case of incomplete credit markets, the damage is limited to the "race for the bottom," i.e. the default of the creditor, the case of incomplete foreign exchange markets has broad repercussions economy-wide. The decrease in the reserves of the central bank registers in the capital account as an imbalance, but only because the dollars have ended up under the mattress or in a Mexican's US bank account on the other side of the Rio Grande. Currency substitution is often the preamble to capital flight that hemorrhages private savings and represents a dysfunctional integration into the world economy (Collier, forthcoming).

Currency substitution: the transmission of a monetary phenomenon to the real world of resource misallocation and poverty

The devaluation that normally follows an epidemic of currency substitution not only is gratuitous as a remedy of the macro-fundamentals, but it also results in further distorting the allocation of resources in the economy by misaligning the exchange rate and inducing a misallocation in favor of the tradable sector.[20] Whether the extant allocation of resources is optimal or not, the rational-expectations signal the producer of non-tradables receives from the devaluation of the peso is that his resources that so far produced, say, the equivalent of one dollar's worth of tradables, will yield less than one dollar in the future. Rational expectations would have the peso devalue further in the future, and in anticipation the economy becomes more "dollarized" by shifting more resources to the production of tradables (which trade in dollars) whether the *ex ante* allocation of resources was the correct one or not. Currency substitution is the perfect recipe for misallocating resources.[21]

Why is this case of currency substitution-induced financial crisis so pivotal for the asymmetries of globalization? It epitomizes the importance of the gradations that are introduced to classical commodity trade and to the Ricardo-Mill version of comparative advantage by the experience gained in the current round of globalization. The result of reputational asymmetry-induced currency substitution for asset-holding purposes can afflict any and all currencies since they are by definition "worse" than the "best" reserve currency. Notwithstanding the experience of England, Spain and Italy in the serial devaluations episode of 1992, currency substitution-induced devaluations commonly impact "soft," which is developing-country, currencies. The risk of endemic devaluations bears a number of adverse effects for developing countries that become part of the systematic asymmetries of globalization (and of free flows of financial capital).

The assets of the central bank in a devaluing country are in foreign exchange while its liabilities are in the local currency. Devaluation results in changing the relative prices of the bank's assets and liabilities and thus in higher interest rates that have a contractionary effect on the economy on the one side, while on the other side attract free-floating portfolio capital that is expensive to service in foreign exchange. Hot money, far from promoting domestic investment, constitutes instead the fuel that, given a spark, leads to the conflagration of a (highly-leveraged) currency substitution and on to the next devaluation of the domestic currency. This serial relationship between currency substitution and devaluation can only find temporary relief in developing countries shoring up their reserves by borrowing dollars at exorbitant rates of interest (Stiglitz, 2003).

Again at the economy-wide level, as devaluation makes exports cheaper and imports costlier, the terms-of-trade and the balance-of-payments effects tend to work against the developing countries, given the usual assumptions about price and income elasticities of their exports vis-à-vis their imports. This tends to weaken further the fundamentals of the economy and thus increases the risk of an ensuing devaluation.

The reallocation of resources has also socioeconomic class-specific implications. When resources are being increasingly allocated in favor of sectoral outputs denominated in dollars (exports, including tourism, etc.) as opposed to sectors that produce the indigenous non-tradable goods that are transacted in the local currency, the cost of production of non-tradables escalates (assuming a significant import component).[22] The result is that the cost of living of the lower economic classes increases. By the same process of shifting the allocation of resources from non-tradables to tradables, often in an irreversible manner, poorer people in developing countries tend to suffer twofold losses: one, as long as their preferences are tilted towards cheaper, non-tradable goods, they suffer utility losses; two, to the extent this conversion hurts the environmental resource base of the developing countries and their poor citizens, they suffer a further loss of utility.[23]

The ancillary effect of currency substitution-induced devaluations is that they can easily evolve into full-scale financial crises. The adverse effects of crises on the real economy of developing countries are well documented and do not need to be rehashed here.

Conclusion: globalization and the divide of inequality between and within countries

The transparent theme of *The Asymmetries of Globalization* is that free markets and free trade work as long as they are supported by an intricate and extensive institutional structure. And since institutions do not come springing from the trees, the outcomes of globalization are more likely to be asymmetric, favoring the countries that are wealthy and institution rich, at the expense of those that are poor. This argument is not to deny the universality of the benefits of free trade. It simply signals that comparative advantage trade becomes unattainable for countries that do not have the requisite institutional infrastructure in place.

The more subtle and novel theme of this volume revolves around the idea that the systematic outcomes of globalization depend on the degree of commodification of the trade in question. Trade in the classical commodities, agricultural primary goods and manufactures, can be reduced to Ricardian comparative advantage trade that delivers its benefits to consumers and to the least-cost producers, without any viable asymmetries in the outcomes between rich and poor countries. Given the (enhanced) Smithian institutional infrastructure, free trade and comparative advantage can act as a homeostatic mechanism that lifts the poorer countries up by their bootstraps. This is consonant with the Washington Consensus.

In the current era of globalization trade in services, that only recently entered world trade and the WTO writ, has become the most rapidly growing component of international trade. Trade in services differs from the traditional commodity trade by its characteristic of instantaneous perishability and the requirement for a degree of person-to-person interaction, both being consumed jointly with trust and reputation in the provision of services. Patents and intellectual property rights have entered the scene, and so has advertising in the attempt to establish brand names, all in an effort to create and cement trust, thus reinforcing the free trade inhibiting characteristics of the non-contestable markets in which services are transacted. Trust becomes the foundation of trade in services and it is rewarded with monopoly returns and ancillary economic rents that accrue to "reputation." International exchange that incorporates a component of reputation does not deal in comparative advantage anymore, because reputation is a positional good and it is subject to ordinal measurement only, based on the ranking of a service from best to worst. What is necessary in the trade of services becomes applicable also in the trade of the erstwhile (pure) commodities that are becoming increasingly decommodified by the incorporation of components of economic rents. In fact, the "trade in ideas" that solidifies trust, whether reflected in intellectual property rights and their monopoly returns, or in advertising and brand names that yield economic rents, has expanded the role of reputation to apply in a continuum of decommodification between the two extremes of the traditional "pure" commodities and "pure" services. The novel contribution of this volume is to signal the growing importance that the reputation component implies for the expanded domain of world trade. Far from delivering mutual benefits, trade in positional goods rewards the rank ordering which gets reshuffled when the runner-up wins in the competition with the leader, or the leader loses to anybody else in the order. The message for trade in services is that winning the reputation game in competition with the developed countries is not as automatic for the developing world as it is having a comparative advantage in the trade of commodities. The reason is that reputation is an attribute of wealth and power which the developed countries can take to the bank, as opposed to the developing countries that have to build reputation from scratch.

Another unorthodox insight gleaned from the previous two sections of this chapter relates to the need for intervention in the trade of the reserve currency for asset holding purposes. Given the asymmetric reputation of any of the world's currencies relative to the reserve currency, the outcome of a free market in currencies is a race for the bottom, in an exact parallel to the incompleteness of the credit market. The difference is that the origin of incompleteness in asymmetric information has become, instead, asymmetric reputation in the case of currency substitution. Even worse, the race for the bottom in this latter case does not end with the default of the creditors as in the case of asymmetric information. In the worst case it can end in serial devaluations that wreak havoc on LDCs.

While this chapter focused mainly on the increasing divide that separates rich and poor countries in the era of globalization, on occasion the impact of free trade on poverty within the LDCs was also examined and yielded systematic asymmetries that increase the divide between rich and poor people. Yet, both the poor and the rich within a country are consumers of the goods purveyed by globalization at bargain prices. To that extent, poor and rich alike must be benefiting from globalization. Why should the divide between socioeconomic classes increase?

The analytical mechanism that turns the poor into losers, whether in developed countries or in LDCs, is simple: the poor have too little, while the rich have too much. The argument refers not to equality, or to the sense of justice, but to an economic asymmetry between the consumption and the production processes. The difference between the poor and the rich lies in the fact that the poor were previously the producers of those one-euro Chinese blouses when they were produced locally, at the textile factories of Prato in Italy or of Thessaloniki in Greece. Those jobs in the local industry were paying decent wages and they were feeding the workers' dreams of stepping on the escalator that would propel them from poverty to the middle classes. With globalization these jobs have disappeared and the unemployed have lost their wage checks. By not being producers any more, they can no longer afford the consumers' cornucopia and the one-euro blouses that globalization offers.[24]

The rich, on the other hand, have no problem of losing their jobs to imports nor do they face an income constraint, since they have wealth. They profit from the cheap commodities of globalization trade but mainly they profit from the freedom to import the decommodified standards of living of their rich brethren in the First World. Their graduation from consumers in the Third World, where they live, to consumers of the First World, in terms of what imports they can afford to buy, has become the problem of the central bank that finds its international reserves depleted by the economic imbalance of producing like a poor country and consuming like the rich!

Although this chapter has focused on the risk that globalization becomes the epitaph of growth in the Third World, the increasing divide between the rich and the poor within the developed countries may prove even more ominous for the future of globalization. Unless the gains from free trade are shared more equally between rich and poor countries, and among the rich and the poor within them, the future of this second globalization may be short lived.

Notes

1 I am grateful for comments to Samar Datta, Jeff Nugent, Kolleen Rask, Donato Romano, Yasuyuki Sawada and T.N. Srinivasan.
2 Kreps (1994) defines "institutions" as the set of the rules of the game.

3 For more exacting conditions of the Arrow-Debreu world and its application in this essay see Pagano (Chapter 2).

4 The need for intervention in cases of market failure is not new, dating at least as far back as the early years of the modern economics of development when government planning of the economy was still respectable and Rosenstein-Rodan was formulating his theory of the big-push (Rosenstein-Rodan, 1961: 57–81; Yotopoulos and Nugent, 1976: Chs 20 and 21). The "new" element in development economics is the extension of the need for intervention in cases of market incompleteness that comes in an era when the alternative of government planning has been finally buried and free markets are enthusiastically promoted as the only way to run an economy.

5 In contemporary business parlance the euphemism for the process of creating and capturing economic rents is "moving up the value-added chain."

6 For an example of such decommodification in developing country agriculture cf. D'Haese *et al.* (Chapter 9).

7 In extending this literature and viewing customization as a process of creating "positional goods" I postulate that the rank ordering of customized goods in general and of services in particular, is based on more elements than the tangible "quality characteristics" of the good that are identifiable *ex ante*.

8 These components that establish reputation may be attributed to better institutions and more resources that are at the disposal of developed countries, and may result, arguably, to producing better services, defined in terms of average higher quality and/or lower quality variation.

9 Bergstrand (1991) endogenizes the effect of advertising in a model that assigns income elasticity of demand for services greater than one and for commodities lesser than one. This makes developing countries better able to produce services. See also Romano (Chapter 10).

10 Restrictions of trade in the form of regional (or national) standards are effective in containing these network effects. For example, the need to customize IT products for European standards in business systems fuelled the success of the Irish software industry in the 1990s. Similarly, the difference in standards for the US cellular phone industry as compared to those adopted in Europe and in most Asian countries has protected the respective regional interests.

11 In case the temporary stay is converted to permanent residence the foreign exchange gains of LDCs become more significant, but at the expense of a costly brain drain for the country of origin.

12 Cf. Liu *et al.* (Chapter 6), for examples of commodification of these types of services.

13 One, of course, could define such investments as part of the (extended) Smithian infrastructure that is requisite for comparative advantage trade. It would still strike me as an attempt of excessive word-smith-ing in the altar of mainstream conventional wisdom.

14 Cf. Miniesy and Nugent and Sawada and Yotopoulos (Chapters 4 and 3, respectively).

15 Pagano (2006 and Chapter 2) refers to "legal disequilibria" in the case of "pan-positional" goods when the legal framework of "rights" does not also assign clear "responsibilities" for their enforcement. Such is the case of WTO "legislation" on intellectual property rights, with the residual responsibility for enforcing the law falling on hapless governments in the Third World that may or may not have the resources or the will to do that. In such cases the economic system works suboptimally. See also Romano (Chapter 10).

16 Pagano (Chapter 2, fourth section) generalizes the model of positional competition in terms of the cumulative causation between reputation and liquidity.

17 This is precisely the reason why restrictions in the capital account that limit or totally prohibit holdings of foreign monetary assets have had a long history in international

finance. They were abolished in the United Kingdom only in 1979 – just in time, one might observe, for the pound to be hit by a historical currency substitution crisis in 1992! In China, on the other hand, the currency until early 2006 had been convertible on the current account only – and not on the capital account.

18 For the modeling and testing of this case cf. Sawada and Yotopoulos (2005).
19 It is noted that this has been a long-venerated practice in development planning in most countries prior to the 1980s, and in China until more recently. On the other hand, gold held for asset-holding purposes has served India well for more than a century. For reasons of illiquidity and of storage cost gold becomes an expensive way of buying insurance against future devaluations and thus its use for that purpose is more limited than of the foreign exchange alternative. But what is even more important, an increase in imports of gold is treated like any other item in the current account, with its demand and supply adjusting, subject to the exchange rate. An increase in the demand for dollar assets, on the other hand, triggers the devaluation of the peso, which changes the prices of all items in the balance of payments, plus the relative prices of tradables and non-tradables in the economy. This is a huge change in the real world that follows the mere repositioning of liquid assets (by the wealthy).
20 Yotopoulos and Sawada (2006) provide an empirical test of the proposition that the damage from the misalignment of the exchange rate originates in the free market for foreign exchange to be used as an asset.
21 For the modeling and quantification of these allocative inefficiencies see Yotopoulos (1996: 51 and Ch. 7) and Sawada and Yotopoulos (2005).
22 Moreover, since luxury tourism is normally transacted in dollars in poor countries, the revaluation of the dollar would have offset the result of the devaluation of cheap tourism becoming cheaper and more attractive for the backpack crowd. In addition, where luxury tourism is controlled by foreign multinationals, its profits enhance the GDP but are not part of the national product, having fled the country.
23 Contrary to normal regulatory treatment that applies to developed countries, developing countries cannot claim benefits for the environmental goods they produce, nor can they demand compensation for the environmental damage they inflict on themselves through their export activities.
24 Memories in economics are short sometimes. The Japanese "dollar-blouse" trade war with the United States in the late 1950s ended with an American tariff against Japanese imports. This, in turn, propelled the Ministry of Industry and Trade to launch a new strategy of "articulated development" that propelled Japanese industrialization until 1992 (Yotopoulos, 1996: 193 and Ch. 9). It seems that China might have digested this strategy while the West is again toying with "tariffing-away" the Chinese "threat."

References

Baldwin, Richard and Philippe Martin (1999), "Two Waves of Globalization: Superficial Similarities and Fundamental Differences." In Horst Siebert, ed., *Globalization and Labour*. Tübingen: J.C.B. Mohr, for Kiel Institute of World Economics, pp. 3–59.

Bhagwati, Jagdish, Arvind Panagariya and T.N. Srinivasan (2004), "The Muddles over Outsourcing," *Journal of Economic Perspectives*, 18 (4): 93–114.

Bergstrand, Jeffrey H. (1991), "Structural Determinants of Real Exchange Rates and National Prices Levels: Some Empirical Evidence," *American Economic Review*, 81 (1): 325–34.

Collier, Paul (forthcoming), "Africa and Globalization." In Ernesto Zedillo, ed., *The Future of Globalization: Explorations in Light of Recent Turbulence*. London: Routledge.

Frank, Robert H. (1985), *Choosing the Right Pond*. New York: Oxford University Press.

Frank, Robert H. and Philip J. Cook (1976), *The Winner-Take-All Society: Why the Few at the Top Get So Much More Than the Rest of Us*. New York: Penguin.

Friedman, Thomas (2006), "Op-Ed," *New York Times*, 19 May. Online, available at nytimes.com (accessed 19 May, 2006).

Fuchs, Victor R. (1968), *The Service Economy*. New York: National Bureau of Economic Research and Columbia University Press.

Hill, T. Peter (1997), "On Goods and Services," *Review of Income and Wealth*, 23 (December): 315–38.

Hirsch, Fred (1976), *Social Limits to Growth*. Cambridge, MA: Harvard University Press.

Kreps, David (1994), "Corporate Culture and Economic Theory." In James Alt and Kenneth Shepsle, eds, *Perspectives on Positive Political Economy*. Cambridge: Cambridge University Press, pp. 90–143.

Lewis, W. Arthur (1978), *The Evolution of the International Economic Order*. Princeton, NJ: Princeton University Press.

Linder, Steffan (1961), *An Essay on Trade and Transformation*. Stockholm: Almqvist and Wicksell.

Mill, John S. (1844), *Essays on Some Unsettled Questions of Political Economy*. London: Parker.

Mundell, Robert A. (2000), "The Euro and the Stability of the International Monetary System." In Robert A. Mundell and Armand Cleese, eds, *The Euro as a Stabilizer in the International Economic System*. Boston: Kluwer Academic, pp. 57–84.

Pagano, Ugo (1999), "Is Power an Economic Good? Notes on Social Scarcity and the Economics of Positional Goods." In Samuel Bowles, Maurizio Franzini and Ugo Pagano, eds, *The Politics and Economics of Power*. London: Routledge, pp. 63–84.

Pagano, Ugo (2006), "Legal Positions and Institutional Complementarities." In Fabrizio Cafaggi, Antonio Nicita and Ugo Pagano, eds, *Legal Orderings and Economic Institutions*. London: Routledge, pp. 54–83.

Ricardo, David (1817), *On the Principle of Political Economy and Taxation*. London: John Murray.

Rosenstein-Rodan, Paul N. (1961), "Notes on the Theory of the 'Big Push'." In Howard S. Ellis and Henry C. Wallich, eds, *Economic Development for Latin America*. New York: St Martin's Press.

Samuelson, Paul A. (2004), "Where Ricardo and Mill Rebut and Confirm Arguments of Mainstream Economists Supporting Globalization," *Journal of Economic Perspectives*, 18 (3): 135–45.

Sawada, Yasuyuki and Pan A. Yotopoulos (2005), "Corner Solutions, Crises, and Capital Controls: Theory and Empirical Analysis on the Optimal Exchange Rate Regime in Emerging Economies." Stanford Institute for Economic Policy Research, Paper no. 04–037 (September 2005). Online, available at siepr.stanford.edu/Papers/pdf/04–37.html (accessed 13 September 2005).

Stiglitz, Joseph E. (2003), *The Roaring Nineties: A New History of the World's Most Prosperous Decade*. New York: W.W. Norton.

Stiglitz, Joseph E. and Andrew Weiss (1981), "Credit Rationing in Markets with Imperfect Information," *American Economic Review*, 71 (June): 393–410.

WTO (2004), "International Trade Statistics, Statistical Database." Online, available at www.wto.org/english/res_e/statis_e/statis_e.htm (accessed 29 December 2004).

Yotopoulos, Pan A. (1996), *Exchange Rate Parity for Trade and Development: Theory, Tests, and Case Studies*. Cambridge and New York: Cambridge University Press.

Yotopoulos, Pan A. and Jeffrey B. Nugent (1976), *Economics of Development: Empirical Investigations*. New York: Harper and Row.

Yotopoulos, Pan A. and Yasuyuki Sawada (1999), "Free Currency Markets, Financial Crises and the Growth Debacle: Is There a Causal Relationship?" *Seoul Journal of Economics*, 12 (Winter): 419–56. (Available also online at siepr.stanford.edu/papers/pdf/99–04.html).

Yotopoulos, Pan A. and Yasuyuki Sawada (2006), "Exchange Rate Misalignment: A New Test of Long-Run PPP Based on Cross-Country Data," *Applied Financial Economics*, 16 (1): 127–34.

2 Positional goods and asymmetric development[1]

Ugo Pagano

Introduction

Standard international trade theory considers the case in which countries specialize in the production of private goods. In an open economy, countries specialize in the production of the private goods in which they have a comparative advantage. In this way, all countries gain from trade and improve their welfare and their level of development. This theory has even more optimistic implications when public goods are included in the picture. Most catch-up theories of development were based on the idea that the wealthier and more advanced countries were likely to specialize in knowledge-intensive processes and, therefore, make substantial investments in public goods that could also be used by poorer countries. International trade would have either implied symmetric benefits or even repaired pre-existing asymmetries between developed and developing countries.

In this chapter, I will argue that this picture changes substantially when we introduce positional goods into the analysis. Positional goods can be viewed as a case polar to that of public goods. If "First World" countries specialize in goods sharing a positional nature, this optimistic view of global development changes and international trade may lead to forms of increasing asymmetric development. In the following section, I consider the characteristics of positional goods. In the next section, I give a very short account of the role that positional goods like status and power can play as a possible cause of asymmetric development. In the fourth section, I argue that also money (the most typical example of a positional good) can be an important cause of asymmetric development. In the fifth section, I build on the Hohfeld-Commons analysis of legal relations and argue that legal disequilibrium can be the cause of the asymmetric effects that competition systematically generates in various countries, notably the developed as opposed to less developed. In the final section, I consider the role of the global legal positions defined by intellectual property and I maintain that they have an important role in causing diverging paths of international specialization. I argue that the recent process of globalization can be seen as a shift from an international order, in which the public goods supplied by developed countries had an important developmental role to play, to a new global order that is mainly driven by the developed countries' specialization in positional goods.

The nature of positional goods and welfare theory

Positional vs private and public goods

In his famous book, Hirsh (1976) argued that positional goods pose social limits to growth. Hirsh argued that, while some goods could be produced without limitations, other goods, which he labeled positional goods, were only available in limited supply. Economic development implied an increasing price of positional goods and was inevitably constrained by the scarcity of these goods.

Under the umbrella of positional goods Hirsh included two types of goods. The supply of the first set of goods was limited by their natural scarcity. By contrast, the second set included goods like power and status, whose supply was limited by their social scarcity. In both cases, the possibility of acquiring these goods was related to the relative standings of the individuals and a process of development could not improve everybody's chances of getting them. The importance of relative positions induced Hirsh to use the term positional goods for both types of goods. However, the two types of goods have different characteristics and, in my view, only the second category deserves the label of positional goods.

Goods, such as natural resorts that cannot be reproduced, are positional only in the weak sense that the relative positions of the individuals matter to acquire them. Natural scarcity implies that a form of social scarcity, related to the relative standings of the different individuals, does indirectly matter. However, these goods could be consumed independently of the behavior of other individuals and, indeed, more easily without their interference. Moreover, an egalitarian consumption of these goods is not impossible and it is indeed a likely outcome when there are no relevant differences in the social standing, the relative wealth and the preferences of the different individuals.

The positional nature of the second category of goods is much stronger: in the act of consumption, individuals must necessarily divide themselves into two different groups of "positive" and "negative" consumers. Consider the case of status and power. Any positive amount of power and prestige must be jointly consumed with negative quantities of it. It is impossible for some individuals to exercise power if other individuals do not undergo the exercise of this power or, in other words, it is impossible for somebody to dominate if somebody is not dominated: positive power must be jointly consumed with negative power.[2] In a similar way, it is impossible for somebody to consume prestige or "social superiority" if others do not consume some social "inferiority." Again positive and negative amounts of the good must be jointly consumed. No (European) soccer team in a tournament can consume three points of advantage if another team is not consuming three points of disadvantage. Unlike the features of unique natural resorts, the positional characteristics of these goods are intrinsic to their nature. In this case, it is impossible to consume positive amounts independently of the behavior of some other individuals who must undergo a negative consumption of the same goods. Moreover, the egalitarian consumption of these goods is seriously limited by their intrinsic positional nature. If everybody can be somebody, nobody can be somebody: it is impossible for all the members of a group of individuals to be equally powerful and prestigious without spoiling the very meaning of these goods that do necessarily imply divisive consumptions with two opposite signs.

Therefore, we define as positional goods only the second category of goods, which are somehow related to the legacy of Veblen (1899). We will observe that, unlike the first category (which does not differ from the standard scarce economic goods), the second category of goods requires an extension of the standard economic classification into private and public goods.

Private goods are characterized by the fact that other individuals consume a *zero amount* of what a certain individual consumes. The other individuals are excluded from the consumption of these goods. The exclusion from positive amounts of consumption is impossible in the case of public goods and, indeed, in the case of a pure public good all the agents will consume the *same positive amount*.

In the case of positional goods, like status and power, when some individuals consume these goods other individuals must be included in consumption of related negative quantities. A pure positional good can be defined as a good such that an agent consumes the same but negative amount of what another agent consumes. In this respect pure positional goods define a case that is polar to the case of pure public goods.[3]

Consider the case of Robinson Crusoe's island. At the beginning, before Friday's arrival, Robinson will not observe any relevant difference among the goods that he consumes. He cannot perceive the distinction between private and public goods. The impossibility of exclusion, that distinguishes public goods from private goods, cannot be perceived in a situation where there are not other individuals and positional goods cannot be consumed at all if nobody else is included in their negative consumption. When Friday arrives, the distinction between public and private goods becomes evident and, according to the common prejudices of his time, the white civilized Robinson can start to consume positive amounts of positional goods such as status and power.

Referring to the simple case of the two individual Robinson–Friday economy the relation between the signs of these goods can be summarized as in Table 2.1.

It is not surprising that the problems of positional goods are opposite to the problems of public goods. In the case of public goods we have the standard under-investment problem in their supply (and in their abatement when they are public bads). It may turn out to be impossible to exclude the individuals from externalities having the "same sign" of the good. By contrast, in the case of positional goods, we have a problem of over-investment. All the agents may try to consume positive amounts of these goods and include other individuals in the corresponding negative consumption. For this reason, "positional competition" is much harder, and sometimes more violent, than competition for "private" goods. It is also wasteful because individual efforts do often offset each other. In some cases, they may end up with the same outcome that they would have

Table 2.1 Consumption according to the nature of goods

	Robinson	*Friday*
Public good	+	+
Private good	+	0
Private good	0	+
Positional good	+	−
Positional good	−	+
Public bad	−	−

achieved if they had not dedicated any effort to the improvement of their relative positions.

Positional goods and welfare

The standard maximum welfare conditions can be generalized to include the case of positional goods. Let us assume that we have two goods: one good y, which is 'a priori' defined as a private good, and another good x that has many 'a posteriori' definitions according to the values taken by the fraction t_{ih} of x that individual i consumes when individual h consumes a quantity x_h.

We can, therefore, distinguish among the following three "pure" cases:

1   t_{ih} is equal to 0: this is the standard case of private goods where no individual i consumes fractions of the goods that are also consumed by other individuals h.
2   t_{ih} is positive: this is the case of (semi)public goods where individuals i consume positive fractions of the good consumed by each individual h. When, for all the individuals i and h, t_{ih} is equal to 1, x is a pure public good. When t_{ih} is equal to 1 for some individuals and 0 for other individuals, we have the standard case of local public goods.
3   t_{ih} is negative: in this case x is a (semi)positional good. Other individuals i consume negative fractions when h consumes a positive amount x_h. When t_{ih} is equal to −1 for all the individuals i different from h, we have a case symmetric to the pure public good case and we can label x a pure "pan-positional good." An advantage in a soccer team ranking is an obvious example of a pure pan-positional good. Also positional goods can have the characteristics of "local" positional goods. A particular case of such positional goods are the bi-positional goods where, when h consumes x, only one individual consumes a fraction equal to −1 of the positional good while all the other individuals consume 0 quantities of the good. A master–servant relation can be considered as an example of these types of bi-positional goods.

While pure cases may be interesting, semi-public and semi-positional goods are likely to be more common cases. Moreover one cannot exclude cases of goods that are public goods for a group of individuals and are, at the same time, positional goods for another group of individuals. National security is one of these goods. It is considered to be the classic textbook case of a pure public good in the sense that when an individual h of a nation consumes additional units of national security, the other individual i consumes the same amount ($t_{ih}=1$) of the good. In this sense, the undersupply of national defense would be the outcome of a stateless nation and national defense is the classic public good requiring state intervention. However, the consumption of national security by the individuals of some nation can involve a corresponding consumption of national insecurity by the individuals of another rival nation ($t_{ih}=-1$ for these individuals) and be an example of a pure positional good. For this reason, investments in national security are also said to be characterized by oversupply and can easily degenerate in wasteful arms races.

We can generalize the standard model of welfare economics to deal with all these cases by assuming that each individual i will consume a quantity y_i of the private good and quantities $t_{ih}x_h$ of good x. Let us denote by μ_i the weight given to the utility function of individual i in the social welfare function and by $T(x,y)$ the social transformation function between the two goods.

The maximization problem for society taken as a whole is:

$$\max W = \mu_i U_i(y_i, t_{i1}x_1 + t_{i2}x_2 + \ldots + t_{ii}x_i + t_{ih}x_h + \ldots + t_{in}x_n) +$$
$$+ \Sigma_h \mu_h U_h(y_h, t_{h1}x_1 + t_{h2}x_2 + \ldots + t_{hi}x_i + t_{hh}x_h + \ldots + t_{hn}x_n)$$

$$h = 1,\ldots,n \quad h \neq i$$

subject to $T(x,y)=0$.
We yield the following condition:[4]

$$t_{ii}MRS^i(x_i,y_i) + \Sigma_h t_{hi} MRS^h(t_{hi}x_i,y_h) = MRT(x,y) \tag{1}$$

The condition in equation (1) expresses the most general case and it is also compatible with cases, such as national security, in which t_{hi} is positive for some individuals and negative for other individuals.

In the case of private goods (t_{ih} is equal to 0 and t_{ii} is equal to 1), condition (1) becomes:

$$MRS^i(x_i,y_i) = MRT(x,y). \tag{2}$$

In the case of pure public goods (t_{ih} and t_{ii} are both equal to 1) condition (1) becomes:

$$MRS^i(x_i,y_i) + \Sigma_h MRS^h(x_i,y_h) = MRT(x,y). \tag{3}$$

In the case of bi-positional goods (t_{ih} is equal to -1 for $h=j$ and otherwise equal to 0; t_{ii} is equal to 1) condition (1) becomes:

$$MRS^i(x_i, y_i) - MRS^j(-x_i, y_h) = MRT(x, y). \tag{4}$$

Finally, in the case of pan-positional good (t_{ih} is equal to -1 for all individuals h; t_{ii} is equal to 1) condition (1) becomes:

$$MRS^i(x_i, y_i) - \Sigma_h MRS^h(-x_i, y_h) = MRT(x, y). \tag{5}$$

In the case of private goods the fact that an individual consumes units of the good has no effect on the level of goods consumed by the other individuals who can be excluded from the consumption of the good. By contrast, in the case of pure public goods non-rivalry in consumption and the impossibility of exclusion implies that the marginal rates of substitution of other individuals have to be added to that of the individual consuming the good. Finally, in the case of positional goods, the necessity of including the negative consumption by other individuals implies that their marginal rates of substitution have to be subtracted from the marginal rate of substitution of the individual consuming the (corresponding positive amount of the) good.

A comparison of this extended set of maximum welfare conditions with those of standard competitive markets shows that, while public goods are going to be under-supplied, positional goods are going to be over-supplied (Pagano, 1999). In the first case, there are missing markets to bargain with the individuals who cannot be excluded from a joint consumption of positive amounts of the good. By contrast, in the second case, there are missing markets to bargain with all the individuals who must be included in the corresponding negative consumption.

The role of status and power in economic development

For too long, status and power have been totally overlooked in economic reasoning. They are very important for the issues concerning economic development. One can even argue that the stagnant nature of agrarian societies and the dynamism of capitalist societies are related to this characterization of positional goods. The agrarian societies turn out to have different relations between these "sociological dimensions" (resulting from an enlargement of the space of "economic goods" to values where t_{hi} assumes negative values) and the investments in both human and non-human capital.

In agrarian societies, coercive power and status determine the access to wealth and to education. The positions of individuals in society in terms of power and status are relatively fixed and are usually given by birth. They determine the access of individuals to education and to wealth. The opposite direction of causality (from education and wealth to power and status) is much weaker and it is often explicitly repressed.

In capitalist societies, causation flows often in the opposite direction. The positions of the individuals are not given in terms of power and status while access to education, to occupations and to wealth accumulation is not explicitly forbidden to any individual. While status and power can sometimes favor the access to some occupations and to the accumulation of wealth, this relation is rather weak and is not typical of a capitalist society. The opposite is true. The accumulation of wealth and of human capital becomes now the key that unlocks, for individuals, power and status.

We could simplify the argument by saying that, while in an agrarian society a given distribution of status and power determines the distribution of wealth and the access to education, in a modern capitalist society the acquisition of wealth and education determines the distribution of status and power. In other words, under the two social arrangements, causation between power and status on the one hand and physical and human capital on the other flows in two opposite directions.[5]

In an agrarian society the distribution of power and status is fixed by birth and determines the access to wealth and education. For this reason there is little incentive to innovate and to accumulate wealth and the society is often stuck in stagnant conditions. Here, social scarcity constrains natural scarcity in a strong way because the fixed allocation of power and status positions destroys the incentives that can generate a process of economic development. The accumulation of human and physical capital is constrained by not allowing changes in the distribution of power and status. Thus, in welfare terms we are likely to have an "under-accumulation" of wealth.

In a capitalist society the distribution of power and status is not fixed by birth in the sense that there is no given percentage of blue blood that guarantees a given position in society and a given access to the wealth produced by society. The opposite is rather true. Access to wealth via productive and innovative activities gives access to temporary positions of power and status. However, unlike wealth, power and status are zero-sum goods and the increase in the positive consumption of positional goods by some individuals brings about an increase of negative consumption by some other individuals. Here, social scarcity, far from limiting the incentive to produce and innovate, brings about a drive to accumulate physical and human capital that is often unrelated to the aim of increasing present or future consumption of material wealth. While the desire of the rich may well be limited by the human capacity to enjoy wealth, social scarcity may well bring about an unlimited drive to accumulate. When wealth is only aimed at the acquisition of positional goods, more wealth means a temporary advantage for somebody and a corresponding disadvantage for others that can be cancelled only by accumulating an even greater amount of wealth. The result is an "over-accumulation" of physical capital that is in sharp contrast with the "under-accumulation" that characterizes agrarian societies. A similar argument holds for the accumulation of human capital. While the necessity of keeping the fixed ranks of agrarian societies limits the access of education to their own elites, in capitalist societies the access to education is not only open to everybody but it is one of the means by which one can gain access to socially scarce positions. As it was observed by Hirsch (1976), an over-accumulation of education may take place because only the relative level of education matters for the access to a given social position. Thus, whereas agrarian societies are characterized by the under-accumulation of human and physical capital, modern capitalist societies often tend to over-accumulate both forms of capital.

While this way of reasoning may be too schematic to provide a satisfactory account of asymmetric patterns of economic development, it shows that the relations between positional goods and other economic variables can easily push economic systems towards different directions. More insights in these effects can be gained by considering money, probably the purest case of positional good.

The positional nature of money and of other reputational goods

In real-life market economies, the goods that have a reputation for higher marketability command a higher value. In a world characterized by positive transaction costs, commodities have different degrees of liquidity and individuals are ready to pay more for those commodities that have money-like attributes. Commodities are ranked according to their reputation for liquidity and governments can guarantee this differential reputation also for commodities that have otherwise no use value.[6]

In a globalized world, where commodities move across national borders, differential reputation for liquidity has dramatic self-reinforcing effects. If the liquidity reputation of a commodity is high, it is used as intermediary in a greater number of transactions and, in this way, it further increases its liquidity reputation. Currency represents the prototypical case of this liquidity that is based on differential reputation and is rewarded with more extensive use. While all currencies do service as media of exchange in their home transactions, only a handful of currencies, the reserve and some hard currencies, are most widely used for international transactions. The winners in this fierce competition of differential reputational advantage enjoy the fruits of the cumulative causation between reputation and diffusion for a rather long time.[7] The extreme case of this positional competition among currencies occurs when currency is used as an asset, as opposed to its transactional service alone. In a globalized environment where (financial) capital sloshes across national borders and where exchange rates are free, the currency at the top of the positional ladder is bound to be chosen broadly around the world for asset holding purposes by the elites and the wealthy who wish to buy insurance against devaluation of their liquid assets held in the local currency. And since exchange rates are flexible, superimposing the asset demand for the reserve currency, on top of the transactions demand for servicing the current account, is bound to strain the reserves of the local central bank and lead to devaluation of the local currency. This process of substituting the foreign reserve (hard) currency for the domestic in holding liquid assets constitutes, in turn, a self-fulfilling prophecy. Whether the dollars that were purchased to buy insurance against devaluation are kept under the mattress, or they became part of the capital flight that seeks refuge in a more reputationally advantaged environment, the ensuing devaluation has rewarded the perpetrators of the devaluation. Yotopoulos, in this volume, signals this type of incomplete market because of asymmetric (currency) reputation as a deleterious case of "bad" competition for providing the wrong incentives of undermining the local currency. Currency substitution for the soft currency brings about its devaluation and the expectation of future devaluations fuels even further currency substitution in a cumulative circular causation process.

In the case of currencies positional competition is highly wasteful. The currencies that challenge the winner have to follow rather restrictive policies that compensate the greater liquidity of the dominant currencies with the hardness of their own currency. Even this costly strategy is not available to the weaker currencies. They suffer indirectly from the positional struggle happening at the top and are trapped in a vicious circle of currency substitution and devaluation. While the country of the winning currency is able to obtain for free (against the paper employed in the production of their currency) real goods and services, poor countries have to supply these goods without getting much in exchange as a result of their devalued currencies.

While currencies are perhaps the most extreme case of a reputational good, the decentralization to developing countries of the production of famous Western trademarks can be partially seen in a similar way.[8] Also in this case a reputational positional good (the trademark) is exchanged for standard economic goods.

In general the traditional international trade model must be modified to consider the fact that many goods of the First World, far from competing in traditional competitive markets, trade instead in non-contestable (restricted) markets. They acquire characteristics of monopolistic uniqueness. They become decommodified in the sense that an exclusive right of production is assigned to certain producers while others' economic liberties are severely limited by traditional economic means, such as monopoly power and investments in reputation. Markets also become restricted and non-contestable by the fact that only some agents in the world hold the legal rights to produce certain goods. In this situation, international trade takes place among countries holding very asymmetric legal positions. Some countries specialize in decommodified goods protected by international legal trademarks, while other countries specialize in the standard commodities for which there is a very strong competition in world markets.

The international protection of the trademarks is one aspect of the global dimensions of intellectual property rights that give rise to these asymmetries. We are going to consider other dimensions of asymmetries in the following sections.

Legal relations and positional competition

Building on the work of Hohfeld (1919), Commons (1924) proposed a table that highlights the positional nature of legal relations (Table 2.2).[9]

In this simple two-individual world the set of actions for which x has rights do not only define the duties of y. They define also the remaining actions for

Table 2.2 First order legal relations

Right of x	Duty of y
Exposure of x	Liberty of y

which y has the liberty to act (i.e. the set of actions for which x has no right to interfere and is exposed to the liberties of y). In other words, in this simple framework, the legal relations entail that the boundary between the rights and the exposures of x should coincide with the boundary between the duties and the liberties of y and vice versa.

For instance, ships that are in danger enjoy some legal right to be helped by other ships. This right is necessarily correlated with the duty of other ships not to leave when another ship is in danger. This duty does also necessarily entail that other ships do not have the liberty to leave and that the ship which is in danger is not exposed to the liberty of other ships of refusing help.

In these legal relations there is a social scarcity that is typical of positional goods. The rights of some agents can only be enlarged by restricting the liberties of other agents and 'vice versa' the liberties of other agents can only be enlarged by exposing other individuals to these liberties, that is by limiting their rights to interfere with their actions even when they dislike them.

The positional nature of legal relations implies that rights and liberties can be oversupplied. This is likely to happen if politicians and other agents do not take into account the correlated duties and exposure to liberties that must be jointly consumed with them. Individuals often have conflicting interests about rights and liberties. A disequilibrium may easily arise because the individuals may hold different expectations about their reciprocal legal positions. This disequilibrium is an *ex ante* phenomenon regarding contrasting a priori claims of the individuals. *Ex post* the legal relations that we have considered become identities: one ship x will consume its right to be helped only if the other ship y has fulfilled its duties and x has not been exposed to y's liberty to leave x in trouble. However, *ex ante*, the agents may have different beliefs about their respective rights and liberties. It may well happen that x believes that he has the right to be helped while y believes that she has the liberty to leave.

Wasteful positional competition may well occur when the individuals try to enlarge their own sphere of rights and liberties. This conflict is an inevitable aspect of most societies and, in many cases, it has, even, favored the advancement of civilization. However, legal institutions have also greatly favored human development by helping to find shared solutions to these contradictions and by aligning many *ex ante* expectations about the future interactions of the individuals. According to Hart (1961), law making is a system of second order legal relations (Table 2.3) that involves the power to change and possibly to align the relations that we have just considered in Table 2.2. As Commons (1924) himself, Hayek (1973) and Fuller (1969) also stressed, this change does not involve only the public ordering but also the private sphere. Even in the

Table 2.3 Second order legal relations

Power of x	Liability of y
Disability of x	Immunity of y

private sphere, the employers exercise some power and align the expectations of the rights and the duties that the employees have within their firms (Coase, 1937).

Moreover the second order legal relations entail a symmetric *ex post* correlation between the positions of two (or more) agents. In this case, if the *ex ante* expectations of the agents are *ex post* satisfied, the boundary between the powers and the disabilities of x should coincide with the boundary between the liabilities and the immunities of y (and vice versa).

For instance if public officials have the power to stop me smoking, this implies that I am liable to their orders and I have no immunity against them which implies that the officials have no disability to give me that order. Second order relations can be used to align first order legal positions. If y has no liberty to smoke, this implies that x is not exposed to his liberty. Her right to have y not smoking can be aligned to the corresponding duty of y by resorting to the power of public officials to enforce x's rights. This power implies that y is liable to the authority of the public officials and has no immunity against their actions. When public officials succeed in the alignment of x's and y's legal positions, we have the following Table 2.4 that describes a situation of "legal equilibrium."

In a legal equilibrium the broken line separating the rights and the exposures of x coincides with the power and the disabilities that are granted to public officials (p.o.) to enforce her rights. It also coincides with the broken line separating the duties and the liberties of y, which in turn coincides with the broken line that defines the boundary between the liabilities and the immunities that y has towards public officials.

However, the broken lines of Table 2.4 do not need to be necessarily aligned. In reality a situation of "legal disequilibrium," such as that considered in Table 2.5, may well arise (Pagano, 2006). In Table 2.5, the broken line, defining the boundary between the rights and exposures of x, does not coincide with that defining the boundary between the duties and the liberties of y. In this case the powers of and the liabilities towards public officials fail to correlate the legal

Table 2.4 Legal equilibrium

Power of x via p.o.	↔	Right of x	↔	Duty of y	↔	Liability of y via p.o.
- - - - - -		- - - - - -		- - - - - -		- - - - - -
Disability of x via p.o.	↔	Exposure of x	↔	Liberty of y	↔	Immunity of y via p.o.

Table 2.5 Legal disequilibrium

Power of x via p.o.	Right of x	Duty of y	Liability of y via p.o.
- - - - - - - - - -		- - - - - - - - - -	
Disability of x via p.o.	- - - - - - - - - -	Liberty of y	- - - - - - - - - -
	Exposure of x		Immunity of y via p.o.

entitlements of the two agents. *Ex ante* also the expectations between powers and liabilities can well be divergent and all legal relations can be in disequilibrium. By contrast, a well working legal system, equilibrating the powers and liabilities that agents acquire through public officials, tends also to equilibrate their rights and duties or, in other words, tends to achieve the legal equilibrium considered in Table 2.4.

Because of the positional nature of legal relations, legal disequilibrium tends to be an important real-life phenomenon. From Hobbes onwards, political theory has stressed the waste that is due to positional competition when individuals try to enlarge their rights and powers and limit other individuals' liberties and immunities and vice versa. Unlike standard economic competition, positional competition has no self-equilibrating mechanism and complicated legal institutions are required to limit the tendency of each individual to expand its rights and powers at the expense of the liberties and the rights of the others.

While the Hobbesian tradition has emphasized the vices of unfettered positional competition, the Smithian tradition has emphasized the virtues of competition for the supply of private goods. If legal relations are properly defined, positional competition can be replaced by competition to supply useful private goods. If individuals care about their absolute (not relative) wealth and their legal positions cannot be altered, then they can, only, increase their own welfare by producing goods that are useful for others. In the same vein, the neoclassical Pareto optimality claims of competition can be interpreted as stating the virtues that can be achieved by market equilibria for private goods if the disequilibrium generated by positional competition can be eliminated by the legal system. However, the standard requirement that private property rights are well defined implies itself a complicated set of legal equilibria. The property right is a complex bundle of claim-rights, liberties, powers and immunities.[10] The existence of this bundle of rights involves the establishment of a complicated legal equilibrium. The right of exclusive use of assets by some individuals has to be correlated to the duties of others not to consume these resources; and the liberty that the owners have to choose among different uses of the resources is to be correlated to the exposure of others to this liberty. Moreover, the power that the private owner has to transfer her title has to be aligned to the liability that the other agents have towards these transfers of property; and the immunity of the owner against having his title altered or transferred by the act of another is to be aligned to the disability of others to perform these acts. The economists' term "well-defined property rights" conceals a complicated setting of institutions that are able to equilibrate conflicting legal positions and to overcome wasteful positional competition.[11]

As Romano (Chapter 10) has pointed out, the fact that legal positions have no self-equilibrating tendency implies that countries may widely diverge according to the nature of their institutions. When in some developing countries the equilibrating institutions are lacking, economic competition can easily degenerate into wasteful positional competition. Competition can have asymmetric effects on development in different frameworks.

Global legal positions and intellectual property rights

Legal positions can involve rights, duties and liberties that relate to interactions with our neighbors. They may regard private property rights on well-defined physical objects. In this case, the enforcement can be done "locally" by verifying that others do not interfere with the rights defined over that particular object. The nature of the property of a computer, a car or a house is such that legal relations can be defined at local level. As long as an individual does not interfere with the local space occupied by the objects owned by other people the respect of the property rights of others does not limit her liberties. On the other hand, as long as the objects are not visibly taken away or changed by others an owner can safely assume that his ownership rights are respected. The related legal positions have a local domain geographically limited by the position in space that, at a certain moment in time, is occupied by the material object over which the rights are defined. The material character of the good and its defined location imply a possible overcrowding by potential consumers and are a source of rivalry in consumption. When an individual uses the good, others cannot consume it at the same level and, in many cases, they are likely to consume zero fractions of the good. This circumstance brings such goods very close to the case of the pure private goods considered in the second section of this chapter. In this case, as long as individual i keeps under control the good x in a given physical location, he can be sure that the other individuals are not consuming it and are not violating its (i's) private property. Both the definition and enforcement of private property are specified at local level and they are unlikely to have any relevant implications for the other countries.

Legal positions can also have a global nature. They may involve restrictions for many individuals at various country locations and potentially for all the individuals in the world. Intellectual property rights (IPR), such as they are currently defined by the Trade Related Aspects of Intellectual Property Rights (TRIPS) agreements and enforced by the WTO, have this nature. Their ownership by some individuals involves restrictions for all other individuals. To use the terminology introduced in the second section of this chapter, the global application of IPR has created *pan-positional goods* in the sense that the exclusive rights of an individual or a firm involve for all the individuals duties that are independent of their physical location in the world. The ownership of a house, a car or a field involves some duties for the surrounding individuals who should not interfere with the property rights of the owner and are, only for this reason, limited in the exercise of their liberty. By contrast, the ownership of a piece of intellectual property implies that all the individuals in the world have a duty not to interfere with that legal position. They have to comply with the rights that it creates by limiting their actions in their daily life in multiple ways, irrespective of the country in which they operate. If some individuals happen to produce (or in a relevant case they have already produced) the same knowledge on which the right is granted, their liberty to use the results of their efforts is limited by the monopoly on knowledge that has been already granted to the right holder.[12] The right–duty relation acquires a pan-positional character and the right to exclusive use involves the limitation of liberty of many individuals in many countries.

The strengthening and the extension of IPR have been compared to the enclosure of lands that preceded the industrial revolution.[13] Also in this case, commons were turned into exclusive private property. There is, however, a fundamental difference. In the case of land, the object of privatization was a local common that involved the legal positions of few individuals. By contrast, the privatization of intellectual property changes the legal positions of many individuals and has major implications for the international standings of the various countries.

Here we have a public-positional-good paradox. Because of its non-rival nature, unlike land, knowledge can be used by many individuals without decreasing its value. However, the public-good nature of knowledge makes its privatization much more limiting for the liberty of other individuals. Privatization turns the ownership of a piece of public knowledge into a pan-positional right that involves duties for all the other individuals and has little to do with the traditional rights of exclusive consumption of the owners of material objects. The non-rival symmetric nature of the consumption of knowledge becomes, paradoxically, the cause of a sharp asymmetric division. The domain of the rights of some individuals is greatly extended while the range of the liberties of other individuals is dramatically restricted. To use Jefferson's vivid image, knowledge is like the flame of a candle that can light many other candles without decreasing its own flame.[14] The exclusive ownership of the flame can only mean that others are deprived of the liberty to light their own flames. The rival nature of land implies that its private ownership restricts the liberty of non-owners only in the few cases in which it interferes with the (necessarily local) private uses of a piece of land. The private appropriation of knowledge cannot imply that the liberty of the non-owners should be only limited when it interferes with the consumption of the owners: because of the public nature of knowledge, this never happens. The nature of ownership is here, necessarily, much more restrictive: it means that non-owners have no liberty to "light their taper" and use their own flame without the permission of the owner. This is more restrictive than simply non-decreasing the "flame" of the owner as the analogy with land would imply.

The limitation of the costless liberty to use knowledge is inefficient. It is a well-known piece of economic theory that the non-rival nature of a good should not be the cause of an excessive restriction of liberty but rather a reason to grant to all the individuals the liberty to light their own flames. There is, however, also a well-known argument that can support this restriction: if the person that has borne the cost of lighting the first candle is not compensated for this effort, perhaps the overall flame of knowledge would be weaker. An appropriate incentive for the inventor requires that she becomes the owner of the knowledge that she has discovered and that the liberty of access of others is restricted. However, this restriction is always costly: after the first discovery, many other candles could have been lighted, in some cases also independently, without decreasing the flame of the first candle.

The cost of depriving other candles of the flame increases when the knowledge is "basic" in the sense that it comes upstream in the production of other knowledge or it is "complementary" to other pieces of knowledge. For this reason, it is undesirable to impose private property restrictions to farther upstream or basic knowledge. Since early times, public institutions like universities have provided alternative systems of compensating the producers of open-access science. Publications, based on peer reviews, and careers and prizes that are based on these publications, are the most typical types of incentives offered by universities to promote effort and universal disclosure of knowledge. Unsurprisingly, a great deal of the funding of these institutions has traditionally come from public sources.

Where should one draw the line between more upstream knowledge produced and freely transmitted by universities and the more downstream knowledge that can be privately owned by its discoverers? There is no precise answer to this question but, wherever the line lies, it will change when we move from a closed economy, ruled by one single state, to an open economy with many independent states.

A world government (or, in similar way, a state isolated from the world economy) could try to draw the line between the production of "open access knowledge" (funded by tax revenue) and the production of "closed access knowledge" (that is left to the profit motive of private firms) in such a way as to maximize the benefits accruing to its citizens.

However, the real economy is different. No national state can be isolated from the world economy and no world government exists. In this framework, each national state will realize that its citizens get only a fraction of the benefits of the investments in public knowledge while some of them (and all through national taxation) can gain the full benefit of the investments in privately-owned knowledge because the benefits from the latter are not shared with the citizens of the other countries. Thus, in an integrated world economy, characterized by internationally enforced IPR, national states have an incentive to increase the number of "closed access science" research projects over which private property rights are defined and to move upstream the line that separates them from the "open access science" research projects. Institutions, producing and diffusing public knowledge, are increasingly seen as a "waste of money" and there is a widespread tendency to decrease their funding. For the same reason, the same institutions (universities in the first place) are also under severe pressure to betray their nature of institutions mainly dedicated to the production and diffusion of public open-access knowledge and are pushed towards the production of private intellectual property.

Basic knowledge should be a global common. However, the presence of TRIPS and the absence of global cooperation have created an environment with global intellectual private property rights and with local national funding for public research. As a result, we face an inefficient over-development of private knowledge and a corresponding under-development of public knowledge, which necessarily leads to an asymmetric development of the poor, as compared to the rich areas of the world. The increasing privatization of knowledge, which is done by the most advanced countries, turns public goods, shared by all humankind, into private goods characterized by a pan-positional legal right that limits the liberties of all other individuals in the world. In this way, equal and unrestricted global liberties to enjoy the benefits of public goods are replaced by global duties, constraining the development of local systems of knowledge, and creating sharp asymmetries in the paths of development of the different countries.

As the New Property Rights approach has shown (Hart, 1995), private property of the means of production has important incentive effects. A frictionless market for the means of production should imply that this property goes to the most capable individuals. However, the market is far from being frictionless and individuals are usually wealth constrained. For this reason, causation may well work, in a self-reinforcing manner, also in the opposite direction: the owners of the means of production have a greater incentive to develop their capabilities and, for this reason, tend to become the best owners. This incentive effect of ownership is much stronger for intellectual property because the right to exclude involves a restriction of the liberty of all the other individuals to replicate similar means of production (Pagano and Rossi, 2004).

In the case of a machine, an individual, who has learnt to work and possibly to innovate with skills that are partially specific to the machine, is only partially damaged if he is deprived of its use. He keeps the liberty to work with other machines or to build identical machines. The damage is more relevant in the case of an individual who has acquired skills that are specific to a piece of intellectual property and he is denied the access to this piece. The nature of intellectual property implies that he does not keep the liberty to work with or to "rediscover" a similar piece of knowledge. The legal position, concerning an IPR, is a global one and involves a pan-positional right to limit the access of all individuals to the use of all the similar pieces of knowledge, including those that are independently developed. Turning a public good like knowledge into a private good transforms a universal unlimited liberty into an asymmetric legal position limiting non-owners' freedom well beyond the restrictions that stem from the property rights defined on traditional rival goods.

In the current era of globalization, and within the framework of international economic policy, private intellectual property rights have had a major role in creating the systematic conditions for asymmetric global development that favors the developed countries at the expense of the poor. Advanced countries monopolize the frontier of knowledge. Far from sustaining the effort for the provision of a public good that allows the catch-up of other countries, they enjoy a self-reinforcing process of development. The monopolistic ownership of intellectual property encourages the investment in the skills necessary to improve these pieces of knowledge and the skills that are developed make it even more convenient to acquire and produce private knowledge. By contrast, other countries may be trapped in an asymmetric vicious circle of (under-)development where the lack of intellectual property discourages the acquisition of skills and the lack of skills discourages the acquisition of intellectual property.

While the countries at the frontier of knowledge advocate free trade policies, they themselves are specializing in goods whose ownership almost by definition involves an internationally enforced barrier to the entry for other firms. Countries specializing in IPR enjoy a legal protection barrier that works well beyond national boundaries and extends to include the whole world.[15] For this reason they can easily advocate the simultaneous enforcement of open markets and IPR which is the implicit constitution of WTO. This means free trade for the commodities, exported by developing countries, and closed markets, protected by IPR at world level, for the "decommodified" goods produced by the "First World" countries (Yotopoulos, Chapter 1). The global legal positions, associated to private intellectual property create and reinforce the conditions for an increasing asymmetry in the process of development.

Conclusion

The optimistic view of the process of economic development is usually grounded on economic reasoning focusing on the distinction between public and private goods. Global public goods, like knowledge, imply opportunities for symmetric development and for a distribution of costs favoring the less developed countries. Moreover, since Ricardo, economic theories have emphasized the mutual advantages of trade involving private goods.

Taking exception to the optimistic outcomes of conventional theories of trade and development by referring to the standard economic space of public and private goods is familiar in the literature. In this chapter, I have extended the analysis of the approach to free trade as a trigger of growth and development by including positional goods that constitute a large and rapidly increasing share of trade under globalization. Free trade in conventional commodities, as practiced in the nineteenth century version of globalization, is very different from the current profile of trade, that involves a significant and fast increasing component of decommodified goods and services that in many cases enjoy the protection of international property rights.

In the distinction between these two patterns of trade, we identify a tendency of free trade to induce further development of modern capitalist societies while it perpetuates underdevelopment in the rest of the world. The existence of reputational goods can explain these types of unequal exchanges and, in particular, those occurring between countries that have hard currencies with high international reputation and the rest of the countries that have soft currencies that are used mostly for within-the-country transactions. Moreover, positional competition, due to incompletely structured legal relations, can be one of the causes of the asymmetric effects that competition can have within different countries.

Finally, the global privatization of knowledge involves a dramatic shift away from public goods that allows an equal liberty of use in all countries, to a system of pan-positional rights that restricts the liberty of use all over the world and creates a strong asymmetry between countries specializing in decommodified (often IPR-protected) production and the developing world that relies largely on the trade of standardized commodities.

Notes

1 I am very grateful to Sam Bowles, Pan Yotopoulos, Donato Romano and Matteo Rizzolli for their very useful comments.
2 On different concepts of power see Bowles *et al.* (1999), Bowles and Gintis (1999) and Pagano (1999).
3 This definition is given in Pagano (1999). A different definition, based on rank, is given by Frank (1985). Frank's definition is focused on the definition of status and is not also related to the definition of the exercise of power.
4 For a more detailed analysis, see Pagano (1999).
5 This section draws on Gellner contributions (1983, 1998, 1999). For an account of Gellner's work see Pagano (2003).
6 The importance of the relative status that commodities have in terms of liquidity disappears in abstract theoretical constructions, such as the Arrow-Debreu model, where all goods are equally liquid and can be used as means of exchange. The absence of a specific good with the role of money does not imply that the Arrow-Debreu model is a barter economy. In barter economies, no commodity is liquid and exchange requires a double coincidence of wants. By contrast, the Arrow-Debreu model applies in a "super-monetary economy" where all goods are perfectly liquid and have got the status of money. In order to get closer to reality, the real issue is not the "introduction of money" into general equilibrium but it is rather the elimination of the too many money-like commodities existing in this theoretical construction.
7 This point, as well as much of this section, draws from the work of Yotopoulos (1996), Yotopoulos (Chapter 1) and Sawada and Yotopoulos (Chapter 3).
8 Also on this point, see Yotopoulos (Chapter 1).
9 For a modern analytical defense of Hohfeld, see Kramer (2001).
10 For instance, a landowner typically enjoys the claim-right that others do not trespass his land boundaries, the liberty to walk on his land, the powers to transfer title to others, and the act of immunity against having his title altered or transferred by the act of another (Simmonds, 1986).
11 Nicita *et al.* (2006a) show how, while there has been much literature on incomplete contracts, many rich consequences stem from incomplete property.
12 An account of cases in which traditional knowledge is stolen by multinationals is given by Shiva (2001).
13 For instance, see Shiva (2001: 44–8).

14 "He who receives an idea from me, receives instruction himself without lessening mine; as he who lights his taper at mine, receives light without darkening me." Thomas Jefferson, letter to Isaac McPherson, "No Patents on Ideas," 13 August 1813. Sometimes paraphrased as "Knowledge is like a candle. Even as it lights a new candle, the strength of the original flame is not diminished."

15 On the relation between IPR and anti-trust law in an incomplete property rights framework see Nicita *et al.* (2006b).

References

Bowles, Samuel and Herbert Gintis (1999), "Power in Competitive Exchange." In Samuel Bowles, Maurizio Franzini and Ugo Pagano, eds, *The Politics and the Economics of Power.* London: Routledge, pp. 13–31.

Bowles, Samuel, Maurizio Franzini and Ugo Pagano (1999), "Introduction: Trespassing the Boundaries of Politics and Economics." In Samuel Bowles, Maurizio Franzini and Ugo Pagano, eds, *The Politics and the Economics of Power.* London: Routledge, pp. 1–11.

Coase, Ronald H. (1937), "The Nature of the Firm," *Economica*, 4 (16): 386–405.

Commons, John R. (1924), *Legal Foundations of Capitalism.* Clifton: Augustus M. Kelley Publishers.

Frank, Robert H. (1985), "The Demand for Unobservable and Other Non-positional Goods," *American Economic Review*, 75 (1): 101–16.

Fuller, Lon L. (1969), *The Morality of Law.* New Haven and London: Yale University Press.

Gellner, Ernest (1983), *Nations and Nationalism.* Oxford: Blackwell.

Gellner, Ernest (1998), *Nationalism.* London: Phoenix.

Gellner, Ernest (1999), "The Coming of Nationalism, and Its Interpretation. The Myths of Nation and Class." In Samuel Bowles, Maurizio Franzini and Ugo Pagano, eds, *The Politics and the Economics of Power.* London: Routledge, pp. 179–224.

Hart, Herbert L.A. (1961), *The Concept of Law.* Oxford: Clarendon.

Hart, Oliver D. (1995), *Firms, Contracts and Financial Structure.* Oxford: Clarendon.

Hayek, Friedrich (1973), *Law, Legislation and Liberty.* Chicago: University of Chicago Press.

Hirsch, Fred (1976), *Social Limits to Growth.* Cambridge, MA: Harvard University Press.

Hohfeld, Wesley N. (1919), *Fundamental Legal Conceptions.* New Haven and London: Yale University Press.

Kramer, Matthew H. (2001), "Getting Rights Right." In Matthew H. Kramer, ed., *Rights, Wrongs and Responsibilities.* Basingstoke and New York: Palgrave, pp. 28–95.

Nicita, Antonio, Matteo Rizzolli and Maria Alessandra Rossi (2006a), "Towards a Theory of Incomplete Property Rights." University of Siena. Mimeo.

Nicita, Antonio, Matteo Rizzolli and Maria Alessandra Rossi (2006b), "IP Law and Antitrust Law Complementarity When Property Rights Are Incomplete." University of Siena, Italy. Mimeo.

Pagano, Ugo (1999), "Is Power an Economic Good? Notes on Social Scarcity and the Economics of Positional Goods." In Samuel Bowles, Maurizio Franzini and Ugo Pagano, eds, *The Politics and the Economics of Power.* London: Routledge, pp. 63–84.

Pagano, Ugo (2003), "Nationalism, Development and Integration: The Political Economy of Ernest Gellner," *Cambridge Journal of Economics*, 27 (5): 623–46.

Pagano, Ugo (2006), "Legal Positions and Institutional Complementarities." In Fabrizio

Cafaggi, Antonio Nicita and Ugo Pagano, eds, *Legal Orderings and Economic Institutions*. London and New York: Routledge, pp. 54–83.

Pagano, Ugo and Maria Alessandra Rossi (2004), "Incomplete Contracts, Intellectual Property and Institutional Complementarities," *European Journal of Law and Economics*, 18 (1): 55–76.

Shiva, Vandana (2001), *Protect or Plunder? Understanding Intellectual Property Rights*. London and New York: Zed Books.

Simmonds, Nigel E. (1986), *Central Issues in Jurisprudence. Justice, Law and Rights*. London: Sweet & Maxwell.

Veblen, Thorstein (1899; 1953), *The Theory of the Leisure Class*. New York: Viking Press.

Yotopoulos, Pan A. (1996), *Exchange Rate Parity for Trade and Development: Theory, Tests, and Case Studies*. Cambridge and New York: Cambridge University Press.

3 Growth and poverty reduction under globalization

The systematic impact of currency substitution and exchange rate misalignment[1]

Yasuyuki Sawada and Pan A. Yotopoulos

Introduction

The Millennium Declaration of the United Nations signed by 189 countries, including 147 heads of state, on 8 September 2000, led to the Millennium Development Goals (MDGs). The MDGs formalize the international community's unprecedented agreement on the development goals by 2015 with explicit numerical targets for reducing poverty in the world. The first goal of MDGs is to eradicate extreme poverty and hunger, with the interim explicit target of decreasing by 2015 the extent of poverty by one half, defined as halving the proportion of people whose income is less than one dollar a day, as compared to the same proportion in 1990. With the 1990 baseline for the head count ratio being 27.94 percent of the total, the targeted ratio of a-dollar-a-day for MDGs corresponds to 13.97 percent of the world's population (cf. World Bank, 2004).

The focus of this chapter is on the feasibility of achieving this target and on the appropriate policy instruments for doing so. While direct poverty reduction programs may be effective, their costs could become prohibitive if they were targeted at the communities that are the poorest, and therefore the less easily accessible (Besley and Burgess, 2003). In skirting this dilemma, a good part of the literature advocates a higher rate of economic growth as an alternative and a more effective approach toward a comprehensive poverty reduction program. The empirical literature that supports this view rests on a strong and statistically significant relationship between macroeconomic growth and poverty reduction (Ravallion, 2001; Dollar and Kraay, 2002; Besley and Burgess, 2003).

Globalization, defined as the cross-national integration and interdependence of the world's markets of goods, labor and finance, as well as businesses and cultures, is generally considered an important driving force for enhancing economic growth (World Bank, 2002). This causality, by implication, makes economic growth an effective instrument for reducing poverty in developing countries (Dollar and Kraay, 2002).

The existing literature identifies different channels that lead from globalization to economic growth. First, there is a direct positive relationship between the trade openness of a country and its economic growth (Harrison, 1996; Dollar and Kraay, 2004). Second, foreign direct investment (FDI) has been found to be an important venue for transferring technology; therefore FDI can contribute relatively more to growth than domestic investment. This positive nexus between FDI and growth works especially well when the host economy is endowed with sufficient absorptive capacity for assimilating advanced technologies (Borenzstein *et al.*, 1998). Finally, not only direct investments across countries but also indirect capital flows might affect growth positively.

These virtuous synergies between globalization and growth are subject to the caveats of misalignment of exchange rates. Harrison (1996) and World Bank (1991) found that a black market premium in foreign exchange rates is negatively associated with growth. This observation leads to the implication that chronic misalignment in the exchange rate has been a major source of slow growth in Africa and Latin America through deterring smooth flows of capital, while prudent macroeconomic, trade and exchange rate policies have fostered growth in Asia (Dollar, 1992; Edwards, 1988; Ghura and Grennes, 1993; Rodrik, 1994).

This chapter evaluates the role of economic growth under globalization in achieving the first target of the MDGs, i.e. of decreasing by one-half the headcount of poverty in the world. The second section of the chapter approaches economic growth as the one important instrument that can serve in achieving the above target. We extend the concept of "exit time" of Kanbur (1987) and Morduch (1998) to reach a quantitative assessment of the success or failure of the MDGs by comparing the requisite rate of growth for the target group to exit poverty with the historical growth trajectory (of the years 1960–90) for each country in question. The inevitable result is that more robust growth is necessary for the success of the MDGs as compared to the historical record of growth.

The finding in the second section of the chapter that "growth as usual" could not deliver the MDGs is challenging. In the least it makes a compelling case for the re-examination of the mechanics of growth. The novelty in the third section of the chapter is that it addresses the mechanics of growth by extending the truncated treatment of the subject in the literature of exchange rate misalignment. This is done by accounting for systematic deviations of nominal exchange rates from their purchasing power parity levels and considering the possibility that such deviations could cause systematic distortions in resource allocation leading to growth debacles.[2] Moreover, these same deviations could provoke severe instabilities of the international macroeconomic system, and especially so in the environment of ongoing globalization. Despite the compelling reasons that militate for chronic exchange rate misalignments having strongly negative effects on a country's rate of growth, there is relatively little empirical evidence on the subject, with the only possible exception being the systematic cross-country analysis conducted by Yotopoulos (1996). In an attempt to fill in this gap in the literature we employ the Yotopoulos and Sawada (2006) empirical formulation of chronic misalignment in nominal exchange rates, in order to reassess indirectly the prospects of the target countries for achieving the requisite rates of economic growth for meeting the first MDGs target, given the extant realities of their exchange rate regimes.

In an effort to identify more closely the specific source of exchange rate misalignment we formulate in the fourth section of the chapter, the currency substitution hypothesis that is consistent with the severe exchange rate misalignment and with the faltering of growth that we observe in many developing countries during the current era of globalization.

The final section provides the conclusion on the MDGs and assesses the policy approaches that could increase growth by alleviating the severe negative impact that exchange rate misalignment was found to have on achieving the rates of growth requisite to reach these targets.

The role of economic growth in reducing poverty

In investigating the role of macroeconomic growth in reducing poverty, the well-known article by Dollar and Kraay (2002) showed that economic growth is a necessary condition to achieve poverty reduction. Besley and Burgess (2003) and Ravallion (2001) estimated the poverty reduction elasticity with respect to income by using cross-country data and a micro data set, respectively. Both studies found that the elasticity is significantly negative, although the actual estimates diverged from -0.73 for Besley and Burgess (2003) to -2.50 for Ravallion (2001).

Seeing that these approaches will not provide us with practically relevant parameter estimates for each of the target countries, we employ alternatively the concept of "exit time" of Kanbur (1987) and Morduch (1998). Using this approach we can estimate the growth rate that is required for each country to achieve the first target of MDGs and we compare the result with the country's historical trajectory of growth. By doing so, we will be able to analyze how country-specific economic growth can deliver as the prime actor in effectively achieving poverty reduction.

The exit time, t, is given by the time a person i with income y_i below poverty line z, will exit the poverty situation (Morduch, 1998):

$$t_i = \frac{\ln(z) - \ln(y_i)}{\ln(1 + g)}, \tag{1}$$

where g is the growth rate of income of this person. Kanbur (1987) introduced the exit time of the "average poor" (superscript a) with mean income of the poor, μ_P:

$$t_i^a = \frac{\ln(z) - \ln(\mu_P)}{\ln(1 + g^a)}. \tag{2}$$

Let $P(\alpha)$ be the poverty measure as per Foster *et al.* (1984) where $P(0)$ and $P(1)$ are the poverty headcount ratio and the poverty gap measure, respectively.

Ravallion *et al.* (1991) showed that $P(1)=[1-(\mu_P/z)]P(0)$. Then equation (2) can be rewritten as:

$$t_i^a = \frac{\ln[P(0)] - \ln[P(0) - P(1)]}{\ln(1 + g^a)}. \tag{3}$$

Similarly, with the median income of the poor, μ_m, Morduch (1998) showed that the time to halve the number of the poor can be computed by:

$$t_i^m = \frac{\ln(z) - \ln(\mu_m)}{\ln(1 + g^m)}. \tag{4}$$

By using equation (3), we can compute the required income growth rate for the average poor in 1990 to exit poverty by year 2015:

$$g^a = \exp\left[\frac{\ln(P(0)) - \ln(P(0) - P(1))}{25}\right] - 1. \tag{5}$$

Tables 3.1 and 3.2 show the required economic growth rates as computed from equation (5) using the Global Poverty Monitoring database of the World Bank. Note that the required growth rate for the median poor in 1990 to exit poverty by 2015 based on equation (4) can be interpreted as the required growth rate for the first target of MDGs. Yet, using the fact that $\mu_P < \mu_m$ in the lower tail of a uni-modal income distribution function, it is straightforward to show that this required growth rate based on the concept of the average exit time can be interpreted as the upper bound of the required growth rate to achieve the first target of MDGs (Sawada, 2004).

Our results in Table 3.1 suggest that about one-half of the countries whose per capita income is above US$2,000 can achieve the first target of MDGs by maintaining their historical levels of economic growth rate (1960–90). The same successful-by-one-half record is maintained in Table 3.2 for the countries that had per capita income in year 1990 between US$1,000 and US$2,000. In the same table the second and poorest cohort of countries with per capita income below US$1,000 is a complete failure; no country in this group will be able to reach the first target of MDGs by replicating its past growth record. These findings highlight the importance of accelerating economic growth, particularly for the poorest economies, as a necessary condition of effective poverty reduction.

Table 3.3 again utilizes the exit time concept to compute the required growth rate by region, using the Global Poverty Monitoring data set (World Bank, 2004). The results are comparable with the figures computed by Besley and Burgess (2003), also shown in Table 3.3.

In general, the exit time-based estimates give lower required annual per capita growth rates than the Besley–Burgess estimates except for the Eastern Europe and Central Asia regions. Moreover, according to the same table, growth

Table 3.1 Required annual income growth rate (1990–2015) for exit from poverty by 2015 of an average poor person in 1990 (country per capita income in 1990 > US$2,000)

Country	Per capita income in 1990	(A) Average annual per capita growth rate, 1960–90	(B) Required growth rate	If (B) > (A) = 1 otherwise = 0
Algeria	2,604.88	0.012	0.016	1
Belarus	4,367.79	0.022	0.005	0
Botswana	4,739.68	0.071	0.019	0
Brazil	5,353.13	0.027	0.014	0
Chile	4,810.04	0.017	0.009	0
Colombia	4,714.73	0.021	0.012	0
Costa Rica	5,302.26	0.014	0.020	1
Dominican Republic	3,247.68	0.022	0.009	0
Egypt, Arab Rep.	2,416.04	0.032	0.006	0
El Salvador	2,969.62	0.002	0.029	1
Estonia	8,213.16	0.010	0.014	1
Guatemala	2,847.20	0.012	0.029	1
Honduras	2,062.22	0.009	0.025	1
Jamaica	3,294.35	0.008	0.011	1
Jordan	3,218.61	0.097	0.010	0
Kazakhstan	4,700.79	−0.012	0.002	1
Kyrgyz Republic	2,010.47	0.033	0.026	0
Lithuania	9,134.65	0.051	0.009	0
Mexico	6,197.49	0.021	0.017	0
Moldova	3,089.15	−0.014	0.008	1
Morocco	2,780.90	0.020	0.008	0
Namibia	4,292.65	−0.014	0.021	1
Panama	3,708.73	0.018	0.025	1
Paraguay	3,871.28	0.023	0.010	0
Peru	3,203.10	0.001	0.012	1
Philippines	3,210.93	0.014	0.010	0
Poland	6,083.60	–	0.017	0
Romania	5,412.85	0.017	0.022	1
Russian Federation	8,593.73	0.036	0.012	0
South Africa	8,266.22	0.012	0.007	0
Thailand	3,697.77	0.047	0.010	0
Trinidad and Tobago	5,810.69	0.025	0.013	0
Tunisia	3,755.41	0.029	0.012	0
Turkey	4,332.63	0.021	0.011	0
Turkmenistan	5,370.00	−0.002	0.013	1
Ukraine	7,046.31	−0.004	0.014	1
Uruguay	9,557.52	0.007	0.023	1
Uzbekistan	–	0.015	0.006	0
Venezuela, RB	4,812.02	−0.003	0.010	1
Zimbabwe	2,249.26	0.013	0.015	1

performance that tracks a country's past trajectory will reach unambiguously the first MDGs target only in the group of Asia-Pacific and conceivably also in the Middle East and North Africa group. Therefore, Table 3.3 also reinforces our conclusion of the need for more robust economic growth, as compared to the targeted countries' growth records (1960–90), and especially so for the poorest countries in the sample.

Table 3.2 Required annual income growth rate (1990–2015) for exit from poverty by 2015 of an average poor person in 1990 (country per capita income in 1990 ≤ $2,000)

Country	Per capita income in 1990	(A) Average annual per capita growth rate, 1960–90	(B) Required growth rate	If (B) > (A) = 1 otherwise = 0
US$1,000 ≤ Per capita income in 1990 ≤ US$2,000				
Bolivia	1,740.00	0.000	0.009	1
Central African Republic	1,031.58	−0.007	0.037	1
China	1,331.66	0.037	0.014	0
Cote d'Ivoire	1,497.13	0.009	0.008	0
Ecuador	1,445.87	0.021	0.019	0
Gambia	1,502.09	0.008	0.023	1
Ghana	1,336.06	−0.008	0.010	1
India	1,397.11	0.018	0.014	0
Indonesia	1,875.25	0.037	0.008	0
Lesotho	1,055.13	0.031	0.024	0
Mauritania	1,168.82	0.013	0.023	1
Mongolia	1,606.72	0.023	0.010	0
Nicaragua	1,721.24	−0.011	0.022	1
Pakistan	1,380.35	0.029	0.013	0
Senegal	1,154.82	−0.005	0.023	1
Sri Lanka	1,956.03	0.024	0.007	0
Per capita income in 1990 ≤ US$1,000				
Bangladesh	970.12	0.008	0.011	1
Burkina Faso	631.16	0.009	0.022	1
Ethiopia	479.69	−0.016	0.012	1
Kenya	940.59	0.018	0.019	1
Madagascar	783.78	−0.011	0.021	1
Mali	561.13	0.001	0.020	1
Nepal	846.96	0.007	0.012	1
Niger	732.83	−0.018	0.028	1
Sierra Leone	835.44	0.008	0.051	1
Tanzania	436.87	0.014	0.028	1
Uganda	750.47	0.007	0.018	1
Zambia	805.57	−0.010	0.031	1

Table 3.3 Growth and poverty reduction, 1990–2015 (percent)

	World	Asia and Pacific	Eastern Europe and Central Asia	Latin America and Caribbean	Middle East and North Africa	South Asia	Sub-Saharan Africa
Sawada's exit time required annual per capita economic growth rate to achieve target #1[a]	1.5	1.3	4.1	1.8	0.9	1.3	2.3
Besley and Burgess's required annual per capita economic growth rate to achieve target #1[b]	3.8	2.7	2.4	3.8	3.8	4.7	5.6
Average annual per capita growth rate, 1960–90[b]	1.7	3.3	2.0	1.3	4.3	1.9	0.2

Notes
a Adapted from Sawada (2004).
b Adapted from Besley and Burgess (2003: Table 2, p. 8).

Chronic exchange rate misalignments and economic growth

The previous section lays heavy responsibility for achieving the first target of MDGs on the acceleration of growth in developing countries. A timely acceleration of growth becomes especially critical for the countries at the low end of the distribution, those with GDP per capita less than US$1,000. What are the chances that adequate growth records can be achieved to reach the MDGs? Given the strong results in the literature linking development failures to exchange rate misalignment, such as Dollar (1992), Edwards (1988), Ghura and Grennes (1993), Rodrik (1994) and Yotopoulos (1996), this section delves into the subtleties of the relationship between exchange rate misalignment and growth. The innovation in this chapter is the adoption of a new conceptual framework for measuring exchange rate misalignment and identifying its origin. Why is this necessary?

Misalignment is normally defined as the systematic deviation of the nominal exchange rate (NER) from purchasing power parity (PPP), or in a looser formulation its deviation from the real exchange rate (RER). The relationship between the nominal and the real exchange rate has always been a challenge to economists. The attempt to untie this Gordian Knot dates to the writings of Cassel (1921) and Keynes (1923) who were interpreting the experience of the first globalization (roughly between 1870 and 1914). Only in the recent years of the second globalization have economists adopted an over-simplified conventional framework and have considered the Knot non-existent (Yotopoulos, 1996: Ch. 5).

The standard short cut on which the measurement of exchange rate misalignment is based involves the comparison of a country's i real price level (RPL) at time t with that of the numeraire country, US, in some form of the equation (6):

$$RPL(i,t) = \frac{1}{e(i,t)} \left[\frac{P(i,t)}{P(US,t)} \right], \tag{6}$$

where e and P represent a country's nominal exchange rate and overall price level, respectively.[3] For a number of reasons this formulation is unsatisfactory, the most important being that in cross-country comparisons where exchange rates are involved, any aggregate index that intends to capture relative price levels, while totally disregarding the distinction between tradables and non-tradables, is misleading and deficient. As an example, a change in the exchange rate, whether appreciation or devaluation, will have more (or less) profound effects in the economy, and in the allocative function of prices, depending on the structure of the economy, the level of income, the size of the tradable and the non-tradable sector, and so on. Even worse, since a "successful devaluation" implies an increase in the price of tradables and a corresponding decrease in the relative price of non-tradables (in units of the home currency), in the best of all worlds not much would be registered in equation (6) that reflects a change in the price index or the PPP.

"Country specificity" that is totally absent from the above equation can be introduced by decomposing the price index into its two components, P_T and P_N, denoting prices of tradables and non-tradables, respectively (Yotopoulos, 1996: Ch. 6). As an alternative, and for economy of data and computation, nominal exchange rate misalignment can be captured readily with the following decomposition (Yotopoulos and Sawada, 2006):

$$\frac{1}{e(i,t)} = \left[\frac{P_T(US,t)}{P_T(i,t)}\right]u(t)\varepsilon(i)w(i,t). \tag{7}$$

In equation (7), P_T, is the price of tradables and the price ratio, $P_T(i,t)/P_T(US,t)$, represents the purchasing power parity in prices of tradables. Note that the misalignment of NER from PPP has been decomposed into a common aggregate time-specific component, $u(t)$, a country-specific time-invariant fixed component (i.e. country fixed effects), $\varepsilon(i)$, and another time-variant random component, $w(i,t)$. The time-specific term, $u(t)$, can be interpreted broadly as representing the time trend of exchange rate parity fluctuations of the US dollar.[4] The variable $\varepsilon(i)$ represents the degree of the country-specific *chronic misalignment of the nominal exchange rate*, NER, which can be attributed to systematic factors, such as country-specific structural characteristics of an economy, chronic market imperfections, transaction costs, and/or government (dis)intervention in the foreign exchange market in country i. In other words, $\varepsilon(i)$ is a long-term, (i.e. chronic) deviation of NER from PPP.

The variable $\varepsilon(i)$ is intended to capture the effect of any systematic characteristics of (developing) countries that bear on exchange rate misalignment and are not specifically accounted for in equation (6). The Ricardo principle, also known as the Samuelson-Balassa equation, states that the relative prices of tradables to non-tradables decrease in the process of development (Ricardo, 1817; Balassa, 1964; Samuelson, 1964). This systematic relationship, whether it originates in productivity differentials (as per Ricardo) or in factor proportions (as per Samuelson or Balassa) constitutes a structural characteristic of an open economy in the process of development. The systematic component of the relationship is almost axiomatic. Whether as a result of labor being cheap in low-income countries (the productivity approach), or labor being plentiful in relation to capital (the factor proportions approach), the prices of non-tradables relative to tradables tend to be cheap in developing countries and increase as development occurs. By the same process, not only the internal terms of trade (the real exchange rate) improve, but the law of one price dictates that the prices of tradables tend to converge across countries. The result of these two effects should be that misalignments, defined as deviations of the real exchange rate (formed in the price domain of tradables and non-tradables) from the nominal exchange rate (formed in the domain of tradables alone) are likely to be smaller in the developed countries and greater in the developing ones.

The discussion of the Ricardo principle above has an important corollary for the measurement of exchange rate misalignments. Controlling for the nominal exchange rate, the extent of exchange rate misalignment in a specific case is determined by the structural characteristics of a country at a certain stage of development. As a result, misalignment cannot be properly assessed unless the relative prices of both the tradables and the non-tradables are accounted for in the method of measurement. Looking at it in another way, this means that the impact of a change in the nominal exchange rate on the relative prices of tradables and non-tradables is muffled in developed countries where these prices are more closely aligned; in developing countries, on the other hand, the attendant reallocation of resources as a result of the same change in the exchange rate can be sizeable – and what is worse, it can become a potent factor driving the systematic *mis*allocation of resources!

We implement the Yotopoulos and Sawada (2006) procedure in specifying equation (7) for measuring the chronic NER deviation, $\varepsilon(i)$. We use the familiar cross-country data set of Heston *et al.* (2002), for 153 countries, covering a span of 20 years, from 1980 to 2000. We then estimate a standard cross-county growth regression by adding the measure of chronic NER deviation as an additional variable.

In the estimated growth regression in Table 3.4 the dependent variable is the average annual growth rate of real GDP per capita between 1980 and 2000. The variable that measures the chronic exchange rate misalignment comes from the implementation of equation (7) as above. We use the dummy variable for trade openness developed by Sachs and Warner (1995) and we create an openness/exchange-rate-misalignment interaction variable. We hypothesize that the negative impact of exchange rate misalignment on growth is more severe when a country is more open on the external account and thus becomes susceptible to changes in the global economy. Accordingly, the key variable we are interested in is the interaction term of the chronic exchange rate misalignment and openness. The rest of the independent variables in the table are traditional in growth regressions. The data of real GDP per capita are extracted from Heston *et al.* (2002). Following Burnside and Dollar (2000), we consider the policy quality index as formed by a linear combination of the budget surplus, the inflation rate and the trade openness. We add the government share of per capita GDP as another variable. The dummy variables for African, Latin American and high-performing East Asian Countries are included in order to mitigate an omitted variable bias from unobserved heterogeneity.

Table 3.4 presents the estimated results using OLS with White's heteroskedasticity-consistent standard errors. The estimates confirm the results already familiar in the literature. The per capita income and the exchange rate misalignment measure have a negative (but non-significant) impact on growth; the coefficient for the policy quality index is positive and significant; the country dummies for regional groupings have all (highly) significant coefficients, negative for Africa and South America and positive for the high-performing East Asian countries. These results are canonical and unassailable: the coefficients have the expected signs and are consistent with previously estimated cross-country growth regressions such as the studies listed in Durlauf and Quah (1999).

Table 3.4 Growth and exchange rate misalignments

	(1)	*(2)*	*(3)*	*(4)*
Per capita real GDP (in US$1,000,000)	−0.450 (1.52)	−0.420 (1.30)	−0.249 (0.78)	−0.294 (0.92)
Measure of chronic exchange rate misalignments	−0.001 (0.65)	−0.0019 (0.71)	−0.002 (0.79)	−0.002 (0.83)
Measure of chronic exchange rate misalignments × openness		−0.015 (5.12)***	−0.013 (4.38)***	−0.013 (4.29)***
Policy index (in 1,000)			0.028 (1.91)*	0.026 (1.63)
Government share of per capita real GDP				−0.0001 (0.54)
Africa	−0.030 (5.65)***	−0.031 (5.53)	−0.026 (4.38)***	−0.025 (4.29)***
Latin America	−0.017 (3.61)***	−0.019 (3.89)***	−0.016 (3.16)***	−0.016 (3.13)***
East Asia	0.017 (3.61)***	0.018 (3.06)***	0.019 (2.59)**	0.019 (2.52)**
Constant	0.027 (5.86)***	0.026 (4.85)***	0.025 (4.47)***	0.027 (4.11)***
No. observations	86	73	63	63
R-squared	0.415	0.531	0.513	0.517

Notes
The dependent variable is annual growth rate (years 1980–2000) of real per capita GDP. We present t-statistics in parentheses, where White's heteroskedasticity-consistent standard errors are employed.
*Significant at the 10-percent level. **Significant at the 5 percent level. ***Significant at the 1 percent level.

The one novel and surprising result is the misalignment–openness interaction variable that has consistently negative and highly significant coefficients. The inevitable implication is that the more open the economy, the more pernicious is the effect of the chronic exchange rate misalignment and the more punishing is its impact on growth. In other words, the closed economy can achieve more growth, the degree of exchange rate misalignment notwithstanding. The theoretical conundrum is how to explain this negative interaction of openness and misalignment?

The Sachs-Warner dummy variable for openness rests largely on absence of government control on major tradable goods and absence of high (greater than 40 percent on the average) tariffs on machinery and materials. The remaining component of the openness dummy variable is a black market premium of foreign exchange that is less than 20 percent; while any higher premium makes the economy closed in the Sachs-Warner definition. A low black market premium indicates a high degree of globalization and therefore good integration with the global economy. The misalignment of the NER, on the other hand, can also be the outcome of a systematic devaluation due to the softness of the currency. Although the two may be causally related, they are not so in our model since they are not both endogenously determined. So the puzzle remains: how could a low degree of openness interact with misalignment to deliver a positive impact on growth?

Could currency substitution account for the punishing effects of misalignment in an open developing economy?

The discussion in the previous section was hypothesis driven. With the introduction of the distinction between tradables and non-tradables in equation (7) we control for the impact of openness ("globalization") in increasing trade in goods and services of a developing country with its trading partners. At the current state of the empirical evidence there is a dearth of hard data on currency substitution to make its research hypothesis driven.[5] We therefore engage in hypothesis-generating research in the balance of this chapter to discuss the likely impact of currency substitution on exchange rate misalignment to the extent that misalignment can also be exogenous in the sense that it does not originate in the usual shift in demand and supply of foreign exchange for transactions purposes that are registered in the current account.

In the current environment of globalization the concepts of free markets and free trade are extended to apply also to free markets for foreign exchange and to free financial capital flows (portfolio capital), thus allowing for foreign currencies to be bought and held as assets not only by central banks but also, and to a large extent, by individuals, and especially so in developing countries. Unless this currency substitution is otherwise sterilized it results in higher exchange rates than would have been obtained from the current account transactions. However, sterilization through increasing foreign demand for the domestic currency of developing countries is not forthcoming since not all currencies were created equal. While any currency or other fiat money can be used as a consensual medium of exchange, the currency held as an asset trades as a positional good based on *reputation*.[6] In the ordinal reputational ranking of currencies from the "best" to the "worst" that becomes applicable when currencies are held as assets, the reserve currency ranks at the top. The dollar, therefore, systematically substitutes in agents' portfolios for a wide swath of less-preferred currencies. In free currency markets this asymmetric reputation of currencies induces asymmetric demand for holding currencies as assets. Therefore, while residents of developing countries include in their portfolios the reserve/hard currency for asset-holding purposes, residents of hard-currency countries have not a matching interest in holding soft currencies, those of developing countries. In the open economy model of the modern era of globalization the devaluation of the nominal exchange rate in developing countries is more often than not the result of currency substitution, as opposed to the transactions demand for foreign exchange for servicing the current account (Yotopoulos, 1996: 50–1; and Chapter 1).

Ordinarily devaluations are considered benevolent, and especially so for developing countries, since they strengthen the current account and serve to cure allocative inefficiencies. The question arises: why is the exogenous devaluation of a soft currency as a result of currency substitution different and has instead deleterious effects for developing countries leading to a gross misallocation of resources? Yotopoulos (1996) formulates the answer in terms of a time-inconsistency proposition that can trigger currency substitution and parlay it to a sizeable resource misallocation:

> Consider an equilibrium situation in which a bundle of resources produces tradables, *T*, or nontradables, *N*, measured such that one unit of each is worth \$1. Entrepreneurs should be indifferent between producing one unit of *T* or one of *N*. But since the soft currency is more likely to be devalued, it becomes risky for the entrepreneur to produce (or hold) one unit of *N* that could not be converted for later spending into \$1. Expressed in another way, entrepreneurs are attracted to producing *T* because that is the only way they can acquire \$1 they wish to hold for asset purposes. With the relative productivities of the bundle of resources (measured at "normal" prices) remaining unchanged, *N* becomes undervalued and (the allocation of) resources becomes biased towards *T*. This is manifest in a relative price of *N* that is too low compared with productivities, (in other words) too high an RER.
>
> This dilemma does not exist for the D(eveloped) C(country) producer. In hard currency, \$1 of *T* will always be worth \$1 of *N*, as opposed to the soft currency where the expectation of devaluation becomes a self-fulfilling prophecy. Controlling for the other determinants of devaluation in developing countries, the process alone of converting soft currency into hard for asset-holding purposes tends to make the market-clearing NER too high. This is manifest in the relative price of tradables that is too high compared with productivities – again too high an RER.
>
> (Yotopoulos, 1996: 51)

By allowing for the possibility that currency substitution is exogenous, as defined above, we proceed to investigate its possible outcomes on LDCs in terms of exchange rate misalignment.

In a globalized world, the free market in currency exchanges offers the opportunity of conversion of domestic into foreign currency. In the case of developed countries the "reputation" of their reserve/hard currency makes this conversion of their local currency immaterial and unnecessary: the hardness of their currencies allows the producer of non-tradables to exchange his proceeds of domestic currency into tradables, or for that matter into hard assets ("dollars") for future use, with a credible commitment for the stability of relative prices (in terms of the domestic currency). In developing countries, on the other hand, the experience with soft currencies is that they do not simply fluctuate; they depreciate systematically. In an attempt to foreclose future devaluation of their soft-currency assets, agents substitute the hard/reserve currency for the domestic, thus tending to make the devaluation of the soft currency a self-fulfilling prophecy. The current globalization environment with free international movements of financial capital becomes the ideal breeding ground for systematic currency-substitution-induced devaluations and for fostering financial crises in soft-currency (i.e. developing) countries (Yotopoulos, 1996).[7]

This formulation of the hypothesis of currency substitution can be viewed as an extension of the canonical case of market incompleteness for asymmetric information (Stiglitz and Weiss, 1981), but for the fact that in the case of foreign exchange it is *asymmetric reputation* in the positional scale of currencies that anoints only a small and select group of them for also doing service as assets. The canonical policy that becomes applicable in cases of market incompleteness is regulation, most often in the form of rationing. We venture some thoughts on this issue in the concluding section.

Revisiting the cross-country results reported in Table 3.4 to account for currency substitution, we distinguish two components of the negative and highly significant coefficient of the exchange rate misalignment variable regressed on the openness of the economy. The formulation of equation (7) takes care of the component of misalignment that emanates from the Ricardo principle (Yotopoulos and Sawada, 2006). It reduces to a characteristic of the economic structure of developing countries, and it is reflected in a relatively high value for the RER. Controlling for that, the interaction of the misalignment variable with openness captures the effect of any other likely source of deviation that is not captured in the equation, in this case the degree of openness/closeness in the economy in the form of a small/large black market premium of the foreign exchange rate. The negative and significant coefficient of the interaction variable in the growth regression is precisely what the currency substitution hypothesis would predict: high openness of the economy with low transaction costs for currency substitution represents an opportunity for investors (speculators) to profit by buying a cheap insurance policy against the devaluation of the domestic currency. This, in turn, becomes an enabling factor for devaluation; and when devaluation comes it rewards the flight away from the domestic currency. In this environment of "bad competition" with adverse incentives, currency substitution often leads to further devaluations and at times to endemic crises in a process of cumulative causation (Yotopoulos, 1996; Yotopoulos and Sawada, 1999; Sawada and Yotopoulos, 2005). Currency substitution thus becomes a potent factor in increasing the misalignment of the exchange rate for developing countries – the deviation between the NER and its PPP value, the RER.

Whether the target countries of the MDGs were in the cross-country sample for the growth equation or not (some, of course, were) transference of the findings of Table 3.4 to the poorest countries in the MDGs makes the emphatic lesson from the findings of section three of this chapter ever more ominous. The Ricardo principle was applied earlier as an axiomatic mechanism that accounts for systematic deviations of the NER from its PPP value, with the deviations varying inversely with the level of income in a developing economy. The poorer the economy, the greater is the misalignment of its exchange rate, and the lower is its feasible rate of growth. A parallel relationship holds between currency substitution-induced devaluation of the nominal exchange rate and poverty. In a globalization environment the allure of and the opportunities for currency substitution (by the elites who have the liquid assets to insure against devaluation) are so much greater, the poorer the country is. This taste for currency substitution is intermediated by higher exchange rate misalignment leading to a lower growth potential.

If the negative coefficient of the relationship between openness and growth receives the attention it deserves, the best place for the poorest countries to start in enhancing their growth potential is by imposing a modicum of controls on the free convertibility of their currency. A mild form of such restrictions that has been time tested in various countries makes foreign exchange available at the free market rate for transactions in the current account, while holding of foreign monetary assets by individuals is prohibited, or otherwise penalized.[8] This would also have ancillary implications in limiting the free flows of portfolio capital into developing countries.

Conclusions

There is broad agreement in the literature that the objective of the Millennium Development Goals of graduating by year 2015 one-half of the world's denizens who live in abject poverty can best be served by economic growth. Our tests in the first part of the chapter indicate that the set goal can only be met by one-half of the target population (or one-quarter of the poor) unless there is a vigorous acceleration of the historical rate of growth in a large number of countries, especially in those among the poorest in the list. Thus our search is refocused in the second part of the chapter on the lessons from growth analysis with cross-country data in an attempt to identify any neglected factors that might be promising for contributing to higher growth rates.

Exchange rate misalignment has featured in the literature as an important factor with negative implications on growth, although its correct measurement has been elusive. Taking a short cut to the more appropriate specification of exchange rate misalignment as the deviation of the nominal exchange rate from its PPP levels, we conduct an endogenous growth analysis that leads to a surprising result: the significantly negative impact of exchange rate misalignment on growth originates in the openness of the economy. We interpreted this finding as pointing to an incomplete market in foreign exchange in the developing countries of the sample. The market incompleteness arises because of the asymmetric reputation of currencies when they serve for asset-holding purposes and it induces developing country citizens to engage in currency substitution for the purpose of holding hard-currency-denominated assets.

The results of this study may grate on conventional wisdom. The challenge to the unconventional results may arise either with the definition and measurement of the variable of exchange rate misalignment or in doubts about the replicability of the results in another sample. The former issue has been adequately addressed in section three. On the latter issue, the evidence presented ten years ago with one set of data (Yotopoulos, 1996) is in effect replicated in the current analysis with more recent data, the differences in the empirical formulation of the hypothesis notwithstanding. In the original study Yotopoulos makes three points analytically: first, productivity differences between developed and developing countries are smaller for non-traded goods than for traded goods (the Ricardo principle); second, free market forces (in the form of currency substitution) produce nominal exchange rates in developing countries that undervalue the domestic currency, thus leading to high RER, (real exchange rates, i.e. P_T/P_{NT}, for prices of tradables and non-tradables, respectively); and third, the combination of the axiomatic productivity differentials with the nominal exchange rate undervaluation leads to a severe misallocation of resources that takes a toll on economic growth in developing countries. These propositions were subjected to analysis in a growth model (that included a country-specific RER variable) in a combination of cross-sectional and longitudinal data (years 1970, 1975, 1980 and 1985) for 62 developed and developing countries. The data that entered the RER consisted of prices and expenditures for all tradable and non-tradable goods and services, derived from the International Comparisons Project (Kravis *et al.*, 1982, and earlier years) and they were combined with statistics on direction of trade in order to determine the country-specific extent of tradability of each good. As such, the econometric tests engaged the RER as a measure of the exchange rate misalignment variable, based on primary data.

In the present study the proper definition of exchange rate misalignment remains the same as in Yotopoulos (1996), but the model formulation, its empirical implementation and the data are different, and so is the measurement of the misalignment variable. Equation 7 in section three of the current study employs a proxy of the misalignment variable that relies on secondary data. The results, however, of the two approaches are identical on the negative impact of misalignment on growth, despite the different formulation of the variable in the two cases. The coincidence of the two independent studies strengthens our conclusion that interventions in the capital account which are designed to curb the desire of developing-country citizens to hold hard-currency-denominated assets by prohibiting or limiting such holdings, are likely to provide a boost to growth. The simple extension of the standard theory of incomplete markets to apply also to asymmetric reputation of currencies used for asset-holding purposes leads directly to the policy recommendation of a dual exchange rate system for LDCs: a free market for foreign exchange in the current account while currency substitution in the form of purchasing and holding foreign currency assets is prohibited or else it is discouraged with a black market exchange rate premium.

We recognize that for mainstream economists who view exchange rate controls as one of the policies that lead to economic stagnation this conclusion is hard to swallow. We take no exception to the position that the main advantage of a flexible exchange rate regime is that it allows for monetary independence

(McKinnon, 1982; Darrat *et al.*, 1996). But this is no longer true in the presence of currency substitution that makes devaluation as an instrument of adjustment lose its bite. Moreover, restrictions in purchasing and holding hard-currency assets have had a long and effective service record as instruments of monetary policy. They were rightly abolished in some countries because they were no longer needed; in the rest they were also rightly abolished because they were onerous. But if one takes the findings of this study seriously, such controls have become once again necessary for a specific set of developing countries.

As a final caveat it should be mentioned that "good governance," which is captured by the "policy index" in Table 3.4, is a necessary factor for benign interventions to work well. The importance of the appropriate institutional infrastructure, including good governance, for restoring symmetry in the outcomes of globalization has already been emphasized fittingly in other chapters in this volume.

Notes

1 We would like to thank Nick Hope, Odin Knudsen, Jeffrey Nugent and Donato Romano for useful comments on an earlier version of this chapter.
2 As, for instance, exemplified in Yotopoulos and Sawada (1999).
3 Note that this relative price level is the inverse of a simple version of the real exchange rate.
4 Note however that country-specific effects for the numeraire country, the USA, are not captured.
5 Cf. Sawada and Yotopoulos (2005) for an attempt at a hypothesis-driven research on the subject.
6 The parallel literature on "positional goods" identifies the social "pecking order" as "a shared system of social status," where, for example, it becomes possible for an individual (a good) to have a positive amount of prestige (reputation) such as a feeling of superiority, or a "trendy" appeal, only because the other individuals (goods) have a symmetrical feeling of inferiority, i.e. have less or negative reputation (Hirsch, 1976; Frank and Cook, 1976; Pagano, 1999). In extending this literature and viewing foreign exchange as a "positional good" we postulate that in a free currency market, the simple fact that reserve/hard currencies exist, implies that there are soft currencies which are shunned for some (asset-holding) purposes. Cf. also Pagano (Chapter 2) and Yotopoulos (Chapter 1).
7 Yotopoulos, (1996: 141–5) proceeds to test for the hypothesis of the transmission of the effects of exchange rate misalignment from the monetary to the real sector of the economy.
8 Such a policy was in effect in the UK until 1979. Until early 2006 the Chinese yuan was convertible on the current account only; partial and controlled convertibility on the capital account came later.

References

Balassa, Bela (1964), "Purchasing Power Parity Doctrine: A Reappraisal," *Journal of Political Economy*, 72 (6): 584–96.
Besley, Timothy and Robin Burgess (2003), "Halving Global Poverty," *Journal of Economic Perspectives*, 17 (3): 3–22.
Borenzstein, Eduardo, Josè de Gregorio and Jong-Wha Lee (1998), "How Does Foreign

Direct Investment Affect Economic Growth," *Journal of International Economics*, 45 (1): 115–35.

Burnside, Craig and David Dollar (2000), "Aid, Policies, and Growth," *American Economic Review*, 90 (4): 847–68.

Cassel, Gustav (1921), *The World's Monetary Problems*. New York: E.P. Dutton and Co.

Darrat, Ali F., Ahmed Al-Mutawa and Omar M. Benkato (1996), "On Currency Substitution and Money Demand Instability," *International Review of Economics and Finance*, 5 (3): 321–34.

Dollar, David (1992), "Outward-oriented Developing Economies Really Do Grow More Rapidly: Evidence from 95 LDCs, 1976–1985," *Economic Development and Cultural Change*, 40 (3): 523–44.

Dollar, David and Aart Kraay (2002), "Growth is Good for the Poor," *Journal of Economic Growth*, 7 (3): 195–225.

Dollar, David and Aart Kraay (2004), "Trade, Growth, and Poverty," *Economic Journal*, 114 (493): F22–F49.

Durlauf, Steven N. and Danny T. Quah (1999), "The New Empirics of Economic Growth." In John B. Taylor and Michael Woodford, eds, *Handbook of Macroeconomics*. Amsterdam: North-Holland, pp. 235–308.

Edwards, Sebastian (1988), *Exchange Rate Misalignment in Developing Countries*. Baltimore, MD: Johns Hopkins University Press.

Foster, James, Joel Greer and Erik Thorbecke (1984), "A Class of Decomposable Poverty Measures," *Econometrica*, 52 (3): 761–6.

Frank, Robert H. and Philip J. Cook (1976), *The Winner-Take-All Society: Why the Few at the Top Get So Much More Than the Rest of Us*. New York: Penguin.

Ghura, Dhaneshwar and Thomas J. Grennes (1993), "The Real Exchange Rate and Macroeconomic Performance in Sub-Saharan Africa," *Journal of Development Economics*, 42 (1): 155–74.

Harrison, Ann (1996), "Openness and Growth: A Time-series, Cross-country Analysis for Developing Countries," *Journal of Development Economics*, 48 (2): 419–47.

Heston, Alan, Robert Summers and Bettina Aten (2002), "Penn World Table Version 6.1." Philadelphia: Center for International Comparisons at the University of Pennsylvania (CICUP).

Hirsch, Fred (1976), *Social Limits to Growth*. Cambridge, MA: Harvard University Press.

Kanbur, Ravi (1987), "Measurement and Alleviation of Poverty," *IMF Staff Papers*, 34 (1): 60–85.

Keynes, John M. (1923), *A Tract for Monetary Reform*. New York: Macmillan.

Kravis, Irving B., Alan Heston and Robert Summers (1982), *World Product and Income: International Comparisons of Real Gross Product*. Baltimore, MD, Johns Hopkins University Press.

McKinnon, Ronald (1982), "The Order of Economic Liberalization: Lessons from Chile and Argentina," *Carnegie Rochester Conference Series in Public Policy*, 17: 24–45.

Morduch, Jonathan (1998), "Poverty, Economic Growth, and Average Exit Time," *Economics Letters*, 59 (3): 385–90.

Pagano, Ugo (1999), "Is Power an Economic Good? Notes on Social Scarcity and the Economics of Positional Goods." In Samuel Bowles, Maurizio Franzini and Ugo Pagano, eds, *The Politics and Economics of Power*. London: Routledge, pp. 63–84.

Ravallion, Martin (2001), "Growth, Inequality, and Poverty: Looking Beyond Averages," *World Development*, 29 (11): 1815–2001.

Ravallion, Martin, Gaurav Datt and Dominique van de Walle (1991), "Quantifying Absolute Poverty in the Developing World," *Review of Income and Wealth*, 37 (4): 345–61.

Ricardo, David (1817), *On the Principle of Political Economy and Taxation*. London: John Murray.

Rodrik, Dani (1994), "King Kong Meets Godzilla: The World Bank and the East Asian Miracle." In Robert Wade, ed., *Miracle or Design? Lessons from the East Asian Experience*. Washington DC: Overseas Development Council, pp. 13–53.

Sachs, Jeffrey and Andrew Warner (1995), "Economic Reform and the Process of Global Integration," *Brookings Papers on Economic Activity*, 1: 1–118.

Samuelson, Paul A. (1964), "Theoretical Notes on Trade Problems," *Review of Economics and Statistics*, 46 (May): 145–54.

Sawada, Yasuyuki (2004), "MDGs and the Exit Time," Faculty of Economics, University of Tokyo. Mimeo.

Sawada, Yasuyuki and Pan A. Yotopoulos (2005), "Corner Solutions, Crises, and Capital Controls: Theory and Empirical Analysis on the Optimal Exchange Rate Regime in Emerging Economies." Stanford Institute for Economic Policy Research, Paper no. 04–037 (September 2005). Online, available at siepr.stanford.edu/Papers/pdf/04–37.html (accessed 13 September 2005).

Stiglitz, Joseph E. and Andrew Weiss (1981), "Credit Rationing in Markets with Imperfect Information," *American Economic Review*, 71 (3): 393–419.

World Bank (1991) *World Development Report*. Washington, DC: World Bank.

World Bank (2002), *Globalization, Growth, and Poverty: Building an Inclusive World Economy*. New York: Oxford University Press.

World Bank (2004), "Global Poverty Monitoring," Washington, DC: World Bank. Online, available at www.worldbank.org/research/povmonitor/index.htm (accessed 5 July 2004).

Yotopoulos, Pan A. (1996), *Exchange Rate Parity for Trade and Development: Theory Tests, and Case Studies*. Cambridge and New York: Cambridge University Press.

Yotopoulos, Pan A. and Yasuyuki Sawada (1999), "Free Currency Markets, Financial Crises and the Growth Debacle: Is There a Causal Relationship?" *Seoul Journal of Economics*, 12 (Winter): 419–56. (Available also online at siepr.stanford.edu/papers/pdf/99–04.html.)

Yotopoulos, Pan A. and Yasuyuki Sawada (2006), "Exchange Rate Misalignment: A New Test of Long-run PPP Based on Cross-country Data," *Applied Financial Economics*, 16 (1): 127–34.

4 With whom to trade?

An examination of the effects of intra-national and between-country income inequality on bilateral trade[1]

Rania S. Miniesy and Jeffrey B. Nugent

Introduction

In this increasingly globalized world, income inequalities – both between and within countries – deserve center stage in any analysis of the asymmetries of globalization. While recent academic research has investigated many effects of income inequality, it has not looked at those on trade. At the same time, while much attention has been devoted to the conditions under which trade can give rise to polarization and inequality, the reversed relationship from inequality to trade has been largely neglected.

This chapter tries to fill this gap by taking up the theme suggested by Yotopoulos (Chapter 1) and Romano (Chapter 10) that the effects of trade are likely to be most asymmetric when the commodities and services to be traded are subject to reputational differentials. That is, with reputational effects and an uneven infrastructural and institutional playing field between them, the trade partner with the better reputation is likely to gain more from trade than the other partner. Moreover, these asymmetries are likely to be systematic rather than random. Indeed, these authors have argued that the benefits will be more mutually beneficial the more level the playing field between any pair of countries, the more similar the income levels, infrastructure and other institutions, and when both partners enjoy good governance. But, when free trade is practiced between countries that have very unequal incomes, infrastructure and governance structures, the results will tend to give rise to asymmetries.

Since most trade is voluntary at least in the normal sense of the word, *ceteris paribus*, our point of departure is to suggest that this implies also that there would be less trade among countries with different endowments of these types than among countries with more similar endowments. Specifically, this chapter hypothesizes that, controlling for the various factors that have been shown to explain bilateral trade patterns over time and space in standard gravity models, inequality in income both between and within countries tends to reduce trade, as does poor governance, in any one partner. It then goes on to an empirical test of the hypotheses based on an application of an extended version of the standard gravity model of bilateral trade to data on trade matrices and also numerous determinants of trade at the aggregate level for the years 1985, 1990, 1995, 1997 and 2000. The results are used to answer the following question: "If you want to trade in such a way as to avoid being on the short end of asymmetries in trade and to trade more, thereby supporting economic development, with whom should you trade?"

The chapter is organized as follows: the first section derives the basic hypotheses from the trade theories of Steffan Linder (1961); the second section describes the gravity model that is used for this purpose; section three identifies the data used; section four presents the empirical results; and the fifth section concludes with some tentative answers to the question of "with whom to trade?"

Review of the literature on income inequality and trade

In contrast to traditional comparative advantage theory which is primarily driven by supply-side considerations, much of modern trade theory is demand determined. Since reputational considerations on the demand side of items traded internationally have (and are likely to continue to) become more important over time as has been argued quite persuasively in Yotopoulos (Chapter 1), reputational effects on the demand-side considerations are bound to become even more important in the future.

But what does this imply as far as inequality within and between countries is concerned? There were hints of a negative effect of income inequality on imports and exports in the second of Keynes' "psychological laws" (Keynes, 1936). Since both the average and marginal propensities to consume and import could be expected to fall with the level of income, one could expect that a mean-preserving redistribution of income away from equality could reduce aggregate consumption and thus imports in an open economy context. Such expectations have frequently been confirmed in empirical studies.[2]

Another theoretical insight into inequality effects comes from theories emphasizing imperfections and incompleteness of markets for consumer durables and capital goods. In the absence of complete markets for credit, greater income inequality for any given average level of income would imply that more consumers would be credit constrained and hence unable to import bulky goods like capital goods and consumer durables. For the poor in poor countries these credit constraints may be such as to limit spending and imports even of basic consumer non-durables. Once again, this would suggest that countries with weaker and less developed, or even just different, institutions would trade less.

The single most explicit analysis of income inequality effects on trade – and again by way of demand – is that of Linder (1961). Linder argued that a country's exports of manufactures, a type of export that has been occupying an ever-increasing share of world exports, are likely to be quite dependent on that country's own demand for such products. Actual production and export are hypothesized to follow from prior demand. Linder explained this by saying that there would be no production or export of a product unless an entrepreneur would first have seen an investment opportunity. An investment opportunity would be identified only when the entrepreneur realizes that production would satisfy some discernible economic "need." Such a need would be most discernible when it appears in the domestic economy and when the production of the good is based on an invention. Linder concedes that by contrast those "needing" the country's primary exports (especially oil, minerals and tropical agricultural products) are likely to be foreign, explaining why entrepreneurs in these kinds of production and export are likely to be foreign.

The neoclassical factor proportions theory, therefore, may be fairly satisfactory for explaining primary exports but not manufactures (and similarly not for service) exports. Linder derived two important hypotheses. First, manufactures trade is likely to be most intensive between countries that are at similar levels of per capita income. Second, even for countries at the same levels of per capita income, the demand patterns will be most concentrated on overlapping commodities, thereby making for sizeable reciprocal demands for manufactures imports, the lower is income inequality within each country. Hence, income inequality both across countries and within countries is likely to reduce trade.

Linder's theory has also been extended by various authors viewing every commodity produced as going through a product life cycle. As such, like other more recent theories, it puts more emphasis on dynamic factors and changes over time. Much of this work, e.g. Helpman (1981), Helpman and Krugman (1985) and Grossman and Helpman (1991), has formalized the demand-side effects and focused on new products. As such, these authors model consumers' utility as being more affected by the variety of goods they consume than by the quantities of a given number of goods. In treating the extra complications of product differentiation, new products and imperfect competition, however, most of the models – both static and dynamic – have assumed a representative consumer in each country and thus have abstracted from inequality considerations. The exceptional studies that have in fact allowed for multiple consumers have usually made the assumption that the income elasticities of demand are unitary, once again eliminating the possibility of distributional effects arising from changes in inequality. Hence, income inequality effects on trade have been lost sight of in recent years.

A stunning exception is the theoretical paper by Mitra and Trindade (2003) showing that for countries with similar aggregate resource endowments, the trade pattern can be determined strictly by demand patterns, including the concentration of demand on certain commodities that would be expected of countries with low income inequality. They also show that, when intra-national income inequality is combined with endowment differences across countries, the well-known tendency for trade between countries to be only a fraction of that occurring within countries (otherwise known as "the missing trade problem") can be explained. If the two countries or regional aggregates of countries are large, like "east" and "west" or "north" and "south," these factors may also determine both relative factor prices and the international terms of trade.[3] Also, under certain conditions, a policy to redistribute income within one of the regions will also affect the distribution of income in the other region.

The effects of cross-country differences in income have been picked up and analyzed by Markusen (1986) and Thursby and Thursby (1987). Consistent with Linder, they find that countries with similar levels of per capita income and tastes tend to trade more. With respect to intra-national income distribution, Hunter and Markusen (1988) and Hunter (1991) have shown aggregate demand functions to be non-homothetic and that the non-homotheticity of these demand functions has the effect of reducing trade volumes by as much as 25 percent. While non-homotheticity in demand functions is a necessary condition for income distributional effects on international trade, these studies did not explicitly examine the effects on trade of either intra-national income inequality or its interaction with international income inequality.

Gravity model and its specification and estimation

To examine the effect of both intra-national and between-country income inequality on bilateral trade flows, we make use of what has become the work-horse of empirical studies of international trade, namely the gravity model. The gravity model is especially attractive in this context because of its demonstrated applicability to many different kinds of countries and regions, its robustness over time, and to various different specifications.[4] According to this model, trade flows between any pair of countries should be affected by their mass (the product of their respective GDPs) as well as by the distance between them.[5] The latter is because transport and transaction costs can be assumed to rise with distance. Since factors such as exchange rate variability, common language, common colonial or other historical experience, common currency, free trade agreements and sharing a common border can affect these transaction or transportation costs, all such variables can be included in the gravity model.[6]

The model is specified as follows:

$$Ln\ (Bilat_{ijt}) = \beta_0 + \beta_1\ Ln\ GDP_{ijt} + \beta_2\ Ln\ GDPPC_{ijt} + \beta_3\ Ln\ Dist_{ij} +$$
$$+ \beta_4\ Ln\ Areas_{ij} + \beta_5\ LL_{ij} + \beta_6\ Border_{ij} + \beta_7\ Lang_{ij} + \beta_8\ Regional_{ijt} +$$
$$+ \beta_9\ Nation_{ij} + \beta_{10}\ Colonizer_{ij} + \beta_{11}\ Colonial_{ij} + \beta_{12}\ ERV_{ijt} + \beta_{13}\ CU_{ijt} +$$
$$+ \alpha_1\ Gov\_ds_{ijt} + \alpha_2\ CPY_{ijt} + \alpha_3\ CPE_{ijt} + \alpha_4\ Gini2_{ijt} + \alpha_5\ M2GDP_{ijt} +$$
$$+ \alpha_6\ DiffGDPPC_{ijt} + \alpha_7\ OneFTA_{ijt} + \alpha_8\ Year\ Dummy\ Variables + \varepsilon_{ijt}$$

where subscripts i and j denote the countries trading with each other and t denotes time. The variables are grouped in two sets, one with coefficients α and the other with coefficients β. The β-coefficient group relates to the standard gravity model where geographical and historical locations play a major role. The α-coefficient group intends to capture institutional factors and, more specifically, the income distribution and inequality characteristics of the trading partners that may affect the direction and the volume of trade.

The variables of the β-coefficient group are defined as follows: $Bilat_{ijt}$ is the nominal value of bilateral trade between i and j at time t; GDP and $GDPPC$ are the nominal value of gross domestic product (GDP) and GDP per capita, respectively; $Dist_{ij}$ is the great circle distance between i and j in miles; $Areas$ is the sum of the areas of i and j in square kilometers (hence a proxy for distance within the country to the border); LL_{ij} is a dummy variable, which is 0 if no countries are landlocked, 1 if one partner is landlocked, and 2 if both are land-locked; $Border_{ij}$ is a binary variable, which is 1 if i and j share a border and 0 otherwise; $Lang_{ij}$ is a binary variable, which is 1 if i and j share an official language and 0 otherwise; $Regional_{ijt}$ is a binary variable, which is 1 if i and j belong to a regional trading agreement in year t; $Nation_{ij}$ is a binary variable, which is 1 if i and j are part of the same nation; $Colonizer_{ij}$ is a binary variable, which is 1 if i and j shared the same colonizer in or after 1945; $Colonial_{ij}$ is a binary variable, which is 1 if i colonized j or vice versa; ERV_{ijt} is the volatility of the bilateral nominal exchange rate between i and j in period t; CU_{ijt} is a binary variable, which is 1 if i and j use the same currency at time t.

The variables in the α-coefficient group are defined as follows: Gov_ds_{ijt} is the sum of the governance indices of i and j at t; CPY_{ijt} is a dummy variable, which is 0 if neither partner was centrally planned at year t, 1 if only one country was, and 2 if both countries were centrally planned in year t; CPE_{ij} is a dummy variable, which is 0 if no country was ever centrally planned, 1 if only one country was ever centrally planned, and 2 if both countries were ever centrally planned; $Gini2_{ijt}$ is the sum of the Gini coefficients of the two countries; $M2GDP_{ijt}$ is the product of the two countries' $M2 - GDP$ ratios (where the money supply and GDP are proxies for financial deepening); $DiffGDPPC_{ijt}$ is the difference in per capita income between i and j; $OneFTA$ is a dummy variable measure of trade diversion defined as 1 if only one of the countries is in a regional trading arrange-ment (and 0 otherwise); the *Year Dummy Variables* are for 1990, 1995, 1997 and 2000 (1985 being the omitted variable); and ε_{ijt} is the error term.

As indicated by the form of the equation, the model is log-linear in some, but not all, of the continuous variables. Some explanatory variables are categorical ones with only two or three scores. A distinct novelty among the α-coefficient variables is the inclusion of the difference in per capita income (*DiffGDPPC*) to capture the inter-country income inequality, of *Gini2* to capture the effect of intra-national income inequality and of *Gov_ds* to capture institutional factors. Furthermore we will also add an interaction term (*Gini*DiffGDPPC*) between the two types of inequality, intra-national inequality (*Gini2*) and inter-country inequality (*DiffGDPPC*). The inclusion of this interaction term represents what we believe to be an important extension of the Linder model. Although he did not explicitly make this argument, by his logic one should expect such an influ-ence to be positive. This is because the greater the difference in the per capita incomes of two trading partners and the lower are their domestic income inequality indexes, the less overlap there would be in the demand patterns between the two countries. But, as intra-national inequality increases, the degree of overlap could be expected to increase, thereby stimulating reciprocal demand and trade between the two partners.

As a result, there are three inequality effects on bilateral trade to be tested: (1) that of cross-country income inequality (*DiffGDPPC*); (2) that of internal income inequality (*Gini2*) and (3) that of the interaction between the two types of inequality (*Gini*DiffGDPPC*).

The data

The trade data for well over 100 countries for all years except 2000 were taken from Feenstra (2000).[7] Missing data in this source in these years as well as 2000 trade data were taken from the International Monetary Fund's Direction of Trade Statistics (DOTS) CD-Rom (IMF, 2003). For simplicity, as well as because the IMF's DOTS CD-Rom has only aggregate data, we confine our attention to explaining variations in aggregate values of bilateral trade across pairs of trading partners and over time. Data on *GDP*, *GDPPC* and *M2GDP* were taken from the World Bank's 2003 World Development Indicators' CD-Rom (World Bank, 2003). Some missing values for GDP and population were taken from UN (2003). Data on *Areas*, *LL*, *Border*, *Lang*, *Nation*, *Colonizer*, *Dist* and *Colonial*, are taken from the US Central Intelligence Agency's website (CIA, 2004) and in a few cases from Rose (2000). The variables *Regional* and *OneFTA* were constructed on the basis of information about the commonly recognized trade agreements obtained from the World Trade Organization's website (WTO, 2004).

Exchange rate volatility between countries *i* and *j* at time *t* (*ERV*) was calculated in the way suggested by Rose (2000) as the standard deviation of the first-difference of the monthly natural logarithm of the bilateral nominal exchange rate (using the IMF's International Financial Statistics (IFS) Line ae) in the five years preceding the date of the bilateral trade observations. For the *CU* variable, information on the use of a common currency by the two trading partners is taken from Rose (2000) and corrections thereof in Glick and Rose (2002). *CPY* and *CPE* were constructed on the basis of knowledge about the use of central planning in the past. In some cases, that would involve membership in Council for Mutual Economic Assistance.

For *Gini2*, a combination of two sources was used: (1) Deininger and Squire (1997) and (2) WIDER (2000). The higher the value of *Gini2*, the greater is income inequality.

The governance indicator *Gov_ds* is a broad measure capturing (1) the process by which governments are selected, monitored and replaced, (2) the capacity of the government to effectively formulate and implement sound policies and (3) the respect of citizens and the state of the institutions that govern economic and social interactions. These three dimensions of governance are operationalized on the basis of six different sub-indicators as suggested and constructed by Kaufmann *et al.* (2002)[8] based on subjective indicators taken from the International Country Risk Guide.[9] The six different indicators were combined into a single index via a principal components analysis. Since the various indicators make use of somewhat different scales, they were also standardized into a similar scale. Furthermore, since all the resulting country-specific indexes were highly correlated with *GDPPC*, a separate auxiliary regression of the standardized weighted governance variable of the individual countries was run on *GDPPC* and then the deviation between the predicted governance and the actual governance variables was used to come up with an index for each country. Putting these together for trading partners, the governance variable (a deviated standardized weighted sum) was finally reached.[10]

Empirical results

The trade matrices have one potentially important pitfall: there are numerous missing values. As noted above, we have tried to fill in these missing observations by making use of data from additional sources. Nevertheless, that by no means solves the problem since even after this there remain many cases for which it is difficult to know whether the values are actually zero or missing. Most analysts have simply assumed that these cases represent missing values and hence estimate the gravity equations from the non-missing values by ordinary least squares (OLS). Alternatively one can assume that these values are zeros and estimate the equations by OLS or more appropriately by TOBIT, recognizing that the observations are bounded from below (negative values are "censored"). Elsewhere we have found the results to be quite sensitive to the choice of assumptions and hence in this chapter we estimate the gravity models both ways.

In Table 4.1 we present the results for the pooled data on bilateral trade for all countries and years (15,756 observations) under the assumption that the missing observations are zeros. For this reason we provide both OLS and TOBIT estimates. Moreover, we do so for two different specifications of the model, one without and one with the extra interaction term involving the two types of inequality that, as noted above, we feel is needed to complete the Linder model.

Note that in both specifications of the model and by both estimation procedures, many of the parameters of the standard gravity model in Table 4.1 have the expected signs and are statistically significant. In particular, those for *GDP*, *Lang*, *Colonizer*, *Regional* and currency union (*CU*) are all positive and highly significant,[11] and those for *Distance*, *Areas*, *LL*, and *ERV* are all negative and significant. Of the non-standard variables that we have added to the gravity model, *OneFTA* and *CPY* have significant negative effects on bilateral trade, demonstrating the presence of a trade diversion effect of regional trading arrangements and the negative effect of central planning on bilateral trade. As expected, the effect of *Gov_ds* is positive and significant. Slight surprises are the fact that the coefficients for per capita income (*GDPPC*) are not significant and that colonial relationship has a negative effect.

Of special relevance, of course, are the results for *Gini2*, *DiffGDPPC* and the interaction term (*Gini*DiffGDPPC*) that combines the two types of inequality. While from the results of the first specification without the interaction term, each of the inequality terms has negative coefficients, the effects are rather small and in the case of the between-country inequality (*DiffGDPPC*) not statistically significant. Yet, when the interaction term is included as in the second and fourth columns of the table, the negative values of the coefficients of these

Table 4.1 Determinants of bilateral trade for the pooled data set including observations with zero trade

Variables	OLS		TOBIT	
Gini2	−0.02***	−0.15***	−0.02***	−0.18***
	(0.01)	(0.02)	(0.01)	(0.02)
Gini*diffGDPPC		0.02***		0.02***
		(0.00)		(0.00)
DiffGDPPC	−0.04	−1.49***	−0.02	−1.79***
	(0.05)	(0.21)	(0.06)	(0.26)
GDP	2.45***	2.45***	2.72***	2.71***
	(0.04)	(0.04)	(0.05)	(0.05)
GDPPC	0.07	0.10**	0.05	0.08
	(0.05)	(0.05)	(0.06)	(0.06)
Distance	−2.59***	-2.65***	−2.82***	−2.89***
	(0.09)	(0.09)	(0.11)	(0.11)
Areas	−0.90***	−0.91***	−1.06***	−1.07***
	(0.06)	(0.06)	(0.07)	(0.07)
LL	−0.86***	−0.78***	−1.01***	−0.92***
	(0.12)	(0.12)	(0.13)	(0.13)
ERV	−3.46***	−3.58***	−4.11***	−4.25***
	(0.84)	(0.84)	(0.84)	(0.87)
Border	0.27	0.14	0.13	−0.02
	(0.32)	(0.33)	(0.48)	(0.48)
Lang	2.18***	2.19***	2.48***	2.49***
	(0.17)	(0.17)	(0.22)	(0.22)
Colonial	−2.58**	−2.75**	−3.25*	−3.46**
	(1.18)	(1.18)	(1.69)	(1.69)
Colonizer	1.97***	1.97***	2.28***	2.28***
	(0.24)	(0.24)	(0.27)	(0.27)
Regional	0.66*	0.59	0.43	0.35
	(0.36)	(0.36)	(0.67)	(0.66)
OneFTA	−0.72***	−0.68***	−0.88***	−0.84***
	(0.12)	(0.12)	(0.15)	(0.15)
CU	5.00***	5.20***	5.60***	5.84***
	(0.54)	(0.60)	(0.94)	(0.94)
M2GDP	−0.00003	−0.00003	−0.00007*	−0.00007*
	(0.00003)	(0.00003)	(0.00004)	(0.00004)
Gov_ds	0.45***	0.43***	0.52***	0.50***
	(0.04)	(0.04)	(0.05)	(0.05)
CPY	−2.68***	−2.76***	−3.13***	−3.23***
	(0.85)	(0.86)	(0.78)	(0.78)
CPE	0.12	0.09	0.16	0.12
	(0.14)	(0.14)	(0.16)	(0.16)
Constant	−70.14***	−58.66***	−78.50***	−64.45***
	(1.63)	(2.42)	(1.87)	(2.77)
No. observations	15,756	15,756	2,197[a]	13,559[b]
R^2	0.47	0.55		
Pseudo R^2			0.08	0.08
Log likelihood			−50,784	−50,761

Notes
***Significant at $p = 0.01$; **Significant at $p = 0.05$; *Significant at $p = 0.10$.
a Left-censored, cf. p. 73.
b Uncensored, cf. p. 73.

separate types of inequality become much larger and more significant. As hypothesized, the coefficient of the interaction term is positive. These results rather dramatically demonstrate the importance of our extension of the Linder model and also the significance of the two types of inequality in affecting the level of bilateral trade. Separate analyses by year, though not reported here, also showed the values of all parameters except the constant terms to be quite stable over time, thereby justifying the inclusion of year dummies in the specification used throughout this chapter.

The European Union's (EU) "cohesion" policies represent a much more serious attempt to level the playing field for trade among its members through redistributive transfers to its poorer members and in homogenizing governance and other institutions. Therefore in Table 4.2 we present the corresponding OLS and TOBIT estimates for the preferred specification (inclusive of the interaction term) for the European Union (689 observations) and for all other countries separately.

If these homogenizing actions of the EU have had any influence, one might expect the estimated coefficients from the EU sample to differ from those obtained from the non-EU sample. To that end, notice that bilateral trade among EU countries is much less negatively affected by the transaction cost variables *Distance*, *Areas* and *LL* and also by *ERV*, *OneFTA* and *DiffGDPPC* and much less positively affected by mass (represented by *GDP*) than bilateral trade among all non-EU countries. We interpret these results as indicating that the EU has done much to succeed in reducing the effects of these naturally asymmetric differences among countries of different size, levels of development and governance institutions.

Table 4.3 presents the corresponding OLS estimates for the preferred specification of the extended gravity model of bilateral trade for all countries, and then the EU and all non-EU countries separately for the more conventional case in which the missing/zero observations are treated as missing. In this case the full sample consists of 13,559 observations, the non-EU sample 12,870 observations and the EU sample the same as it was before (689 observations). Notice that for both the full sample and the non-EU sample the R^2 value is quite a bit higher than it was when the missing/zero observations were treated as zeros as in Tables 4.1 and 4.2. There are also numerous examples of considerable differences in the coefficients estimated according to the two different assumptions about the missing/zero observations. For example, the coefficients of *GDP*, *Colonizer*, *Lang* and *CU*, are all smaller (though still positive) in Table 4.3 compared with Table 4.1 while the negative coefficients for *Distance*, *Areas*, *LL* and *ERV* are all smaller in absolute terms. On the other hand, the positive influence of *Regional* is now larger and much more significant. Yet, once again, with the inequality interaction term included, the results for all three inequality measures are qualitatively similar to those in Tables 4.1 and 4.2. In other words, both intra-country inequality (*Gini2*) and inter-country inequality (*DiffGDPPC*) have negative and significant effects on bilateral trade whereas *Gini*DiffGDPPC* has a positive and significant influence. Once again, all three hypotheses are supported.

Table 4.2 Determinants of bilateral trade among EU and non-EU countries based on data that includes observations with zero trade[a]

Variables	EU			Non-EU		
	OLS	TOBIT	TOBIT	OLS	TOBIT	TOBIT
Gini2	−0.19***	0.01**	−0.19***	−0.14***	−0.02***	−0.17***
	(0.05)	(0.01)	(0.05)	(0.02)	(0.01)	(0.02)
Gini_diffGDPPC	0.02***		0.02***	0.02***		0.02***
	(0.00)		(0.01)	(0.00)		(0.00)
DiffGDPPC	−1.34***	0.27***	−1.33***	−1.43***	−0.12**	−1.73***
	(0.37)	(0.06)	(0.42)	(0.22)	(0.06)	(0.28)
GDP	0.91***	0.91***	0.91***	2.48***	2.76***	2.76***
	(0.05)	(0.04)	(0.04)	(0.04)	(0.05)	(0.05)
GDPPC	0.21***	0.23***	0.21***	0.15***	0.11	0.14**
	(0.05)	(0.05)	(0.05)	(0.05)	(0.07)	(0.07)
Distance	−0.79***	−0.81***	−0.80***	−2.72***	−2.94***	−2.99***
	(0.08)	(0.08)	(0.08)	(0.09)	(0.11)	(0.11)
Areas	−0.13***	−0.14***	−0.13***	−0.92***	−1.08***	−1.09***
	(0.05)	(0.05)	(0.05)	(0.06)	(0.07)	(0.07)
LL	−0.36***	−0.34***	−0.35***	−0.78***	−1.01***	−0.92***
	(0.13)	(0.12)	(0.12)	(0.13)	(0.14)	(0.14)
ERV	−0.10	−0.12	−0.10	−3.83***	−4.44***	−4.57***
	(0.72)	(0.68)	(0.68)	(0.86)	(0.90)	(0.90)
Border	1.01**	0.95*	1.00**	−0.02	−0.10	−0.22
	(0.42)	(0.48)	(0.48)	(0.34)	(0.49)	(0.49)
Lang	(dropped)	(dropped)	(dropped)	2.20***	2.50***	2.51***
				(0.18)	(0.23)	(0.23)
Colonial	(dropped)	(dropped)	(dropped)	−2.94**	−3.55**	−3.72**
				(1.15)	(1.73)	(1.73)
Colonizer	(dropped)	(dropped)	(dropped)	2.04***	2.38***	2.38***
				(0.24)	(0.28)	(0.27)
Regional	(dropped)	(dropped)	(dropped)	0.57	0.38	0.31
				(0.38)	(0.69)	(0.69)
OneFTA	0.39***	0.41***	0.39***	−0.77***	−0.98***	−0.95***
	(0.11)	(0.11)	(0.11)	(0.13)	(0.15)	(0.15)
EU	0.35***	0.25	0.35			
	(0.13)	(0.58)	(0.57)			
CU	(dropped)	(dropped)	(dropped)	5.09***	5.53***	5.74***
				(0.60)	(0.96)	(0.96)
M2GDP	0.00017***	0.00016***	0.00016***	−0.00002	−0.00007*	−0.00007
	(0.00003)	(0.00004)	(0.00004)	(0.00003)	(0.00004)	(0.00004)
Gov_ds	0.05	0.06*	0.05	0.44***	0.53***	0.51***
	(0.03)	(0.03)	(0.03)	(0.04)	(0.05)	(0.05)
CPY	−0.59	−0.34	−0.58	−2.72***	−3.11***	−3.21***
	(0.66)	(0.58)	(0.58)	(0.88)	(0.81)	(0.81)
CPE	0.48***	0.40***	0.48***	0.09	0.16	0.13
	(0.14)	(0.15)	(0.15)	(0.15)	(0.16)	(0.16)
Dum_1985	(dropped)	1.12***	(dropped)	(dropped)	0.92***	0.92***
		(0.20)			(0.27)	(0.27)
Dum_1990	−0.98***	0.22	−0.97***	−0.32	0.59**	0.61**
	(0.17)	(0.17)	(0.16)	(0.26)	(0.26)	(0.26)
Dum_1995	−1.31***	−0.13	−1.31***	−0.37	0.55**	0.55**
	(0.19)	(0.16)	(0.16)	(0.23)	(0.22)	(0.22)

continued

Table 4.2 Continued

Variables	EU			Non-EU		
	OLS	TOBIT	TOBIT	OLS	TOBIT	TOBIT
Dum_1997	−1.41***	−0.21	−1.41***	−0.85***	(dropped)	(dropped)
	(0.17)	(0.15)	(0.16)	(0.23)		
Dum_2000	−1.21***	(dropped)	−1.21***	−1.08***	−0.24	−0.26
	(0.18)	(0.20)	(0.24)	(0.21)	(0.21)	
Constant	−11.09***	−27.84***	−11.19***	−59.66***	−79.61***	66.92***
	(4.06)	(1.77)	(4.34)	(2.44)	(1.95)	(2.87)
No. observations	689	689	689	15,067	15,067	15,067
		688	1[b]		12,870[b]	2,197[c]
R^2	0.8032			0.4699		
RMSE	1.1211			7.3520		
Pseudo R^2		0.3436	0.3483		0.0823	0.0826

Notes
***Significant at $p = 0.01$; **Significant at $p = 0.05$; *Significant at $p = 0.10$.
a Variables deliberately omitted are indicated as blank cells. Variables that resulted as linear combination of other variables have been dropped.
b Uncensored, cf. p. 73.
c Left-censored, cf. p. 73.

Conclusions

While some earlier empirical studies have examined the effects of cross-country income inequality (i.e. differences in per capita income between trading partners or *DiffGDPPC*) on bilateral trade, to the best of our knowledge no such study has focused on the effects of intra-national income inequality (*Gini2*) or its interactions with *DiffGDPPC* on such trade. Yet, the results presented here based on pooled data in Tables 4.1–4.3 show that, overall, the effects of both inter-country inequality and within-country inequality are both negative and highly significant. But this is primarily the case only after one includes also the interaction term between the two types of inequality (*Gini*DiffGDPPC*). These results are quite robust to differences in treatment of the missing/zero observations and to the choice of estimation technique.

The inspiration for both such effects was the famous essay of Linder (1961). He argued that both such effects on bilateral trade should be negative, at least in the case of trade in manufactures. He recognized, however, that primary trade would be likely to have rather different determinants, indeed, along the lines of comparative advantage based on relative factor endowments. Hence, the fact that in our study the negative and significant effects of both intra-national and between-country income inequality hold even for *total* bilateral trade in commodities is quite important.

In view of the strength of these findings, one can only wonder why the effects of inequality on trade have been so much neglected. One possible clue can be obtained by comparing the results of the first two columns in Table 4.1. In

Table 4.3 Determinants of bilateral trade excluding observations with zeros or missing data[a]

Variables	All countries		EU		Non-EU	
Gini2	0.00072	−0.04***	0.01**	−0.19***	−0.00084	−0.04***
	(0.00159)	(0.01)	(0.01)	(0.05)	(0.00164)	(0.01)
Gini*diff GDPPC		0.00495***		0.02***		0.00449***
		(0.00073)		(0.00)		(0.00075)
DiffGDPPC	0.01	−0.41***	0.27***	−1.34***	0.00	−0.38***
	(0.01)	(0.06)	(0.07)	(0.37)	(0.01)	(0.06)
GDP	1.10***	1.10***	0.91***	0.91***	1.11***	1.11***
	(0.01)	(0.01)	(0.05)	(0.05)	(0.01)	(0.01)
GDPPC	0.05***	0.06***	0.23***	0.21***	0.06***	0.06***
	(0.01)	(0.01)	(0.05)	(0.05)	(0.01)	(0.01)
Distance	−1.35***	−1.37***	−0.81***	−0.79***	−1.40***	−1.41***
	(0.03)	(0.03)	(0.08)	(0.08)	(0.03)	(0.03)
Areas	−0.15***	−0.15***	−0.13***	−0.13***	−0.16***	−0.16***
	(0.02)	(0.02)	(0.05)	(0.05)	(0.02)	(0.02)
LL	−0.26***	−0.24***	−0.34***	−0.36***	−0.26***	−0.24***
	(0.03)	(0.03)	(0.13)	(0.13)	(0.04)	(0.04)
ERV	0.32	0.29	−0.12	−0.10	0.27	0.24
	(0.23)	(0.23)	(0.72)	(0.72)	(0.24)	(0.24)
Border	0.82***	0.79***	0.95**	1.01**	0.76***	0.74***
	(0.11)	(0.11)	(0.45)	(0.42)	(0.11)	(0.11)
Lang	0.62***	0.63***			0.60***	0.61***
	(0.05)	(0.05)			(0.05)	(0.05)
Colonial	0.65*	0.59*		0.56	0.52	
	(0.34)	(0.32)		(0.35)	(0.33)	
Colonizer	0.58***	0.59***		0.58***	0.58***	
	(0.07)	(0.07)		(0.07)	(0.07)	
Regional	1.36***	1.34***		1.34***	1.33***	
	(0.13)	(0.13)		(0.13)	(0.13)	
OneFTA	0.01	0.02	0.40***	0.39***	0.03	0.03
	(0.03)	(0.03)	(0.12)	(0.11)	(0.04)	(0.04)
EU			0.25*	0.35***		
			(0.13)	(0.13)		
CU	1.61***	1.67***	(dropped)	(dropped)	1.60***	1.66***
	(0.24)	(0.24)			(0.24)	(0.24)
M2GDP	0.00015***	0.00015***	0.00016***	0.00017***	0.00014***	0.00014***
	0.00001	0.00001	0.00003	0.00003	0.00001	0.00001
Gov_ds	0.13***	0.12***	0.06*	0.05	0.13***	0.13***
	(0.01)	(0.01)	(0.03)	(0.03)	(0.01)	(0.01)
CPY	−0.26	−0.28	−0.34	−0.59	−0.24	−0.26
	(0.19)	(0.19)	(0.64)	(0.66)	(0.20)	(0.20)
CPE	−0.06	−0.07*	0.40***	0.48***	−0.09**	−0.10**
	(0.04)	(0.04)	(0.14)	(0.14)	(0.04)	(0.04)
Dum_1985	(dropped)	(dropped)	1.11***	(dropped)	(dropped)	(dropped)
			(0.18)			
Dum_1990	−0.37***	−0.36***	0.22	−0.98***	−0.35***	−0.34***
	(0.07)	(0.07)	(0.15)	(0.17)	(0.07)	(0.07)
Dum_1995	−0.58***	−0.58***	−0.13	−1.31***	−0.56***	−0.56***
	(0.06)	(0.06)	(0.14)	(0.19)	(0.07)	(0.07)
Dum_1997	−0.76***	−0.76***	−0.21*	−1.41***	−0.75***	−0.75***
	(0.06)	(0.06)	(0.12)	(0.17)	(0.07)	(0.07)

continued

Table 4.3 Continued

Variables	All countries		EU		Non-EU	
Dum_2000	−0.51***	−0.52***	(dropped)	−1.21***	−0.52***	−0.52***
	(0.06)	(0.06)		(0.18)	(0.07)	(0.07)
Constant	−24.82***	−21.45***	−27.77***	−11.09***	−24.65***	−21.63***
	(0.45)	(0.69)	(1.99)	(4.06)	(0.46)	(0.70)
No. observations	13,559	13,559	689	689	12,870	12,870
R^2	0.72	0.72	0.80	0.80	0.71	0.71
RMSE	1.89	1.89	1.13	1.12	1.92	1.91

Notes
***Significant at $p = 0.01$; **Significant at $p = 0.05$; *Significant at $p = 0.10$.
a Variables deliberately omitted are indicated as blank cells. Variables that resulted as linear combination of other variables have been dropped.

particular, the results given in the first column of Table 4.1 show that, when the two inequality measures (*Gini2* and *DiffGDPPC*) are included by themselves, the inter-country inequality term has a negative but not significant effect on bilateral trade. Only when the third inequality measure, namely *Gini*DiffGDPPC*, is included in the specification, do the other effects become strongly negative. Since the interaction term was ignored by Linder and hence by all empirical researchers trying to test Linder's hypotheses, one can begin to see why the Linder hypotheses have found only scant support in the literature.

Should these results hold up to further replication and testing with new data, some interesting implications, including some for policy, may follow. First, since the characteristics of the countries one trades with can have especially important effects on the quantity of trade in the increasingly important reputational goods, the choice of trade partners may have considerable long-term impacts on the total volume of realizable trade. Therefore, if trade is actually good for growth and development for all trading partners, as suggested by Frankel and Romer (1999) and many (but by no means all) scholars working on "openness and growth" or "exports and growth," then policy efforts to reduce inequality, both between nations and within nations, could have an additional justification.

Second, the positive effect on bilateral trade of the interaction of the two types of inequality (*Gini*DiffGDPPC*) suggests that intra-national inequality hurts trade most among countries at similar levels of income per capita. Hence, in the context of economic integration, it might suggest that countries should try to integrate with countries at similar levels of development and with low levels of income inequality. Since the governance index has also been shown to have highly significant positive effects on bilateral trade, the results also suggest that countries would do well to choose trading partners with good governance institutions. Put differently, the results would suggest that efforts to reduce trade and transaction cost barriers would be most effective among trading partners with similar levels of average income, low inequality and good governance.

Moreover, given a regional trade arrangement, the results would imply that trade can be promoted by measures designed to mitigate inequalities both within and between countries. At a global level, the model would suggest that efforts to increase trade through tariff and other liberalization measures would be more successful when preceded or at least accompanied by measures designed to reduce these same inequalities. It would also suggest that efforts to improve governance among countries one trades with would also be trade promoting. Further evidence in support of these last implications can also be seen by comparing the means of the different inequality and governance measures for each of the different sample years in Table 4.4. Note for example the fact that the values of *Gini2* and *DiffGDPPC* are both lower for the EU trading partners than for those of the *NAFTA, CACM, CARICOM, ASEAN* or *Non-FTA* samples.[12] Even the average difference in Gini coefficients (*Gini2diff*) between trading partners is smaller than those of all other regions except *CARICOM*. Although the governance index among each pair of EU members fell with expansion of the EU in the 1990s, the index has increased since 1995 and remains higher in 2000 than those of trading partners in all but one other region.

The fact that our results hold for aggregate commodity trade that includes agricultural and other primary commodities for which Linder conceded that his model would not apply implies that the results should hold a fortiori for manufactured goods. However, in view of the increasingly close linkage between agriculture and food processing, supermarket distribution and patenting of agricultural varieties, it is not inconceivable that the same considerations may now be applying even to agriculture. This would be interesting to test using more disaggregated data.

Also, some of the same brand name, product differentiation and network influences lying behind the Linder-oriented trade in manufactures might well apply to trade in services. However, to the extent that industry concentration would appear to be greater in many services, it is less obvious that the same coincidence of greater income equality and greater trade would also prevail in services. Since trade in services is now accounting for over half of total trade flows, this issue deserves careful investigation.

Table 4.4 Means of variables by group of trading partners[a]

	EU	NAFTA	Non-FTA[b]	CARICOM[b]	CACM	ASEAN[b]	All Other[b]
1985							
No. observations	36		9,728	36	10	36	106
GDPPC	16,452		6,992	6,226	2,231	6,027	6,687
Gov_ds	5.26		−0.57	−3.30	−3.10	−0.40	−1.08
Gini2	64.80		180.30	85.90	102.00	80.10	85.30
Gini2diff	4.54		11.53	4.42	6.88	8.68	7.77
DiffGDPPC (%)	15.80		63.60	57.70	23.45	78.86	57.13
1990							
No. observations	55		10,268	36	10	45	117
GDPPC	33,898		10,883	6,916	2,042	6,478	9,306
Gov_ds	3.19		−1.40	−3.17	−2.61	−1.52	−2.02
Gini2	63.30		81.00	82.70	103.30	80.00	84.70
Gini2diff	3.50		11.80	1.70	8.10	9.40	7.90
DiffGDPPC (%)	19.66		68.68	58.36	44.96	76.17	53.53
1995							
No. observations	91	3	12,507	36	10	45	122
GDPPC	45,961	33,724	12,129	7,310	3,099	10,837	12,182
Gov_ds	−0.14	−0.55	0.01	0.42	0.33	0.77	0.23
Gini2	63.70	82.30	80.90	81.90	103.40	79.10	83.50
Gini2diff	5.70	15.20	11.70	3.70	6.10	7.80	7.30
DiffGDPPC (%)	18.53	48.58	71.34	56.82	45.63	73.77	55.76
1997							
No. observations	91	3	12,356	28	10	45	114
GDPPC	43,834	36,950	12,205	6,171	3,386	11,385	12,607
Gov_ds	1.66	0.10	0.99	1.29	1.42	1.37	1.05
Gini2	65.10	86.77	81.16	81.10	104.45	80.24	84.54
Gini2diff	5.40	14.20	11.10	4.50	6.60	8.70	7.60
DiffGDPPC (%)	15.15	47.04	70.06	46.62	44.69	72.98	53.57
2000							
No. observations	91	3	12,365	36	10	28	105
GDPPC	42,409	42,432	11,653	10,162	3,733	7,920	12,560
Gov_ds	1.68	0	0.80	0.93	2.28	1.06	1.13
Gini2	65.23	86.77	81.45	81.10	105.46	79.44	84.44
Gini2diff	5.40	14.20	11.00	4.50	7.10	8.30	7.60
DiffGDPPC (%)	14.76	45.31	70.52	53.21	46.02	82.21	50.79

Notes

a NAFTA: North America Free Trade Area; CACM: Central American Common Market; CARICOM: Caribbean Community and Common Market; ASEAN: Association of Southeast Asian Nations.

b Some variables have fewer observations than the number indicated for the year shown.

Appendix

Table 4.a.1 List of countries/territories included in the analysis

1 Afghanistan	44 Cyprus	84 Iran
2 Albania	45 Czech Rep.	85 Iraq
3 Algeria	46 Fm. Czechoslovakia	86 Ireland
4 Angola	47 Denmark	87 Israel
5 Argentina	48 Djibouti	88 Italy
6 Armenia	49 Dominican Rep.	89 Jamaica
7 Australia	50 Ecuador	90 Japan
8 Austria	51 Egypt	91 Jordan
9 Azerbaijan	52 El Salvador	92 Kazakhstan
10 Bahamas	53 Eq. Guinea	93 Kenya
11 Bahrain	54 Estonia	94 Kiribati (includes
12 Bangladesh	55 Ethiopia	Tonga)
13 Barbados	56 Falkland Islands	95 Korea Dem. P. Rep.
14 Belarus	57 Fiji	(North)
15 Belgium-Luxembourg	58 Finland	96 Korea Rep. (South)
16 Belize	59 Fm. German Dem.	97 Kuwait
17 Benin	Rep. (East)	98 Kyrgyz Rep.
18 Bermuda	60 Fm. USSR	99 Laos P. Dem. Rep.
19 Bhutan	61 Fm. Yugoslavia	100 Latvia
20 Bolivia	(includes Croatia,	101 Lebanon
21 Bosnia and	Slovenia)	102 Liberia
Herzegovina	62 France	103 Libyan Arab Jamahiriya
22 British Indian Ocean	63 French Guiana	104 Lithuania
Territories	64 Gabon	105 Macedonia
23 Brazil	65 Gambia	106 Madagascar
24 Brunei	66 Georgia	107 Malawi
25 Bulgaria	67 Germany	108 Malaysia
26 Burkina Faso	68 Ghana	109 Maldives
27 Burundi	69 Gibraltar	110 Mali
28 Cambodia	70 Greece	111 Malta
29 Cameroon	71 Greenland	112 Mauritania
30 Canada	72 Guadeloupe (includes	113 Mauritius
31 Cayman Islands	Martinique)	114 Mexico
32 Central African Rep.	73 Guatemala	115 Moldova
33 Chad	74 Guinea	116 Mongolia
34 Chile	75 Guinea-Bissau	117 Morocco
35 China	(includes Cape Verde)	118 Mozambique
36 Colombia	76 Guyana	119 Myanmar (Burma)
37 Comoros	77 Haiti	120 Nepal
38 Congo	78 Honduras	121 Neth Antilles
39 Congo, Dem. Rep. of	79 Hong Kong	122 Netherlands
(Zaire)	80 Hungary	123 New Caledonia
40 Costa Rica	81 Iceland	(includes French
41 Cote D'Ivoire	82 India	Polynesia and
42 Croatia	83 Indonesia (including	Vanuatu)
43 Cuba	Macao)	124 New Zealand

125 Nicaragua	147 Sierra Leone	165 Tajikistan
126 Niger	148 Singapore	166 Tanzania
127 Nigeria	149 Slovak Rep.	167 Thailand
128 Norway	150 Slovenia	168 Togo
129 Oman	151 Solomon Islands	169 Trinidad-Tobago
130 Pakistan	152 Somalia	170 Tunisia
131 Panama	153 South Africa	171 Turkey
132 Papua New Guinea	154 Spain	172 Turkmenistan
133 Paraguay	155 Sri Lanka	173 Turks Caicos Isl.
134 Peru	156 St Kitts Nevis	174 Uganda
135 Philippines	(includes Dominica,	175 Ukraine
136 Poland	St Lucia, St Vincent	176 United Kingdom
137 Portugal	and Grenadines,	177 United Arab Em.
138 Qatar	Grenada)	178 Uruguay
139 Reunion	157 St Pierre Miqu	179 USA
140 Romania	158 St Helena	180 Uzbekistan
141 Russia	159 Sudan	181 Venezuela
142 Rwanda	160 Surinam	182 Vietnam
143 Saudi Arabia	161 Sweden	183 Western Sahara
144 Senegal	162 Switzerland	184 Yemen
145 Serbia and Montenegro	163 Syrian Arab Rep.	185 Zambia
146 Seychelles	164 Taiwan	186 Zimbabwe

Table 4.a.2 Descriptive statistics on variables used in the analysis from maximum sample size

Variable	No. observations	Mean	Standard Deviation
Totaltrade2	76,14	5.40	13.04
Gini2	33,63	80.85	13.90
Gini*diffGDPPC	31,58	633.30	162.29
DiffGDPPC	58,15	7.86	1.80
GDP	58,15	46.48	3.14
GDPPC	58,15	14.99	2.21
Distance	75,91	8.27	0.74
Areas	76,14	13.13	1.63
LL	76,14	0.34	0.53
Border	76,14	0.01	0.13
Lang	76,14	0.12	0.32
Regional	76,14	0.01	0.11
Colonizer	76,14	0.07	0.27
Colonial	76,14	0.00	0.07
ERV	57,19	0.08	0.11
CU	76,14	0.00	0.09
Gov_ds	35,40	0.01	2.33
CPY	76,14	0.04	0.20
CPE	76,14	0.40	0.56
M2GDP	42,60	1,653.95	1,965.63
OneFTA	76,14	0.38	0.48

Notes

1 The authors express their appreciation to Fahyre Loiola de Alencar for her research assistance in finding relevant papers and preparing tables, and to an anonymous referee, Yujiro Hayami, Odin Knudsen, Donato Romano and especially Pan Yotopoulos for their useful comments on an earlier draft of the chapter.

2 See especially Deaton and Muellbauer (1980) for a detailed analytical survey. However, systematic error in stated income measurement across income groups is another possible explanation. In particular, people with low incomes are often self-employed and likely either to deliberately or to inadvertently understate their income in surveys.

3 See also Matsuyama (2000). Matsuyama, however, did not introduce income distribution into the analysis.

4 Use of the gravity model has become even more popular after Anderson (1979), Bergstrand (1989) and others provided a theoretical underpinning for it.

5 Leamer and Levinsohn (1995) attribute to the gravity model "some of the clearest and most robust empirical findings in economics."

6 Prices and tariffs are not used as explanatory variables because of the very limited availability and low quality of data on them.

7 The countries are listed in Table 4.a.1 in the Appendix.

8 These are of "Voice and Accountability," "Political Stability," "Government Effectiveness," "Regulatory Quality," "Rule of Law" and "Control of Corruption." Data on these governance components were taken from the International Country Risk Guide (ICRG) produced by the Political Risk Services (PRS) group, where the components of the political risk index were used, which report subjective assessments of the factors influencing the business environment in the countries studied. Several of these components were, in turn, based on additional sub-indicators. Specifically, "Voice and Accountability" was based on two sub-components from ICRG data: Military in Politics and Democratic Accountability; "Political Stability" was based on one sub-component, Internal Conflict; "Government Effectiveness" on both Government Stability and Bureaucratic Quality; "Regulatory Quality" on Investment Profile; "Rule of Law" on Law and Order; and "Control of Corruption" on Corruption. The ICRG data has two very desirable features: (1) its large sample of developed and developing countries (130+) and (2) its length of coverage over time (1982–current). The ICRG data depends on polls of experts. The central advantage of polls of experts is that they are explicitly designed for cross-country comparability, and great effort is put into the benchmarking process to ensure this.

9 While the aforementioned aspects of governance are admittedly subjective, there are several reasons for believing their use to be beneficial. First, objective data, e.g. on corruption, are almost by definition very difficult to obtain. Second, while a country may enjoy a set of sound institutions according to some objective standards, the confidence of residents of this country in these institutions is required if those residents are to participate in and contribute to good governance. Thus perceptions of the quality of governance may be as important as objective differences in institutions across countries (Kaufmann *et al.*, 1999a). Third, subjective perceptions might have greater explanatory power for future economic outcomes than past objective data. For example, Kaufmann *et al.* (1999b), in the context of the East Asian financial crisis, found that investor perceptions of future financial instability had significant explanatory power for future actual volatility. Fourth, the data are not intended to constitute absolute measures but only "indices." As such their aim is primarily to sort countries into broad groupings according to levels of governance and to indicate changes over time.

10 Descriptive statistics on all the variables are given in Table 4.a.2.

11 The dummy variable for a regional trading arrangement between the two trading partners (*Regional*), however, though positive, is not statistically significant.

12 For more detailed analyses and comparisons of the effects of different regional trading agreements, see Miniesy *et al.* (2004).

References

Anderson, James E. (1979), "A Theoretical Foundation for the Gravity Equation," *American Economic Review*, 69 (1): 106–16.

Bergstrand, Jeffrey H. (1989), "The Generalized Gravity Equation, Monopolistic Competition and the Factor Proportions Theory in International Trade," *Review of Economics and Statistics*, 71 (2): 143–53.

CIA (2004), "The World Factbook," Langley, VA: US Central Intelligence Agency. Online, available www.odci.gov/cia/publications/factbook/index.html (accessed 3 June 2004).

Deaton, Angus and John Muellbauer (1980), *Economics and Consumer Behavior*. Cambridge: Cambridge University Press.

Deininger, Klaus and Lynn Squire (1997), "Measuring Income Inequality: A New Data Base." Washington, DC: World Bank.

Feenstra, Robert C. (2000), *World Trade Flows, 1980–1997*. Davis, CA: Center for International Data, Institute of Governmental Affairs.

Frankel, Jeffrey A. and David Romer (1999), "Does Trade Cause Growth?" *American Economic Review*, 89 (3): 379–96.

Glick, Reuven and Andrew K. Rose (2002), "Does a Currency Union Affect Trade? The Time Series Evidence," *European Economic Review*, 46 (4): 1125–51.

Grossman, Gene M. and Elhanan Helpman (1991), *Innovation and Growth in the Global Economy*. Cambridge: The MIT Press.

Helpman, Elhanan (1981), "International Trade in the Presence of Product Differentiation, Economies of Scale and Monopolistic Competition," *Journal of International Economics*, 11 (August): 305–40.

Helpman, Elhanan and Paul R. Krugman (1985), *Market Structure and Foreign Trade: Increasing Returns, Imperfect Competition and the International Economy*. Cambridge: The MIT Press.

Hunter, Linda C. (1991), "The Contribution of Nonhomothetic Preferences to Trade," *Journal of International Economics*, 30 (2): 345–58.

Hunter, Linda C. and James R. Markusen (1988), "Per-Capita Income as a Determinant of Trade." In Robert C. Feenstra, ed., *Empirical Methods for International Trade*. Cambridge: The MIT Press, pp. 89–109.

IMF (2003), *Directon of Trade Statistics (DOTS) 2003*, CD-Rom. Washington, DC: International Monetary Fund.

Kaufmann, Daniel, Aart Kraay and Pablo Zoido-Lobatón (1999a), "Aggregating Governance Indicators." Policy Research Working Papers no. 2195. Washington, DC: World Bank.

Kaufmann, Daniel, Gil Mehrez and Sergio Schmukler (1999b), "Was the East Asia Crisis Predictable?" Washington, DC: World Bank.

Kaufmann, Daniel, Aart Kraay and Pablo Zoido-Lobatón (2002), "Governance Matters II." Policy Research Working Papers no. 2772. Washington, DC: World Bank.

Keynes, John M. (1936), *The General Theory of Employment, Interest and Money*. New York: Harcourt, Brace and World.

Leamer, Edward E. and James Levinsohn (1995), "International Trade Theory: The Evidence." In Gene M. Grossman and Kenneth Rogoff, eds, *Handbook of International Economics*, vol. III. Amsterdam: Elsevier-North Holland.

Linder, Steffan (1961), *An Essay on Trade and Transformation*. Stockholm: Almqvist and Wicksell.

Markusen, James R. (1986), "Explaining the Volume of Trade: An Eclectic Approach," *American Economic Review*, 76 (5): 1002–11.

Matsuyama, Kiminori (2000), "A Ricardian Model with a Continuum of Goods under Nonhomothetic Preferences: Demand Complementarities, Income Distribution and North-South Trade," *Journal of Political Economy*, 108 (6): 1093–120.

Miniesy, Rania S., Jeffrey B. Nugent and Tarik M. Yousef (2004), "Intra-regional Trade Integration in the Middle East: Past Performance and Future Potential." In Hassan Hakimian and Jeffrey B. Nugent, eds, *Trade Policy and Economic Integration in the Middle East and North Africa: Economic Boundaries in Flux*. London: Routledge Curzon, pp. 41–65.

Mitra, Devashish and Vitor Trindade (2003), "Inequality and Trade," NBER Working Paper no. 10087. Cambridge, MA: National Bureau of Economic Research.

Rose, Andrew K. (2000), "One Money, One Market: Estimating the Effect of Common Currencies on Trade," *Economic Policy*, 15 (April): 7–46.

Thursby, Jerry G. and Marie C. Thursby (1987), "Bilateral Trade Flows, the Linder Hypothesis and Exchange Risk," *Review of Economics and Statistics*, 69 (3): 488–95.

UN (2003), "National Accounts Statistics: Main Aggregates and Detailed Tables (1985–2000)." New York: United Nations. Online, available unstats.un.org/unsd/nationalaccount/nasp.htm (accessed 5 June 2004).

WIDER (2000), "World Income Inequality Database (2000)." Helsinki: United Nations University/World Institute for Development Economic Research. Online, available www.wider.unu.edu/wiid/wiid.htm (accessed 5 June 2004).

World Bank (2003), *World Development Indicators 2003*, CD-Rom. Washington, DC: World Bank.

WTO (2004), "Regional Trade Agreements Notified to the GATT/WTO and in Force," Geneva: World Trade Organization. Online, available www.wto.org/english/tratop_e/region_e/eif_e.xls (accessed 5 June 2004).

Part II
Institutional asymmetries

5 Communities and markets for rural development under globalization

A perspective from villages in Asia[1]

Yujiro Hayami

Introduction

The current surge of globalization is creating the opportunity to increase income for the rural poor by conveying demands from advanced economies for such high-valued products as flowers, fruits and vegetables to the hinterlands that have hitherto been bypassed in development currents. However, rural producers in low-income economies will not be able to capture this opportunity unless adequate channels exist for connecting them with distant urban markets and/or centers for exports. It is well known that rural markets in low-income economies are underdeveloped, being characterized by high transaction costs owing to imperfect information and high risk as well as absence of effective mechanisms to protect property rights and to enforce contracts. Under these constraints it has often been feared that small producers and petty traders in rural hinterlands tend to be exploited by foreign or urban traders who have monopoly access to global information – the so-called "asymmetric information problem."

The major thrust of this chapter is to show that the trust and cooperation mechanisms existing in rural communities in developing economies could form a basis for the efficient functioning of markets that channel global demands to producers in the hinterlands. The conceptual framework shall be based on recent theoretical developments in institutional economics, and shall be further supported by concrete examples from case studies on the marketing of peasants' produce in Asia.

Community trust: a conceptual framework

In this use of the word, a "community" is a group of people tied by mutual trust based on intense personal interactions. Theoretically, communities range from the family to the national community and further to the global community. However, the communities discussed in this chapter are those in between this range, characterized by personal relationships closer than the arm's length relation. In developing economies they are typically identified as tribes and villages tied by blood and locational affinities.

The community in this definition can be considered one major component of the economic system. As aptly pointed out by Adam Smith, advancement in the productive power of human society is brought about by progress in the division of labor. As people specialize in various activities, a system is required to co-ordinate them. The "economic system" in its present definition is a combination of the economic organizations that coordinate various economic activities so as to achieve a socially optimum division of labor. The market is the organization that coordinates profit-seeking individuals through competition under the signal of parametric price changes. The state is the organization that forces people to adjust their resource allocations by the command of government. On the other hand, the community is the organization that guides community members to vol-untary cooperation based upon close personal ties and mutual trust. In other words, the market operates by means of competition based on egoism, the state operates by means of command based on legitimate coercive power, and the community utilizes cooperation based on consent to coordinate the division of labor among people towards a socially desirable direction (Hayami and Godo, 2005).

The comparative advantage of the community lies in the supply of "local public goods" whose benefit is limited to a particular group, as compared with the market's advantage in the supply of private goods and the government's advantage in the supply of global or pure public goods (Pagano, Chapter 2). The local public goods that the community normally supplies may be classified into three categories. The first is the provision of social safety nets for rescuing dis-advantaged members from eventual subsistence crises. This role of the commun-ity has long been emphasized since Thomas More's *Utopia* (Hayami, 1989). The second is the conservation of common-pool or common-property resources, such as forests, grazing lands, irrigation systems and village roads. This role has increasingly been advocated recently (Feeny *et al.*, 1990; Ostrom, 1990; Baland and Platteau, 1996). In contrast, the third possible role of community to facilitate market transactions by aiding to enforce trade contracts has received relatively little attention (Aoki and Hayami, 2001).

The community's contribution to market development is based on the same characteristic as is its contributions to the provision of social safety nets and to the conservation of common-pool resources: the power of the community rela-tionship to prevent free riders from trying to profit by violating contracts. For the community-based safety nets to be effective, all the members must contribute due insurance premiums according to the principle of reciprocity dictated by customs and norms. The same applies to community members' contributions to the conservation of common-pool resources. However, it is very tempting for any member to be a free rider, for example, by utilizing a village road built by others' collective work without his participation in the project. Therefore, if one is allowed to be a free rider, all others tend to follow, with the result of no new local public goods being supplied.

The community has the power to suppress one's incentive to be a free rider by means of cooperative spirit nurtured through intensive social interactions among its members and their fear of being ostracized. The cost of being subjected to social opprobrium and ostracism as the result of acting as a free rider can be very high especially in a small closed community, such as a tribe or a village in low-income economies where exit options are severely limited. If this cost, plus the psychological cost of violating social norms and established moral codes, is higher than the expected gain from exercising opportunism, the community has elided the free rider problem.

The same mechanism can apply to the enforcement of trade contracts. The free rider problem in market transactions often takes the form of the so-called agency problem arising from information asymmetry. For example, a farmer grows tomatoes under a contract with the trader who promised to purchase his entire crop at a certain price. Should this farmer be suddenly confronted with the buyer's demand to accept a lower price for his tomatoes after the harvest, the farmer will hesitate to enter the same contract again, however profitable that might be for both parties when it is faithfully enforced. Likewise, the trader will hesitate to advance credit to the farmer before harvest, if he foresees the risk of the farmer's failure to deliver the tomatoes at the agreed upon quantity and quality. It may appear that these market failures stemming from agents' opportunism against principals can be corrected by contract enforcement through legal procedures. However, the costs involved in formal court proceedings are large, often exceeding the expected gains from dispute settlement on the small transactions that are typical in low-income economies. Moreover, where judges and police are not necessarily the faithful agents of citizens' rights, it can happen that the market failures stemming from information asymmetry not only fail to be corrected but may even be enlarged by government failures.

Under such conditions, trade tends to be limited between buyers and sellers who are embraced by common community relations. Farmers prefer to sell their crops to traders who come from their same village or to those who have relatives and close friends in that village, so that the parties are bound by the respect and reputation they have cultivated in their community which will be jeopardized in case either one defaults on his obligations. The same stands for the traders, so that both parties expect that the community mechanism of cooperation and ostracism will effectively force their trade partners to honor their contracts. The trade circle based on community relationships may originally be small as it is constrained by blood and locational ties in traditional rural communities such as farming villages. It can be gradually expanded to form a wider trade network beyond the traditional community by relying on the initial introduction by other members of the village community who have had transactions with a broader network of traders operating at the town level or the level above it, the city level. Initially the farmer will approach the outside trader gingerly, and the latter may need a guarantee from a trader who has closer ties in the village community, for signing the contract for growing the crop. With repetitive transactions, however, trust develops and the "outside" trader can come to enjoy the same trust that a community trader would enjoy.

Indeed, long-term regular transactions have long been recognized by anthropologists as being effective in forging mutual trust and cooperation that

prevents opportunism from being exercised between transacting parties beyond
the confines of a narrow community like a rural village. This process has been
called "clientelization" by Geertz (1978). In his example, a jeweler in town
bazaar may be strongly tempted to cheat a first-time new customer in his shop
by selling low-quality jewels at high prices. However, for a regular customer he
would be inclined to feel guilty and not willing to lose a long-lasting business
opportunity for a one-shot moral hazard. This anthropological explanation is
matched by the theory of repeated games or the Folk theorem (Kreps and
Wilson, 1982; Fudenberg and Maskin, 1986; Abreu, 1988). Mutual trust created
by long-term continuous transactions can further be reinforced by interlinked
transactions (Bardhan, 1980; Bell, 1988; Hayami and Otsuka, 1993). For
example, a trader not only purchases a commodity from a particular producer
regularly year after year, but also supplies him with materials and credits.
Mutual trust enhanced by intensified interactions as well as by fear of losing a
multifaceted cooperation relationship is a strong force in curbing moral hazard
for both parties. The psychological basis of mutual trust could further be
strengthened by incorporating personal elements in business transactions, such
as exchanges of gifts and attendance at weddings and funerals.

The strength of such a community relationship in support of market transactions has been demonstrated by the success in trade and finance of Jewish
traders in medieval Europe and of Chinese traders in modern Southeast Asia, to
mention only few examples. These ethnic groups were able to establish dominant positions in commercial and financial activities, as they were successful in
reducing transaction costs across distant trading posts among the traders and
bankers bound by the same ethnic community ties (Landa, 1981; Greif, 1989,
1993; Hayami and Kawagoe, 1993). This model of cooperation is repeated
across other ethnic communities throughout.

The role of trust in peasant marketing

The trade channels through which rural producers in developing countries are
integrated with markets are various and differ across different agrarian structures. Here, the emphasis will be on small family farms ("peasants") familiar
from our field observations in Southeast Asia as well as from documentary
knowledge of Japanese history.

One common channel is direct sales from producers to consumers. Women
from farm households selling their products in open bazaars or peddling them
around house by house in the town are a familiar sight in any developing
country. They may be selling vegetables harvested from their backyards, pota-
toes from their fields or snacks they themselves processed from beans. At first
sight, the scene of intensive bargaining in bazaars may give the impression of
the familiar spot cash transactions among the casual sellers and buyers that
populate the world of neoclassical economics. Yet, a closer look will reveal the
case of mostly regular clientele that is well-known to the merchant. Whether it is
the bazaar or the street stall, the seller's territory is well determined and this is

confirmed by the fact that the peddler often sells to the regular customers on credit. Typically, a new peddler is given a small territory from an established peddler from the same village that he gradually expands by cementing and enriching the clientele circle that he was handed. A peddling woman said to the author: "If I am honest with a customer, she will introduce her friends to me, but if I would cheat her, I will not only lose her alone but lose other customers who are friends to her." The power of mutual trust forged through long-term regular (i.e. repetitive) trading to reduce transaction costs is evident even in such rudimentary trade cases. It is also evident that long-term transactions contribute to expand community relationships beyond the confines of a traditional community such as a village.

The direct sales of producers to consumers within a narrow location as explained above are largely limited to (a) sideline enterprises for farm households producing small amounts of marketable surplus which family members can handle and (b) perishable commodities for which quick delivery from production to consumption is necessary.

Marketing channels for major crops such as rice, which can find outlets in wider markets, are much more complicated. The analysis here will attempt to illustrate their characteristics based on the case study for the Laguna province in the Philippines (Hayami *et al.*, 1999; Hayami and Kikuchi, 2000). The marketing flow of rice in the study area is as shown in Figure 5.1. Paddy retained for farmers' home consumption is milled at a piece rate in small village mills (*kiskisan*). The surplus that is destined for the market is milled at large commercial mills (*cono*) located in towns or which have easy access along highways. A relatively small portion of paddy that was consigned to the mills is purchased directly from farmers. The majority is assembled by middlemen called "collectors," who are typically residing in villages and are known to the farmers. It is common that a collector employs several commissioned agents in his operation who can better cement his relationship with the farmers. The independent trader buys, stores and sells paddy at his own risk. Considerable skill is necessary for them to judge the qualities of paddy. Since sale prices to mills vary for different varieties and moisture contents, miscalculation on the quality of paddy in offering prices to farmers may entail major losses. Further, the trader must carry the market-price risk which becomes large when he engages in stock-holding operations. He also needs substantial capital investment in owning a truck for hauling the paddy. In contrast, the commission agent is largely free from the trader's risks as he is paid a percentage of the paddies he procured irrespective of price. His capital requirement is low because he uses his principal's truck to haul paddy from farmers' houses. Therefore, villagers who wish to enter the collection business, usually start as commission agents and work toward becoming independent traders.

The hierarchy of traders from commission agents to independent traders, and further up to rice millers, is a common form of the marketing system of peasant agriculture. It is founded on the fact that small farmers have small surpluses to sell, which increases the transaction cost per unit of product collected by the

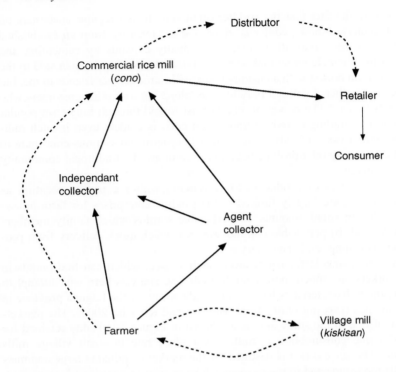

Figure 5.1 Channels of local rice marketing in Laguna, Philippines (source: Hayami et al., 1999).

middleman. An independent trader, who has the sunk costs of his equipment (truck) and his trade skill that he needs to amortize, would rather hire the poor among the peasants who have low opportunity cost to have them contact their neighbor farmers so that he could produce a contract of a full truckload that the trader needs. This condition applies more strongly to rice millers in their dealings with collectors. For the sake of increasing the rate of utilization of their large fixed capital consisting of milling and drying facilities together with a fleet of trucks, they must endeavor to maximize the procurement of paddy from various farms with different harvesting seasons. This condition determines the inevitability of the millers' reliance on the services of collectors. Leaving the task of paddy collection to independent self-employed agents is much more efficient than the vertical integration of the process of collection and of milling. The formal employment of workers by the mill for paddy collection entails high labor management costs since the task is characterized by high seasonality and a large number of small-lot transactions over a wide space.

Given the critical importance of maintaining an assured supply of paddy, rice millers employ various methods to develop a long-term trade relationship with collectors. Credit tying is one method used for this purpose. Millers often advance to collectors short-term credits, from a few days' to a few weeks' duration, with the agreement that paddy procured by the debtors shall be delivered to the lenders, who will deduct the corresponding portion of debt repayment from the loan. This method is also occasionally practiced by independent traders in lending to commission agents as well as to farmers. It should be noted that the incidence of credit advancement from collectors to farmers is smaller than that from farmers to collectors: typically, collectors pay the price of paddy to farmers after they haul and sell the paddy to rice mills and subsequently they pay off their loans. The trust between farmers and collectors in the same village that underlies the practice of paddy sales on credit is an important factor in decreasing the cost of working capital for the collectors.

Rice millers usually act as wholesalers in the distribution of milled rice to local retailers, although some also ship a part of their produce to metropolitan markets via specialized wholesale agents. It is therefore of vital importance for the rice-milling business to secure a stable flow of business from retailers holding stores in town. To this end, millers become inventive in developing and cementing the trust with retailers. One such approach is through advancing interest-free loans to regular customer retailers in the form of sales on credit. This credit operation is said to be risky, because a mutual trust relationship with town retailers is more difficult to establish than with farmers and village-based collectors. A manager of a cooperative owning a rice mill remarked that the coop milling was often interrupted by shortage of demand from retailers. This remark reflects the lack of an incentive mechanism to motivate such risky credit operations, since coop managers are not claimants for residual profits, unlike the private mill operators. Coop managers tend to allocate greater efforts in obtaining subsidies from governmental and non-governmental aid agencies than toward winning competition in the market.

In contrast to the motivation of employees of a business enterprise, private traders are more focused on surviving market competition through the effective use of a community relationship. Indeed, competition is stiff, especially among collectors, because the low capital requirements for this business open the entry virtually to any villager. Rice mills compete in procuring paddy so as to maximize the utilization of their capital. They have to contest business over a wide area, because they have to procure paddy from different locations with different harvesting seasons in order to even out the paddy supply over time. This condition precludes the possibility of any large mill exercising local monopsony power. Intense competition also applies to the wholesaling of rice to retailers as well as to retailing to consumers.

The participants in this competitive market endeavor of crafting stable long-term trade relationships with their partners are driven by the motive of reducing risk and of saving in the transaction costs that arise from the possibility of moral hazard under information asymmetry. Farmers, middlemen and consumers continue to maintain long-term trade relationships as long as it is beneficial to them, but they are quick to switch trade partners if the current relationship is found to be unsatisfactory. As such, long-term trade relationships supported by traditional community norms in rural villages promote rather than constrain market competition for crops produced by small producers, in small lots, for which the time of harvest and delivery is difficult to predict and quality standardization is difficult to establish. Data of marketing margins and of costs collected from our field survey did not show evidence of existence of monopoly/monopsony profit in any segment of rice marketing in the study site.

According to our extensive observations in Asia, the structure of rice marketing outlined in the case of the Philippines is common not only for rice but also for traditional peasant crops in general. The exception is in cases where government market interventions create major distortions by rendering the large institutional rents to a certain favored group that is appointed to transact the marketing. Moreover, this system has not significantly changed for many years. In the Laguna study site, for example, major changes have occurred since the Second World War. The means of transportation have changed from *carabao* and pony-drawn wagons to trucks, paralleled with improvements in infrastructure, such as highways and telephone systems. The dramatic innovations of the "green revolution" that diffused modern varieties since the late 1960s contributed to more than doubling the average rice yield per hectare. Large-scale modern mills have increased their market shares relative to the traditional *kiskisan* mills. Yet, according to the recollections of veteran farmers, collectors and millers, the marketing structure has remained essentially unchanged. Thus, the system observed *in loco* and outlined above can be considered a "prototype" of peasant marketing.

Is there a role for community trust under globalization? From peasant marketing to modern "just-in-time agriculture"

Although the system of peasant marketing outlined in the previous section may be largely efficient in marketing traditional peasant crops for local demand, it is doubtful that it can also serve as an appropriate channel to connect small family farms with wide national and international markets that deal in new commodities. These new agricultural commodities that are in great demand in world markets, such as vegetables or fruits and flowers, are perishable, which means that timely delivery from producers to consumers or to processing plants is critically important. For this purpose farm-level production, from planting to harvesting, must be much more closely coordinated with the schedules of marketing and processing than is the case of the prototype peasant marketing system, in which production plans, including the choice of crops and varieties as well as the planting and harvesting periods, are left to the decentralized decisions of individual farm producers.

A traditional approach to achieving sufficient coordination between farm production and marketing/processing for delivery of tropical agricultural products to international markets is the vertical integration in the form of plantations (Hayami, 1994, 2002). A typical example is the case of black tea. The manufacturing of black tea at a standardized quality for export requires a modern fermentation plant in which fresh leaves must be fed within a few hours after plucking. The need for close coordination between farm production and large-scale processing underlies the traditional use of the plantation system for black tea manufacture. Unfermented green tea, in contrast, remains predominantly the product of family farms in China and Japan. Another example is bananas for export. In this case, harvested fruits must be packed, sent to the wharf, and loaded on a refrigerated boat within a day. A boatful of bananas that can meet the quality standards of foreign buyers must be collected within a few days. Therefore, the whole production process from planting to harvesting must be precisely controlled so as to meet the shipment schedule. Thus, the plantation system has a decisive advantage for bananas for export, but not for bananas for domestic consumption, which, in turn, are usually produced in family farms.

A large plantation system based on hired wage laborers under centralized management was a necessary and efficient organization for opening new lands for export crop production, because of its ability to build necessary infrastructure such as road and harbor. The family farms, on the other hand, have no incentive to invest in infrastructure because their operational sizes are too small to internalize gains from infrastructural investment. However, after the land-opening stage was over and the infrastructure was built, the plantation system became increasingly more inefficient relative to the peasant system, because of high costs to supervise hired wage laborers as compared to the peasant farm that relies on family labor that requires no supervision. Because of the high costs of monitoring hired labor in spatially dispersed and ecologically diverse farm operations, plantations usually practice monoculture. Complicated intercropping and the crop–livestock combination are more difficult to manage by the command system, implying that both labor input and income per hectare are lower in plantations. Moreover, continuous cultivation of a single crop over a wide space increases the incidence of damage from pests, and the counteracting application of chemicals tends to pollute the environment.

The approach that has been recently advocated as a substitute for the plantation system is the "contract farming" system in which an agribusiness enterprise or a cooperative that manages the processing and marketing contracts with small growers for the assured supply of farm-produced raw materials. The contract may include stipulations not only on the time and quantity of material supply but also on prices, credit and technical extension services. In this way the advantage of agribusiness in large-scale marketing/processing and the advantage of the peasant system in farm-level production can be combined (Hayami, 2002).

Contract farming has recorded several significant successes, notably in pineapples for processing by multinational agribusiness in Thailand, on the basis of which Thailand rose to become the world's top exporter of pineapple products, surpassing the Philippines that remains based on the plantation system. However, many failure cases have also been reported. The failure usually stems from the difficulty of agribusiness or coop management to enforce contracts with a large number of smallholders concerning the quantity, quality and timing of their product delivery to processing plants and/or marketing centers. In this regard, one wonders if the skills of enforcing contracts by effective use of community trust, in peasant marketing could be extended to develop "modern" contract farming. In what follows I will try to illustrate this possibility with the case of commercial vegetable marketing in an upland village in Java, Indonesia (Hayami and Kawagoe, 1993: Ch. 4).

The study village is located in a hilly plateau near the border between West and Central Java, about 300 kilometers east of Jakarta. Typical of upland villages, the village was characterized by meager endowments of land resources and, hence, low incomes as compared with lowland villages that were endowed with irrigated rice lands. Average farm size was only 0.4 hectares, a half of which was under tenancy. Farmers traditionally eked out bare subsistence by mixed cropping of upland crops, such as corn and soybean and upland rice, with very low shares of marketable surplus.

In about five years in the mid 1980s, this village economy underwent a major change with successful introduction of commercial vegetable production mainly geared for metropolitan markets. With this innovation, average farm income per hectare increased as much as eight times, surpassing the income level of irrigated rice farming in lowland areas. The cool, high altitude environment in this village and its surroundings is suitable for vegetable production. Rapidly increasing urban demands for fresh vegetables, corresponding to the success of labor-intensive industrialization in Indonesia that was based on liberalization in trade and foreign direct investment in the 1980s, had spilled over to benefit this hinterland. However, the opportunity for marginal farmers in this area would have not been captured unless a new marketing system had been developed to deliver a large bulk of perishable product to the Jakarta metropolis, some 300 kilometers away. It is remarkable to find that this marketing system was organized not by ethnic Chinese traders who held a dominant share in inter-regional trade in Indonesia, but by indigenous entrepreneurs based in rural communities.

The vital consideration in marketing vegetables is how to minimize the time required for delivering them from producers to consumers. The traditional approach relied on the farm women bringing their harvests to sell at morning bazaars in nearby towns. In the village study, some vegetables went through this channel, but more than 70 percent was shipped to distant markets in Jakarta and other major cites. For an entrepreneur to organize this long-distance shipment, it is critically important to assemble a full truckload of vegetables since a half load would effectively double the cost of transportation. But, unlike the case of storable commodities, for fresh vegetables the shipper cannot wait for long until the full truckload is assembled. For this reason vegetable marketing must be very tightly coordinated with production and harvest. In their ability to establish coordination with farm producers, the indigenous entrepreneurs living in villages had a decisive advantage over ethnic Chinese traders who were based in cities and towns.

Organizers of the long-distance shipment of vegetables are called "inter-village collectors" who assemble vegetables through smaller collectors called "village collectors." For developing a concrete image, an inter-village collector who operated in the study village will be portrayed. He owned about five hectares of farmland (quite large in the context of Java), of which a part was cultivated under his direct administration and the rest was leased out. He contracted with some 20 village collectors for assembling vegetables for shipment mainly to Jakarta markets.

His daily operations are as illustrated in Figure 5.2. In the early morning farmers harvest vegetables and deliver them to village collectors' houses, which serve as, and are also commonly called "*depot*." Then, the inter-village collector sends chartered trucks, each with one of his agents, to go around *depots* to load the assembled vegetables. As soon as the truck becomes fully loaded, it immediately proceeds to Jakarta. In about five hours, the truck reaches either one of the two major wholesale markets in Jakarta. The cargo is delivered to a consignee who sells vegetables by the sack to resalers in open space or else in a roofed floor that is leased from the market office. Although formal auction is not practiced, the operation constitutes "de facto auctioning" as many resalers gather together to buy in competition one with another. The resalers bring back their

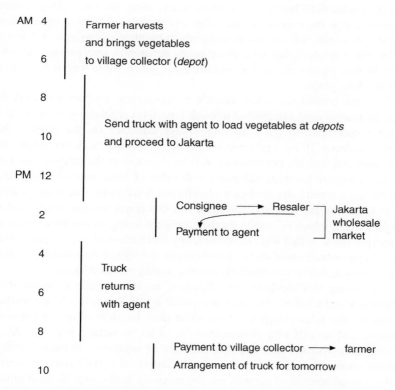

Figure 5.2 Operations of an inter-village collector for vegetable marketing in an upland West Java, Indonesia.

purchase to their stalls within the market and sort out vegetables by grade for sale to retailers, such as grocery shopkeepers and peddlers with carts. As soon as the inter-village collector's agent receives the sales proceeds from the consignee, the truck returns to the village. After receiving the money from the agent, the inter-village collector goes round his village collectors to pay for the vegetables collected by them in the morning, that he sold in Jakarta, deducting first his own commission from the sales proceeds. At the same time, he tries to obtain the village collectors' estimates of the amounts of vegetables to be assembled next morning, using this information to charter the trucks from various sources for the next day's operation.

This is a very tightly scheduled operation designed for quick delivery of perishable commodities to metropolitan consumers with minimum loss in their value. For this marketing system to be viable, the inter-village collector must be able to secure (a) reliable supply from vegetable growers via village collectors and (b) conscientious services of consignees in metropolitan wholesale markets. Taking the latter point first, unlike the case of wholesale markets in developed economies, the consignee in the Jakarta markets is not a formal agent officially licensed to conduct auctions based on some formal rules. With no official record kept of the transactions between consignees and resalers, the inter-village collectors cannot check the veracity of the sales reports handed to their agents from consignees. It is also difficult for their agents to monitor a consignee's dealings with the many resalers that take place in an apparently unorganized, chaotic manner. In fact, agents and drivers usually go to lunch while this de facto auctioning is taking place.

Under such conditions, a consignee's conscientious services can only be secured by mutual trust established through long-term regular transactions. It is easy for a consignee to cheat an inter-village collector on the sales of his cargoes. However, if he under-reports prices too much and too often, the chances improve that his opportunism will be detected as the inter-village collector may compare his trade outcomes with those of other inter-village collectors in the same community dealing with different consignees. This will possibly result in impairing the trust and confidence in this consignee that could lead to loosing his trade, which is suicide for the consignee living on commission on de facto auction sales. In this way, the community mechanism of social opprobrium and ostracism restrains marketing agents outside the village community, such as the consignees in the Jakarta markets, from venturing in moral hazard.

For sustaining this mechanism to function, an inter-village collector must send his truckload regularly to consignees, each in a different wholesale market. Furthermore, the inter-village collector must plan for delivering a number of truckloads, and to different destinations, in order to reduce his risk. As is common with perishable commodities, the price of vegetables fluctuates widely in various wholesale markets based on the deviations of a day's truck deliveries from the normal amount of cargoes usually received. In the specific case of this study, the inter-village collector usually sent his cargoes to four wholesale markets, two in Jakarta and two in other major cities. Correspondingly, his task to secure the reliable supply of vegetables from farmers becomes more difficult because the needed supply not only is large in volume, but must also be regular and predictable for the sake of accurately scheduling truck transportation.

A device for securing the reliable supply is to tie both village collectors and farmers by credit. The inter-village collector advances credit to farmers through village collectors for the purpose of assuring delivery of their collected vegetables. The same mechanism of tying through credit is also in operation occasionally between large wholesalers in towns and small collectors in villages with respect to storable commodities such as corn and soybeans. However, trade credits involved in these crops are short term, ranging from a few days to a few weeks and they seldom flow to farmers. In contrast it is unique for vegetable marketing that this credit tying mechanism is practiced for longer-term production loans to farmers that extend to two or three months and involving two principal agents, the inter-village collector, who advances credit to the village collector and the latter who typically delivers the credit to the vegetable growers in kind, in the form of fertilizer and chemicals, with the agreement that their total harvests shall be delivered to him. Farmers' credit repayments are deducted from the sales proceeds of vegetables over the harvest season. At the end, the village collector delivers to the inter-village collectors on their agreement that all the vegetables assembled shall be marketed by the latter. With the successful conclusion of the season, the renewal of the contract becomes automatic for the next season.

In this contract, interest is not charged explicitly for lending to farmers, nor is it reckoned implicitly by paying lower prices to credit-receiving farmers than to non-credit receivers. Nevertheless, collectors are able to recover their credit costs by taking advantage of the differential in prices paid by collectors and those paid by farmers for various farm inputs. For example, inter-village collectors bought the urea at the wholesale price of Rp185 per kilogram from fertilizer dealers in town. In turn, they had the village collectors charge the farmers Rp200 on their credit repayments, which is less than the farmers would have to pay if they bought their urea at the village grocery stores in small lots. As illustrated in Table 5.1, the average cost of current inputs advanced as credit in kind would have totaled to Rp70,500 per farm according to the 1990 case survey if farmers themselves were to buy in cash, whereas the same inputs could have been purchased by collectors at the cost of Rp65,550. In the credit-tying operation, collectors charged the farmers a total of Rp70,750 for these inputs. If credit is paid back in two months, collectors earned, in effect, an interest rate of 3.9 percent per month. Credit cost for inter-village collectors, who generally own sizeable land assets, should have been close to 1.5 percent per month, which was the official rate of collateral loans from the government Bank (Bank Rakyat Indonesia). Thus, collectors could capture a large margin in this financial intermediation, which is considered a return to their higher credit-monitoring capability with respect to farmer debtors, as compared to the Bank's monitoring capability.

This lucrative credit operation for collectors is also advantageous for farmers.

Table 5.1 Credit costs for vegetable producers under alternative credit arrangements in the Majalengka district, West Java, Indonesia, 1990

	Input cost per farm[a] (Rp)	Effective interest rate for	
		Farmer	Collector
		(percent per month)	
Cash purchase:			
Farmer (in small lot)	70,500		
Collector (in large lot)	65,550		
Credit purchase:			
Collector's trade credit	70,750	0.2	3.9
Fertilizer dealers' sale on credit	73,250	1.9	
Bank loan	75,950	3.8[b]	1.5[c]

Source: Hayami and Kawagoe (1993: Table 4.6, p. 129).

Notes
a   Cost for 150 kg of urea, 50 kg of triple superphosphate, 100 kg of ammonium sulphate, and one liter of Azodrin per 125 bata (0.18 ha).
b   Official interest rate plus transaction costs.
c   Official interest rate for collateral loan.

The input cost in farmers' own cash purchase (Rp70,500), compared with their payment to collectors' credit in kind (Rp70,750), implies an effective interest rate as low as 0.2 percent per month. This rate was much lower than the interest rates farmers would have paid if they were to purchase the inputs on credit from fertilizer dealers (1.9 percent) or if their purchases were based on non-collateral loans from the government bank (3.8 percent), which accounts also for the high transaction costs of the bank for dealing with small credit sizes (Hayami and Kawagoe, 1993: Appendix B). Thus, this credit-tying contract represents a Pareto improvement, benefiting both collectors and farmers.

The credit-tying contract stipulates that a farmer sells his produce exclusively to a village collector at prices offered by the latter during the season under contract.[2] This does not establish monopsonistic power for the collector since the farmer can always shift to another collector in the next season if he considers that he received a bad deal in relation to the market prices. The same relation holds between an inter-village collector and the village collectors. In fact, an inter-village collector who once operated in the study site was cut off from farmers and village collectors, resulting in the closure of his business, as he developed the reputation of paying "unfair" prices.

With the reliable supply of vegetables based on the mutually beneficial contract, inter-village collectors are able to organize efficiently the long-distance marketing of perishable commodities involving high risk and high transaction costs. Enforcement of this contract has to rely solely on community relationships between farmers and collectors living in the same village community. It is difficult to enforce such contracts on traders outside the community, especially ethnic Chinese traders based in town. In Indonesian villages, in particular, Chinese traders are discriminated against and cannot carry incentives from the farmers that would induce them to honor their contracts. They can hardly rely on the mechanism of social opprobrium and ostracism for protecting their interests from moral hazard exercised by people living in rural villages. Also, they cannot expect fair play from governmental agencies, including the police and the court for dispute settlement. There is no wonder, therefore, no ethnic Chinese trader was found operating in vegetable shipments in the study site. Similarly, but certainly not for the same reasons, no village cooperative operated in this field.[3]

In retrospecting on this case study and viewing it in its stepwise sequential development, one may recognize that vegetable marketing in a marginal upland area in Indonesia has the same organizational structure as the institution of contract farming. The ultimate aim is to coordinate efficiently the farm-level production of smallholders with long-distance shipment that is subject to economies of scale for the timely and suitable delivery of highly perishable commodities to the market. The lubricant of this fragile coordination is the reservoir of trust and reputation that binds together the members of a village community and delivers efficient enforcement of a long-term interlinked contract.

It came as a real surprise to find great similarities between this vegetable-marketing system in Indonesia and the modern subcontracting system used by automobile assemblers in Japan (Hayami and Kawagoe, 1993). Typically, a Japanese automobile assembler develops long-term, multi-linked contracts with a relatively small number of part suppliers involving technical guidance and credit guarantees in a "virtual" community relationship. The mutual trust developed between the parties enables the assembler to rely on the supply of the parts in the right quantity and quality and at the right time, so that the assembler does not need to hold any significant inventory of parts (Asanuma, 1985; Wada, 1998; Fujimoto, 1999). This system, known as Toyota's "just-in-time" system (*kanban*), has the same contract structure as the system of vegetable marketing in Java. In both the Indonesian and the Japanese case, the success of the system lay in the arrival of the commodity specified in the contract in the market (in Indonesia) or in the factory for processing (in Japan).[4] This resemblance may not be merely coincidental. In fact, the Toyota automobile company started as a rural-based industry when it was first founded in 1932 as a department of a loom manufacturer. From the beginning it purposively tried to develop a community relationship with parts suppliers according to the model of rural entrepreneurs who were then organizing peasant marketing and putting out contracts widely over Japan (Wada, 1998).

It cannot be over-emphasized that the Indonesian marketing system, which is equally intricate as Toyota's just-in-time system, was appropriately designed and operated by indigenous entrepreneurs rooted in rural villages. If the potential of rural entrepreneurs in low-income economies, as demonstrated by the Indonesian study, can be adequately tapped, it will become an important basis for the development of modern contract farming, which can serve as an efficient mechanism to channel rising global demands for new high-valued commodities to subsistence farmers in the marginal areas of developing economies. With "just-in-time" agriculture the contract farming system could be extended beyond the plantation crops and geographically into the village communities.

Concluding remarks

Rural markets in low-income economies are simply underdeveloped. They often lack the legal infrastructure for dispute adjudication and the police infrastructure for a mechanism of third-party contract enforcement. They are subject to market failures, they are imperfect as opposed to perfectly competitive, and they are also incomplete because of information asymmetries, as a result of which they are subject to moral hazard and adverse selection of risk. Yet they work!

This chapter analyzed the case of vegetable marketing in Indonesia in which rural entrepreneurs have built a sophisticated, "just-in-time" system for delivering to distant markets perishable commodities, utilizing the rural communities' mechanisms for building personal trust. The trust that grows as a result of personal interaction in tightly linked communities can be used to decrease transaction costs and effectively contest markets that were previously not accessible to the producers in these communities.

An important corollary from this application of trust is that it works best when governments keep off and let the markets be contestable. It is critically important in supporting rural entrepreneurs for governments to refrain from distorting incentives of market agents. If markets are competitive, profit-seeking private entrepreneurs in rural areas will try to make the best use of community relationships for reducing transaction costs in order to win in competition. The resulting efficiency improvements in marketing will benefit both consumers and producers, including poor peasants and cottage manufactures under competitive market environments. On the other hand, if the government or other agencies in an attempt to favor the community's efforts of repositioning their resources, deliver special privileges, say, to agricultural cooperatives and village associations, by granting them monopoly rights or exclusive access to subsidized credits and inputs, they risk initiating a monopolistic process of cultivating economic rents. The presence of monopoly will induce the elites to allocate their resources to rent-seeking activities as opposed to activities that reduce costs and improve services in their business that are needed for winning competition in the market.

In organizing contract farming, for example, it is not appropriate to grant an exclusive franchise over a territory to either an agribusiness enterprise or a cooperative in order to force farmers operating in the territory to deliver their products to the center for processing or marketing that is controlled by a particular principal. In contrast, if alternatives exist in processing or marketing, farmers would have an exit option to move to other principals after completing the contract for the present period. Otherwise, contract farming will be an oppressor in support of monopsony to exploit smallholders, irrespective of whether it is organized by a profit-seeking private business or by a non-profit organization like a cooperative.

In concluding, it should be pointed out that community-based trust as addressed in this chapter bears, in part, some symmetry to the function that reputation serves at the global level as discussed in the introductory section of this volume (Yotopoulos, Chapter 1; Pagano, Chapter 2). Reputation is applied in Parts III and IV of this volume at the global level and in uncontestable markets, i.e. on all goods that transcend the definition of commodities which trade on the basis of the minimum cost of production (Fok *et al.*, Chapter 8; D'Haese *et al.*, Chapter 9; and Romano, Chapter 10). The "decommodification" applies to goods and services that involve economic rents and thus trade as "positional goods" in uncontested markets. These markets are uncontested since economic rents are the result of some type of restricted competition, whether it derives from government edict, from a special characteristic of talent or skill, or as a result of advertising and name recognition. Reputation is a generic term for non-contestable market interactions that capture the economic rents embodied in "positional goods."

On the other hand, the community-based trust is efffective in reducing transaction costs, as illustrated in this chapter. This can be instrumental in the development of the community network towards more "modern" exchange relationships (Liu *et al.*, Chapter 6), which can eventually make possible the involvement of the poor and marginal communities of the Third World in global markets.

Notes

1 I would like to thank Pan Yotopoulos for his heavy-handed editing, although I will not absolve him from the collateral responsibility where he might have misunderstood me.
2 Usually the prices offered are determined from the sales proceeds at the metropolitan markets minus a certain percentage in commissions to the village and the inter-village collectors.
3 In fact, a village cooperative once tried it but gave it up. The reason may be the same that underlies the high interest rates that banks charge to farmers. The type of close monitoring of credit contracts that appears to be necessary from the discussion above is costly and difficult for an impersonal enterprise to deliver.
4 The general and generic shortage of space in Japan is equivalent to the perishability condition of the vegetables in Indonesia that makes the "just-in-time" system crucial for the fulfillment of the contract.

References

Abreu, Dilip (1988), "On the Theory of Infinite Repeated Games with Discounting," *Econometrica*, 56 (March): 383–96.
Aoki, Masahiko and Yujiro Hayami, eds, (2001), *Communities and Markets in Economic Development*. Oxford: Oxford University Press.
Asanuma, Banri (1985), "Organization of Parts Purchases in Japanese Automobile Industry," *Japanese Economic Studies*, 13 (Summer): 32–53.

Baland, Jean-Marie and Jean-Philippe Platteau (1996), *Halting Degradation of Natural Resources: Is there a Role for Rural Communities?* Oxford: Oxford University Press.

Bardhan, Pranab K. (1980), "Interlocking Factor Market and Agrarian Development: A Review of Issues," *Oxford Economic Papers*, 32 (March): 82–98.

Bell, Clive (1988), "Credit Markets and Interlinked Transactions." In Hollis Chenery and T. N. Srinivasan, eds, *Handbook of Development Economics*, Vol. 1. Amsterdam: North-Holland, pp. 763–830.

Feeny, David, Fikret Berkes, Bonnie J. McCay and James M. Acheson (1990), "The Tragedy of the Commons: Twenty-two Years Later," *Human Ecology*, 18 (1): 1–19.

Fudenberg, Drew and Eric Maskin (1986), "The Folk Theorem in Repeated Games with Discounting or with Incomplete Information," *Econometrica*, 54 (May): 533–4.

Fujimoto, Takahiro (1999), *The Evolution of a Manufacturing System at Toyota*. New York: Oxford University Press.

Geertz, Clifford (1978), "The Bazaar Economy: Information and Search in Peasant Marketing," *American Economic Review*, 68 (May): 28–32.

Greif, Avner (1989), "Reputation and Coalitions in Medieval Trade: Evidence on the Maghribi Traders," *Journal of Economic History*, 49 (December): 857–82.

Greif, Avner (1993), "Contract Enforceability and Economic Institutions in Early Trade: The Maghribi Traders' Coalition," *American Economic Review*, 83 (June): 525–48.

Hayami, Yujiro (1989), "Community, Market and State." In Allen Maunder and Alberto Valdes, eds, *Agriculture and Government in the Interdependent World*. Aldershot: Gower, pp. 3–14.

Hayami, Yujiro (1994), "Peasant and Plantation in Asia." In Gerald M. Meier, ed., *From Classical Economics to Development Economics*. New York: St Martin's Press, pp. 121–34.

Hayami, Yujiro (2002), "Family Farms and Plantations in Tropical Development," *Asian Development Review*, 19 (2): 67–89.

Hayami, Yujiro and Yoshihisa Godo (2005), *Development Economics: From the Poverty to the Wealth of Nations*, 3rd edn. Oxford: Oxford University Press.

Hayami, Yujiro and Toshihiko Kawagoe (1993), *The Agrarian Origins of Commerce and Industry: A Study of Peasant Marketing in Indonesia*. London: Macmillan; New York: St Martin's Press.

Hayami, Yujiro and Masao Kikuchi (2000), *A Rice Village Saga: Three Decades of Green Revolution in the Philippines*. London: Macmillan; New York: Barnes & Noble; Los Baños, Philippines: International Rice Research Institute.

Hayami, Yujiro and Keijiro Otsuka (1993), *The Economics of Contract Choice: An Agrarian Perspective*. Oxford: Oxford University Press.

Hayami, Yujiro, Masao Kikuchi and Esther B. Marciano (1999), "Middlemen and Peasants in Rice Marketing in the Philippines," *Agricultural Economics*, 20 (March): 79–93.

Kreps, David M. and Robert Wilson (1982), "Reputation and Imperfect Information," *Journal of Economic Theory*, 27 (August): 253–79.

Landa, Janet T. (1981), "A Theory of the Ethnically Homogeneous Middleman Group: An Institutional Alternative to Contract Law," *Journal of Legal Studies*, 20 (June): 349–62.

Ostrom, Elinor (1990), *Governing the Commons*. New York: Cambridge University Press.

Wada, Kazuo (1998), "The Formation of Toyota's Relationship with Suppliers: A Modern Application of the Community Mechanism." In Yujiro Hayami, ed., *Toward the Rural-Based Development of Commerce and Industry: Selected Experiences from East Asia*. Washington, DC: The World Bank Economic Development Institute, pp. 69–86.

6 Export outsourcing

Cost disadvantage and reputation advantage[1]

Bih Jane Liu, Alan Yun Lu and An-Chi Tung

Introduction

The recent bout of globalization has brought about fundamental changes in the nature of international trade. One of the most prominent changes is the integration of world markets. Although neither the extent nor the impact of the globalization is symmetric across countries, the integration of world markets proceeds in all parts of the world through the "free-markets, free-trade, laissez-faire" mechanism, in general, and under the WTO framework, in particular (Yotopoulos, Chapter 1).

It is not surprising that globalization transcends the trade sector and manifests itself also on the production side (Feenstra, 1998). More precisely, production processes that had previously been integrated and performed within a firm have gradually been split up and assigned to different production units (Jones and Kierzkowski, 1989). In many cases, the reassignment of production processes has spread to suppliers beyond national borders due to cost concerns. Furthermore, recent advances in telecommunications, the globalization of finance and reductions in trade barriers have made offshore sourcing more appealing. As a result, foreign outsourcing has been so widespread in the last two decades that it has become "a symbol of globalization" (Jones *et al.*, 2005: 315).

Among all types of foreign outsourcing, an important new mode, export outsourcing has been rapidly expanding in recent years. Export outsourcing is the practice by which firms that receive export orders subcontract part or the entire order to firms in lower-wage countries, while playing the dual role of a middleman and a manufacturer. Aside from their apparent similarities, export outsourcing distinctly differs from three other types of outsourcing, namely: (a) the "output outsourcing" by large firms like Wal-Mart and Nike, usually known as international subcontracting (Sharpston, 1976); (b) the deepening of vertical specialization in manufacturing trade (Hummels *et al.*, 2001); and (c) the outsourcing of service jobs (Garner, 2004). A major feature of export outsourcing is that it involves three parties rather than two, a point that will be elaborated later.

Export outsourcing deserves careful attention for several reasons. First, it has been prevalent among the newly-industrializing economies, especially those in East Asia, since the 1990s (Gereffi, 1999). In Taiwan, for example, almost one-third of all the export orders received in 2004 (in terms of value) were filled and delivered from abroad, increasing from almost none at all in the early 1990s. Second, and more important, as export sourcing is based on asymmetric information among the three parties involved, it is a frequently-used means by which the export-outsourcing firms capitalize on the "reputation" advantage when faced with a cost disadvantage.[2]

This chapter focuses on export outsourcing, which is an important but under-studied area in the literature. The next section introduces the new mode of foreign outsourcing and examines the basis of such a practice. Two issues are explored, namely, why the final buyer would prefer to have the intermediary firms involved, and why these latter firms would agree to take on the middle-man's role. The third section proceeds to look into the pattern of export out-sourcing practiced by Taiwanese firms, while paying special attention to how the buyers' requests exert their influence and why most firms choose to go to China. The case of Taiwanese firms is interesting, not only because their roles have switched in the practice of outsourcing over the years, but also because their sourcing activities have contributed considerably to the recent rise of China as the world's major exporter of textiles, electronics and many other products. In concluding the chapter, the final section discusses the future prospects for export outsourcing in Taiwan as well as its relevance for other economies.

Export outsourcing: concept and basis

Characteristics of export outsourcing

Foreign outsourcing, as mentioned above, has long been used to implement international division of labor based on comparative advantage, but has lately become more diversified and more extensively used. There are four main types of outsourcing. It is important to highlight the differences between export out-sourcing and the other three types, namely, traditional outsourcing (or output outsourcing), input outsourcing and service offshoring. In export outsourcing, the outsourcee, who receives the order and subcontracts to a third party, plays a distinct role in a game of information asymmetry. Table 6.1 illustrates the situation.

The traditional type of outsourcing, output outsourcing, usually involves an outsourcer in the north and an outsourcee in the south (Sharpston, 1976). From the mid 1960s on, many branded firms (e.g. Nike) and large retailers (e.g. Wal-Mart) in industrial economies have contracted production to suppliers in lower-wage countries. A certain portion of the subcontracted final products may be aimed at the export market, but the lion's share usually goes to the home market.[3] Over time, the destination of sourcing has shifted from the middle-income countries whose wages have risen, to countries with lower wages, but the age-honored operation has continued to be managed and controlled by the outsourcers.

Table 6.1 Types of outsourcing

Types	First party	Second party	Third party
Output outsourcing	outsourcer orders	outsourcee produces[a]	–
Input outsourcing	outsourcer orders	outsourcee produces[b]	–
Service offshoring	outsourcer orders	outsourcee provides[c]	–
Export outsourcing	outsourcer orders	outsourcee intermediates	outsourcee produces

Notes
a Final output.
b Intermediate input.
c Services.

Input outsourcing also involves two parties. In a typical case of input outsourcing, an outsourcer subcontracts an intermediate input to an outsourcee, imports the intermediate input and manufactures the final output at home (Hummels *et al.*, 2001).[4] This practice has undergone quantum growth in recent decades with the increase in vertical specialization. Earlier studies have found that the percentage share of imported intermediates in domestic production has risen over time in both high- and middle-income countries (Campa and Goldberg, 1997).

Service offshoring is concerned with the outsourcing of services, instead of commodities. In services ranging from front-office to back-office functions, developing countries around the world, particularly in Asia, have become large suppliers for developed countries. More often than not, the kinds of services that are moved offshore are those at the low end, being labor-intensive, information-based, codifiable and of high transparency (Garner, 2004). These services are "commodified" and contain little rent for the outsourcees to capture (Yotopoulos, Chapter 1).

Export outsourcing distinguishes itself from these three types of outsourcing in that there are three parties involved. Besides the two parties in the first-tier contract, the outsourcee plays the role of a middleman and subcontracts to a third party in the second tier.[5] Furthermore, the intermediation in the two-tier contract functions in a different way from the usual middlemanship. In the traditional type of intermediation, such as the outsourcing of production to Taiwan engaged in by Japanese trading companies three or four decades ago, production experience on the part of the intermediary was not required. In the current type of export outsourcing, the second party exercises the primary role of monitoring product quality and delivery (Gereffi, 1999), and sometimes also provides product design (Hsing, 1999) and managerial functions (Cheng, 2001). All of these functions are based mainly on competence in production. In sum, the intermediary firms not only extend the globalized supply chain by introducing new outsourcees to the game, but also create a new niche by crossing between commodity trade and service trade, thus "decommodifying" the goods in which they trade (Yotopoulos, Chapter 1).[6]

Basis of export outsourcing

Export outsourcing is a new option for exporting firms to respond to the changing configuration of comparative advantage, which has been commonly observed in East Asia. It is worth noting that, during the 1960s and 1970s, these firms were the major receivers of original equipment manufacturing orders for labor-intensive products from the industrial countries. As wage levels in these countries went up, the production sites gradually shifted away. In view of these changes, a firm can respond in one or several non-mutually exclusive ways, such as by engaging in technological upgrading, outward investment or export outsourcing,[7] each of which involves different degrees of resource commitment and flexibility.[8] One particular strategy that these firms adopted was to develop the intermediation function.

Why is there room for intermediation in export outsourcing? The key to this lies in the information asymmetry between buyers and producers (Wan and Weisman, 1999).[9] The middleman has to know what the buyer wants, what the low-end producer is capable of and how to coordinate the two parties. Moreover, the middleman has to establish a level of trust with both the buyer and the low-end producer to smooth the coordination process (Cheng, 2001).

The assets these East Asian firms possess when engaging in this practice include the following three: a long-term partnership with industrial-country buyers, a reputation as a reliable supplier of stable quality and timely delivery, and an ethnic or cultural linkage with certain low-wage countries (such as China and Southeast Asia).[10] As long-term business relationships are formed, foreign clients tend to prefer not to incur the transaction costs associated with changing partners. With superior production competence, the intermediary firm is assured that it has an edge over the low-end suppliers so as not to be replaced right away. Finally, with the proximity in culture or language with low-end producers, the first two advantages can be brought into full play.[11] By serving as middlemen, the high-wage East Asian firms are able to earn the economic rent embodied in these implicit assets, which in turn mitigates or even offsets the loss of business due to high wage levels.

Yet the reputation advantage may gradually fade away, which means that with time the market of the outsourcee becomes more contestable (Hayami, Chapter 5). Through the intermediation, the outsourcer becomes more familiar with production conditions and the final outsourcee improves in terms of manufacturing competence. The possibility of "disintermediation" increases with the narrowing of the information gap between these two parties (Fingleton, 1997). There are plenty of examples of suppliers appealing directly to buyers, and middlemen being replaced in the long run (e.g. Chen and Ku, 2000: 327). Assuming adequate rationality, firms that practice export outsourcing capitalize on the reputation payoff with calculated risk.

Analyzing export outsourcing

To understand when and how export outsourcing works in practice, two inter-connected questions need to be answered. First, why would the clients who desire to outsource go through the middleman firm, instead of approaching the final producer themselves? Second, why would the middleman firm choose to take on this role?[12]

Concerning the first question, the client, whose interest is to have the order filled at minimal expected cost, has three choices, besides producing in-house at high cost. Assume there are three parties: A, a client in the north (say, in the USA), C, a producer in the south (say, in China) and B, a (Taiwanese) firm that has served as A's final outsourcee for many years. Now with a rise in B's wage rate, A can either continue to contract with B but to pay v_0, a price higher than the original one, or hunt for other possibilities. A new option is to contract directly with the low-wage C. Yet as A is unfamiliar with the production conditions, C may act opportunistically and over-charge A at v_1 rather than the true average cost v_2. For simplicity, we assume $v_0 > v_1 > v_2$.

Still another option for A is to contract C through B, who has a reputation for being well-informed of the production conditions. With the knowledge of B, systematic falsehood by C is prevented.[13] Therefore, when B is involved, A only has to pay C at v_2, but has to pay B an intermediation fee v_3. If the net saving in production cost exceeds the intermediation fee, that is, if $v_1 - v_2 > v_3$, A would prefer to have B intermediated.[14] It is worth mentioning that if B and C are closely connected culturally or in some other ways, the saving in production cost can be much larger than in a case where B and C are alien to each other.

The second question concerns the willingness of B to take on the middle-man's role. To intermediate, B has to make some effort in monitoring and tutor-ing, at the (opportunity) cost of v_4. Assuming $v_3 > v_4$, the net receipt from intermediation is $v_3 - v_4$. However, by bringing A and C closer together, B runs a risk of being bypassed in the future. The risk, v_5, means a loss of future profit from a shorter remaining life. If the net receipt exceeds the potential loss, that is if $v_3 > v_4 + v_5$, it is in the interest of B to engage in export outsourcing.

In sum, for A to subcontract C through B, two conditions have to be met. A must be willing to go through B, and B must have a matching interest, such that $v_1 - v_2 > v_3 > v_4 + v_5$. If the intermediation fee, v_3, is too high relative to the saving in production cost, $v_1 - v_2$, A will bypass B and contract directly with C. If the disintermediation risk or the opportunity cost is too high relative to the intermediation fee, B will not choose to serve as the middleman according to the self-selection principle. Only when the intermediation fee is in the right range will export outsourcing become the equilibrium outcome.

This simplified analysis highlights the conditions for a three-party game to take place. In reality, firm B does not usually make a yes/no decision; rather, it decides on what percentage, which segment and when to outsource, based on its own characteristics and external opportunities. Some of these complications will be discussed below, while others will be left for future study.

Export outsourcing: the Taiwan case

Data and measurement

The case of Taiwan is interesting and important as an example of export out-sourcing in two ways. First, the economy has gradually evolved from an out-sourcee in the south into an intermediary between the long-term clients in the north and the new suppliers in the south. What's more, the *Export Orders Survey 2001*, conducted by the Ministry of Economic Affairs in Taiwan, offers a valuable opportunity for us to understand better the pattern of export outsourc-ing, as firm-level data are usually hard to obtain. The survey includes a total of 1,712 respondents, who accounted for 68 percent of Taiwan's total export orders in 2001, and encompass all manufacturing industries and the entire spectrum of firm sizes.

Unlike the outsourcing ratios defined for input outsourcing,[15] the extent of export outsourcing has not yet been formally measured in the literature. Two sets of export outsourcing indices are constructed here. The first group of indices measures the frequency of firms that outsource. The second group calculates the percentage of the value of outsourced orders in either all exporting firms or all outsourcing firms.[16]

Basic statistics

As summarized in the last row of Table 6.2, the frequency of all 1,712 firms engaged in outsourcing activities (OR_1 hereafter) amounted to 36.16 percent, or 619 firms. The ratio of the value of the outsourced export orders (OR_2) was 23.88 percent of all export orders, and the ratio of outsourced orders for out-sourcing firms (OR_3) was higher, at 45.41 percent.[17] These figures demonstrate that export outsourcing is a common practice among Taiwanese exporting firms.

The 1,712 firms are further categorized on the basis of industry or firm characteristics. The first row shows a comparison of firms with and without outward FDI. Export outsourcing turns out to be positively related to foreign investment.[18] Firms with outward FDI had a higher outsourcing ratio than firms without, both in terms of the frequency ratio OR_1 (53.27 percent vs 21.86 percent) and the value index OR_2 (29.30 percent vs 15.49 percent), though there was not much difference in the ratio of outsourced orders among outsourcing firms, OR_3 (46.37 percent vs 42.81 percent). The rationale underlying the strong association between export outsourcing and FDI activities is that FDI firms have the flexibility in choosing between multiple production sites, and can minimize the uncertainty in dealing with unrelated foreign suppliers (Hanson *et al.*, 2003).[19] Another reason is that firms without FDI may possess inadequate know-ledge to perceive outsourcing opportunities and to deal with the outsourcee's opportunism (Helleiner, 1981).

Second, although pure traders outsource abroad more in terms of frequency and percentage of value than manufacturing firms, export outsourcing is already

Table 6.2 Export outsourcing of Taiwanese firms

Types of firms	No. of firms	OR_1 (%)[a]	OR_2 (%)[b]	OR_3 (%)[c]
Firms with FDI	779	53.27	29.30	46.37
Firms without FDI	933	21.86	15.49	42.81
Manufacturers	1,445	33.77	22.78	44.74
Traders	267	49.06	32.76	49.60
Firms of small size[d]	663	38.76	32.09	53.67
Firms of medium size[d]	384	34.64	26.50	60.08
Firms of large size[d]	628	33.92	21.59	41.35
Export-thriving industries[e]	976	40.57	26.88	47.60
Export-sluggish industries[e]	547	29.62	10.85	27.87
Export-declining industries[e]	189	32.28	29.18	63.98
All firms	1,712	36.16	23.88	45.41

Source: authors' calculations based on the Taiwanese *Export Orders Survey, 2001*.

Notes
a OR_1: percentage of firms engaging in outsourcing activity in all 1,712 firms.
b OR_2: percentage of the value of outsourced orders in total export orders for all 1,712 firms.
c OR_3: percentage of the value of outsourced orders for the 619 outsourcing firms.
d Small firms are those with employment of less than 100 persons, medium firms are those with employment between 100 and 200 persons, and large firms those with above 200 people.
e Firms are grouped according to the long-term export growth rate of their respective industries (cf. Table 6.a.1 for details).

widely used among manufacturers. In 2001, 33.77 percent of the manufacturers outsourced abroad. The ratio is smaller than in the case of the pure trading firms (49.06 percent), but the difference in the OR_3 ratio is rather insignificant – 44.74 percent for manufacturers and 49.60 percent for traders. These results are not at all surprising, as manufacturers in general need to worry more about the loss of business secrets to the outsourcees than do traders; in other words, the latter may face a smaller v_5 than the former.

Third, firm sizes do not matter much. In particular, small firms do not shy away from export outsourcing. The frequency ratio OR_1 for small firms (38.76 percent) turned out to be slightly higher than for medium-sized (34.64 percent) and large firms (33.92 percent), while large firms tended to outsource a smaller portion of their export orders than the small- or medium-sized firms. A likely reason is that the services of the middleman here do not include the full range of "headquarter services" as mentioned in Antrás and Helpman (2004), and are therefore less sensitive to economies of scale.

Finally, firms in industries with either high or low growth rates engage more readily in export outsourcing than firms with growth rates at the medium level. In Table 6.2, firms are classified according to the long-run export performance of the industry they belong to.[20] Firms with either the best ("export-thriving industry") or worst ("export-declining industry") export performances have higher values of OR_1, OR_2 and OR_3 than the rest of the firms. One reason is that firms in both the thriving and the declining groups may have a smaller v_5, as it is hard to leak the business know-how out when the technology gap is large, and there is not much to leak out when the industry is at the sunset stage.[21] In sum, these observations are consistent with the economic intuition offered in the second section of this chapter (p. 112).

Buyer's request

We now look into the 619 firms that are engaged in export outsourcing. A special feature of this practice is the function of the buyer's request. Table 6.3 lists the motivating factors specified by the firms in multiple choices, such as the presence of outward investment, the need for flexibility, the ease of securing input, quota or tariff considerations and so on.[22] The factor most frequently identified is cost reduction, which was chosen by 76.09 percent of the 619 firms.[23] In fact, cost saving has been the major concern for all other types of outsourcing as well (Bryce and Useem, 1998; Gereffi and Sturgeon, 2004; Garner, 2004).

What is unique about export outsourcing is that many firms reported that they conducted export outsourcing at the request of foreign clients. The presence of buyer's request confirms that there is a potential conflict of interest between *A* and *B*, as shown in the second section of this chapter (p. 112). Over half (55.25 percent) of the 619 firms specified that they were pushed by the requests of foreign buyers. The actual importance of this factor could be even higher, because the request is not needed if the intermediation is already in position, and a tacit pressure can be exercised in place of an explicit request (Jan, 1989; Fuller, 2005).[24]

Table 6.3 Reasons for export outsourcing: multiple choices by outsourcing firms

Types of firms	Number of outsourcing firms	Cost reduction	Buyer's request	FDI	Need for flexibility	Securing inputs	Tariffs and quotas
Firms with FDI	415	77.35	53.25	61.93	38.55	17.83	10.36
Firms without FDI	204	73.55	59.31	–	33.82	19.61	6.86
Export-thriving industries	396	71.72	57.07	48.23	38.13	19.44	7.58
Export-sluggish industries	162	85.80	49.38	45.06	35.19	15.43	12.96
Export-declining industries	61	78.69	59.02	45.90	34.43	19.67	9.84
Total	619	76.09	55.25	47.17	37.00	18.42	9.21

Reasons for outsourcing (%)[a]

Source: authors' calculations based on the Taiwanese *Export Orders Survey, 2001*.
Note
a The row totals of the percentages do not necessarily add up to 100% due to multiple choices.

Going to China

Another striking feature of the export outsourcing among Taiwanese firms is that the bulk (74.40 percent) of the outsourced orders went to China (Table 6.4). Why do firms go to China? Cost saving unquestionably lies at the core. The average wage rate of workers in Taipei is five or ten times higher than that paid in China (Table 6.5). However, Chinese wages are not the lowest in Asia, and the relocation of export orders to China must have been triggered by other factors as well. Here cultural affinity matters. The intermediation by Taiwanese firms in China has been more effective than in other countries, such as Mexico, in textiles as well as electronics (e.g. Ancelovici and McCaffrey, 2005). Furthermore, Taiwanese firms have also faced fewer barriers than firms of other countries, such as Korea, in intermediating in China in footwear and other industries (Levy, 1991; Lin, 2001).

Given the cost and cultural concerns, why do some firms choose to go to non-China regions? An important consideration is the location of overseas investment.[25] For firms that have already invested abroad, export outsourcing follows FDI in most cases. Firms with past investment in Southeast Asia, for example, sent only 31.28 percent of their outsourced orders to China, which was lower than the percentage sent to their own overseas affiliates (65.94 percent). However, for FDI firms whose investment was driven by non-cost concerns (e.g. investing in the USA as a sales office), and for firms that have not yet engaged in foreign investment, China is again the dominant choice of location for sending the outsourcing orders (with 80.16 percent and 69.93 percent of outsourced orders, respectively).

Table 6.4 Location of export outsourcing for Taiwanese firms

Types of firms	Number of outsourcing firms	Location composition (%)[a]		
		China	Southeast Asia	Other countries
Firms with FDI (mainly in)	415	72.44	13.25	14.32
China	338	77.18	8.09	14.74
Southeast Asia	40	31.28	65.94	2.78
Other countries	37	69.93	9.53	20.54
Firms without FDI	204	80.16	7.45	12.39
Export-thriving industries	396	74.46	10.84	14.70
Export-sluggish industries	162	61.99	24.36	13.64
Export-declining industries	61	93.58	6.17	0.25
Total	619	74.40	11.77	13.83

Source: authors' calculations based on the Taiwanese *Export Orders Survey, 2001*.

Note
a Percentage of total outsourcing value.

Table 6.5 Wages in Asian cities, 2002 (US$)

City	Monthly wage for workers[a]
Taipei, Taiwan	1,028.5
Shenzhen, China	221.0
Kuala Lumpur, Malaysia	208.0
Shanghai, China	207.0
Bangkok, Thailand	163.0
Shenyang, China	155.0
Manila, Philippines	150.0
New Delhi, India	138.0
Chongqing, China	132.5
Ho-Chi Minh City, Vietnam	117.5
Jakarta, Indonesia	108.0
Dalian, China	107.5

Source: authors' calculations based on JETRO (2003).

Note

a Average monthly wage of workers employed in Japanese companies investing in Asia.

Concluding remarks

Export outsourcing, a practice combining middlemanship and manufacturing, has been expanding rapidly in recent decades. As a newly-opened option for exporting firms to respond to the globalization under severe cost competition, the practice raises a series of questions. How does it differ from other types of outsourcing or intermediation? Why is there room for export outsourcing? When will an exporting firm choose to engage in export outsourcing? Will this practice be viable in the long run? Is it a useful model for firms in other countries to follow?

This chapter has answered the first couple of questions using Taiwanese firms as an example. The major findings are summarized as follows. First, export outsourcing distinguishes itself from similar practices in that it extends beyond a two-party game into a three-party one. Second, the middleman firm can capitalize on a reputation payoff, which is derived from its past production experiences as well as the information asymmetry between the three parties. Third, there may be conflicts of interest among the three parties, and intermediation takes place under certain conditions. Fourth, export outsourcing these days is increasingly practiced by Taiwanese firms, and China is the most popular destination, this being due not only to cost concerns but also to cultural linkages.

These findings provide some hints in regard to the last two questions, which are relevant to Taiwan, as well as to firms in other countries in the south. Historically, Japan outsourced export orders to Taiwan in the 1960s and 1970s, at a time when Japanese producers started to suffer from rising wages. Eventually Taiwan has evolved to play a role similar to that which Japan had played by outsourcing export orders to China and other countries, though with certain differences mentioned earlier. During this evolutionary process, Japan has been disintermediated by Taiwan in quite a few instances, especially in industries with low levels of sophistication, such as footwear (Levy, 1991). In the meantime, Japan has upgraded and has stayed in the high-income club.

Will Taiwan follow in Japan's footsteps to become fully developed? A number of Taiwanese firms have managed to climb up the quality ladder, i.e. to trade in decommodified exports, with examples ranging from footwear to electronics. However, the lack of brand reputation and core technology seems to place Taiwanese firms in a weaker position in the global supply chain today than the Japanese firms when they served as the intermediary decades ago. What the future holds for Taiwan is thus not certain.

Then, what are the implications for the rest of the south? It is true that Taiwanese, or more broadly, East Asian firms have a number of unique assets as explained in the second section of this chapter. It is also true that the particular conditions in each economy give rise to different sets of possible responses to the changes in the asymmetric trading world. Taiwan itself is now in a halfway house, being in neither the best, nor the worst of the worlds. To other economies in similar positions, globalization may bring about either the best of times, or the worst of times, should things go really wrong.[26] More research in this area is warranted.

Appendix

An analysis of the three-party game

A simple game theory analysis is offered here to answer the two questions concerned with the three-party game: (1) If outsourcing is desirable for the outsourcer, why does it need the Taiwanese firm to get involved instead of approaching the actual producer by itself? (2) If the involvement of the Taiwanese firm is useful, then why would the firm sometimes choose not to take on the role?

Question 1

To answer the first question as to why the client needs the middleman firm, consider a situation with three parties: *A*, a client in the north (say, in the USA), *B*, a (Taiwanese) firm that has served as the outsourcee to *A* for many years and *C*, a producer in the south (say, in China). There is also *Nature*, which randomly selects the state of the production conditions to be either *g* (good) or *b* (bad), which is identically and independently distributed for each task in each period.

A has diversified needs. Both *B* and *C* are specialized operators, where *B* is one of a number of competing firms with a well-known reputation for being familiar with production conditions for clients like *A*, who is unfamiliar with the production conditions.

The interest of *A* is to have the order filled at a minimal expected cost. The interest of *B* is to maximize its expected present value of profit. The interest of *C* is to maximize its own expected reward by choosing the needed effort level, which is either "high" for the good state, or "low" for the bad state, and reports what that state is (γ for good and β for bad), how much effort is accordingly needed, and then presents the bill for the task. The charge will, of course, be higher if a bad state is reported. The bill will be either accepted (symbol *a*) or rejected (symbol *r*) by *A*.

A is accustomed to outsourcing to *B* before the wage rate rises in *B*. After the wage rise, *A* can either continue to contract with *B* by paying v_0, on average, which is assumed to be lower than *A*'s own in-house production cost, or to respond in one of the following ways.

Case 1: A *contracts directly with* C *(Figure 6.a.1)*

Since *A* is unfamiliar with the production conditions, *C* can act opportunistically. Whether the true state of nature is good (*g*) or bad (*b*), the reported state (by *C*) is always bad (β), leading to two possible nodes, one reached by (*g*, β), and another by (*b*, β). Faced with an information set that consists of both nodes, which represents *A*'s inability to tell what is true from what is false, *A* must either reject all, which is self-defeating, or accept all and acquiesce with the systematical fraud of *C*. The heavy lines in the game tree show the equilibrium outcome. This means an inflated bill at cost v_1 for *A*, rather than the true cost v_2, on the average, and $v_1 > v_2$. For simplicity, assume $v_0 > v_1 > v_2$.

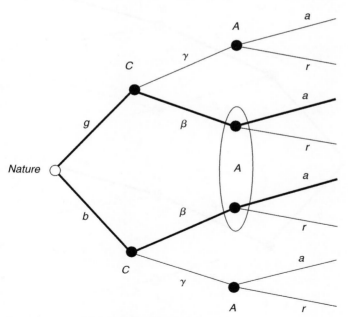

Figure 6.a.1 A places orders directly with C.

Case 2: A places orders indirectly with C, *through* B,
at a market-determined fee v_3 *(Figure 6.a.2)*

The responsibility for monitoring the behavior of *C* now shifts to *B*. Since *B* has the experience of being a specialized operator, *B* knows well the probability that the state of *Nature* is good. Any attempt by *C* to falsely report the state as bad (β) while the true state is good (g) will be rejected by *B*. As such a rejection will inadvertently affect *C*'s record or reputation in the specialized profession, it will be an unacceptable outcome for *C*. So systematic falsehood is prevented.

If the cost saving $v_1 - v_2$, on average, for *A* from working through *B* is higher than the fee paid to *B*, v_3, *A* will prefer having *B* involved. If $v_1 - v_2 < v_3$ instead, *A* will place its order directly with *C*.

Question 2

The second question concerns why the middleman firm sometimes chooses not to get involved. For *B* to engage in the service of providing export sourcing, it must expend some effort, at an opportunity cost v_4, which may be less than v_3, that is, $v_4 < v_3$.

In addition, *B* runs a higher risk of being bypassed by *A* if it plays the middleman's role and brings *A* and *C* together. The capital loss arising from the

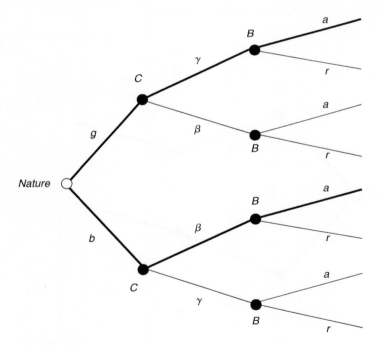

Figure 6.a.2 A places orders indirectly with C.

additional risk is denoted by v_5, which is proportional to the present value of the business based on a certain hazard rate. By staying out of the three-party game, the profit of B is v_4; by staying in, its net profit is $v_3 - v_5$. Therefore, B will take on the middleman's role if $v_4 < v_3 - v_5$; otherwise, it will prefer to engage in other activities.

Remarks

1   The above discussion indicates that, for A to contract C through B, two conditions have to be satisfied. A must be willing to go through B, and B must have a matching interest:

$$v_1 - v_2 > v_3 > v_4 + v_5.$$

If v_3 is too high, A will bypass B and contract directly with C. If v_3 is too low or $v_4 + v_5$ is too high, it is in the interest of A to invite B in, but the latter may not want to play the middleman's role. Unless A is willing to raise v_3 adequately high, B would not "drink poison to quench the thirst" as the Chinese proverb goes.

2   There is another case where the cost disadvantage to B is not very serious as compared with the inflated charge by C, such that $v_1 > v_0 > v_2$. Then, when $v_0 - v_2 > v_3$, it is in the interest of A to have B involved as a middleman *on request*, but not as a producer, especially if B has a higher payoff through production than through intermediation.

Growth of export outsourcing by industry classification

Table 6.a.1 A classification of industries by export performance

Industry types	Average annual export growth rate 1990–2000	Industries covered
Export-thriving industries	≥7% (world average)	Electronics, information and communications, chemicals, basic metals, precision instruments, electrical equipment, plastics and rubber
Export-sluggish industries	<7% but ≥0%	Machinery, transportation equipment, textiles, furniture and miscellaneous manufacturing
Export-declining industries	<0%	Footwear, plywood, household appliances, processed food, toys, games and sports, animal and plant products, leather and ceramic products

Notes

1 The authors would like to thank Pan Yotopoulos for very helpful comments. Bih Jane Liu also acknowledges the financial support of the National Science Council (NSC91–2415–H-002–021–SSS).
2 By reputation, here we mean being known to possess competence or information regarding production (as analyzed in the first part of the appendix to this chapter). Note that the term reputation is used as in Yotopoulos (Chapter 1) and not in the way it is used in game theory, for instance as in the chain-store paradox (Selten, 1978).
3 American retailers, for example K-mart and Wal-Mart, outsource for the main purpose of domestic sales. Nike derived 63 percent of its total revenue in footwear sales from the US market in 1988 (Donaghu and Barff, 1990). The ratio fell to 48 percent in 2004, but was still high (calculated from Nikebiz, 2005).
4 Various other terms, such as "slicing the value chain" (Krugman, 1994), have been used in the literature to address similar but differentiated aspects of vertical specialization (Feenstra, 1998).
5 By contrast, the "triangle manufacturing" practice, as described in Gereffi and Pan (1994: 138), is in essence a two-party game, as the buying offices of American retailers in Taiwan that handle both onshore and offshore production are not independent decision makers.
6 Even after disintermediation, which will be discussed later in the text, this catalytic role remains important.
7 For example, export outsourcing now may serve as the "cash cow" to finance upgrading later.
8 Upgrading requires heavy technological and capital investments. Owning a foreign subsidiary necessitates the commitment of capital, as well as managerial input and technological know-how. In comparison, export outsourcing requires less resource inputs, but carries more uncertainty.
9 Spulber (1999) offers a general and comprehensive discussion on the role of the middleman.
10 The East Asian trader-manufacturer firms differ from the independent traders of rice in the Philippines (Hayami, Chapter 5), who also have these three assets. More specifically, the long-term partnership with buyers in the industrial country, and specifically the reputation that has accrued as a result, has "decommodified" their export products, enabling them to capture also economic rents therefrom. Expressed in more general terms, the East Asian firms have by now improved their production capabilities and are better in adapting in a dynamic world with frequently changing comparative advantage.
11 Taiwan (or Hong Kong) and China, in particular, share the same language and the same race of people.
12 A more detailed game-theoretic analysis of these two issues is presented in the appendix to this chapter.
13 Although not considered here, it is possible that the yield rate of C improves through the tutoring of B.
14 Cf. the appendix to this chapter for another case when the cost disadvantage of B is not very serious as compared with the inflated charge by C.
15 Campa and Goldberg (1997), for example, calculated the ratio of imported intermediate to total intermediate input purchases in four advanced countries. Hummels *et al.* (1998, 2001) computed the imported input content in exports in ten OECD countries and four newly industrialized countries.
16 Note that, based on the rules of origin, the value of export orders produced and transported abroad is recorded under the outsourcee's country.
17 It is understandable that the OR_3 is not 100 percent in the case where firms continue

to manufacture high-end products by themselves to earn v_0, while engaging in export outsourcing to earn v_3 on low-end products.

18 International outsourcing is seen as a substitute for FDI in the literature (e.g. Grossman and Helpman, 2003), for only imports from non-affiliates are included as input outsourcing.

19 For example, when an independent outsourcee fails to meet the quality or punctuality requirement, the owned subsidiary can meet it.

20 Industries are categorized according to their average annual export growth rate in 1990–2000. The export-thriving industries include those industries with a growth rate greater than or equal to the world average of 7 percent. Those with a rate between 0 percent and 7 percent are referred to as export-sluggish industries, and those with a negative growth rate are referred to as export-declining industries. Table 6.a.1 in the appendix gives more details.

21 Other factors, such as the magnitude of the saving in production cost, $v_1 - v_2$, may also be at work.

22 For example, the Multi-fibre Arrangement (MFA, 1974–94) and the Agreement on Textiles and Clothing (ATC, 1995–2004) had governed world trade in textiles and clothing for many years.

23 Note that the reduction in "cost" asked in the survey refers to the costs to B, and is different from the cost saving of $v_1 - v_2$ from A's point of view.

24 Moreover, if firm B refuses to take the order, there would be no observation even if firm A had made the request.

25 There may be a time effect. Those who went offshore in the 1980s had a foothold in Southeast Asia or other locations, and those who made later the FDI decision have tended to go to China.

26 The case of Lesotho illustrates how things could go wrong, when globalization and the abrupt end of the MFA wiped out a major source of foreign exchange (sources: *New York Times*, Asia edn, 18 April 2005: 32; *New York Times*, 31 May 2005: 1).

References

Ancelovici, Marcos and Sara J. McCaffrey (2005), "From NAFTA to China?" In Suzanne Berger and Richard K. Lester, eds, *Global Taiwan: Building Competitive Strengths in A New International Economy*. Armonk, NY: M.E. Sharpe, pp. 166–93.

Antrás, Pol and Elhanan Helpman (2004), "Global Sourcing," *Journal of Political Economy*, 112 (3): 552–80.

Bryce, David J. and Michael Useem (1998), "The Impact of Corporate Outsourcing on Company Value," *European Management Journal*, 16 (6): 634–43.

Campa, José and Linda S. Goldberg (1997), "The Evolving External Orientation of Manufacturing: A Profile of Four Countries," *Federal Reserve Bank of New York Economic Policy Review*, 3 (2): 53–81.

Chen, Tain-Jy and Ying-Hua Ku (2000), "Foreign Direct Investment and Industrial Restructuring: The Case of Taiwan's Textile Industry." In Takatoshi Ito and Ann O. Krueger, eds, *The Role of Foreign Direct Investment in East Asian Economic Development*. Chicago and London: National Bureau of Economic Research, pp. 319–48.

Cheng, Leonard K. (2001), "Li & Fung, Ltd.: An Agent of Global Production." In Leonard K. Cheng and Henryk Kierzkowski, eds, *Global Production and Trade in East Asia*. Boston: Kluwer Academic Publishers, pp. 317–23.

Donaghu, Michael T. and Richard Barff (1990), "Nike Just Did It: International Subcontracting and Flexibility in Athletic Footwear Production," *Regional Studies*, 24 (6): 537–52.

Feenstra, Robert C. (1998), "Integration of Trade and Disintegration of Production in the Global Economy," *Journal of Economic Perspectives*, 12 (4): 31–50.

Fingleton, John (1997), "Competition between Intermediated and Direct Trade and the Timing of Intermediation," *Oxford Economic Papers*, 49 (4): 543–56.

Fuller, Douglas (2005), "Moving Along the Electronics Value Chain." In Suzanne Berger and Richard K. Lester, eds, *Global Taiwan: Building Competitive Strengths in A New International Economy*. Armonk, NY: M.E. Sharpe, pp. 137–65.

Garner, Alan C. (2004), "Offshoring in the Service Sector: Economic Impact and Policy Issues," *Federal Reserve Bank of Kansas City Economic Review*, 89 (3): 5–37.

Gereffi, Gary (1999), "International Trade and Industrial Upgrading in the Apparel Commodity Chain," *Journal of International Economics*, 48 (1): 37–70.

Gereffi, Gary and Mei-Lin Pan (1994), "The Globalization of Taiwan's Garment Industry." In Edna Bonacich, Lucie Cheng, Norma Chinchilla, Nora Hamilton and Paul Ong, eds, *The Apparel Industry in the Pacific Rim*. Philadelphia: Temple University Press, pp. 126–46.

Gereffi, Gary and Timothy J. Sturgeon (2004), "Globalization, Employment, and Economic Development," *Sloan Workshop Series in Industry Studies*. Rockport, MA, 14–16 June.

Grossman, Gene M. and Elhanan Helpman (2003), "Outsourcing versus FDI in Industry Equilibrium," *Journal of the European Economic Association*, 1 (2–3): 317–27.

Hanson, Gordon H., Raymond J. Mataloni and Matthew J. Slaughter (2003), "Vertical Production Networks in Multinational Firms," NBER Working Paper no. 9723. Cambridge, MA: National Bureau of Economic Research.

Helleiner, Gerald K. (1981), *Intra-Firm Trade and the Developing Countries*. London: Macmillan.

Hsing, You-Tien (1999), "Trading Companies in Taiwan's Fashion Shoe Network," *Journal of International Economics*, 48 (1): 101–20.

Hummels, David, Dana Rapoport and Kei-Mu Yi (1998), "Vertical Specialization and the Changing Nature of World Trade," *Federal Reserve Bank of New York Economic Policy Review*, 4 (2): 79–99.

Hummels, David, Jun Ishii and Kei-Mu Yi (2001), "The Nature and Growth of Vertical Specialization in World Trade," *Journal of International Economics*, 54 (1): 75–96.

Jan, Wei-Shiung (1989), "Discoloring of Taiwan's 'Footwear Den'," *Commonwealth*, 102: 134–9 (in Chinese).

JETRO (2003), "The 13th Survey of Investment-related Cost Comparison in Major Cities and Regions in Asia." Tokyo: Overseas Research Department, Japan External Trade Organization.

Jones, Ronald W. and Henryk Kierzkowski (1989), "The Role of Services in Production and International Trade: A Theoretical Framework." In Ronald W. Jones and Ann O. Krueger, eds, *The Political Economy of International Trade*. Cambridge, MA: Basil Blackwell, pp. 31–48.

Jones, Ronald W., Henryk Kierzkowski and Lurong Chen (2005), "What Does Evidence Tell Us about Fragmentation and Outsourcing?" *International Review of Economics and Finance*, 14 (3): 305–16.

Krugman, Paul (1994), "Does Third World Growth Hurt First World Prosperity?" *Harvard Business Review*, 73 (4): 113–21.

Levy, Brian (1991) "Transactions Costs, the Size of Firms and Industrial Policy – Lessons from A Comparative Case Study of the Footwear Industry in Korea and Taiwan," *Journal of Development Economics*, 32 (1–2): 151–78.

Lin, Wei-Jen (2001), "Pao Cheng Footwear: USA as the Mentor," *Commonwealth*, 237: 84–91 (in Chinese).

Nikebiz (2005), "Company Overview, The Facts, Nike Inc." Online, available www.nike.com/nikebiz/nikebiz.jhtml?page=3&item=facts (accessed 28 March 2005).

Selten, Reinhard (1978), "The Chain-Store Paradox," *Theory and Decision*, 9 (2): 127–59.

Sharpston, Michael (1976), "International Subcontracting," *World Development*, 4 (4): 333–7.

Spulber, Daniel F. (1999), *Market Microstructure: Intermediaries and the Theory of the Firm*. Cambridge and New York: Cambridge University Press.

Wan, Henry Y. Jr and Jason Weisman (1999), "Hong Kong: The Fragile Economy of Middlemen," *Review of International Economics*, 7 (3): 410–30.

7 Transition economies and globalization

Food system asymmetries on the path to free markets[1]

Kolleen J. Rask and Norman Rask

Introduction

Asymmetries in agricultural institutions

The emotional and often violent demonstrations accompanying global trade talks underscore the enormity of the transformations occasioned by increasing integration of global markets, especially for developing economies. While these countries try to mitigate the redistribution effects of trade-related changes (thereby often *limiting* trade itself), transition economies are faced with a contrasting fundamental challenge: recreating their economies to conform to global market structures as a *precondition for enhanced* trade.

Common to all markets, whether classified as "free markets" or "command systems," is some level of governmental and institutional presence. Indeed, classical economists were concerned not just with markets, but with how markets work within the broader context of society, stressing that for proper functioning, markets require some limited governmental (as well as moral) foundations (Yotopoulos, Chapter 1). These foundations include legal institutions and trade-enhancing infrastructure, among others. In the United States and in Western Europe the post-war development of agricultural markets was supported by substantial public investment in areas such as research and development of inputs and products, transportation, rising standards for sanitation, quality and safety. Low-income countries could not provide this level of support, resulting in the noted asymmetry of agricultural conditions. In particular, the relative paucity of institutional and infrastructural support in low-income countries places them at a severe disadvantage as they try to participate in world markets. In recent years, this asymmetry has been further exacerbated by the globalization of supporting service industries and by the accelerating shift in agriculture from classical, cost-based competition in homogeneous products (in which low-wage countries would have a comparative advantage) to reputation-based sales of high value-added products under conditions of imperfect competition, in which institutional and infrastructure support plays a bigger role (Yotopoulos, Chapter 1; Romano, Chapter 10).

During the same time a third group, the centrally planned economies with intermediate incomes, focused their government efforts in a different direction –

controlling and subsidizing quantity flows and generating artificially low food prices, thereby significantly enhancing domestic consumption relative to market economies at similar income levels. These differential policies created a further asymmetry in agricultural institutions, and with market economies dominating world trade, the institutions developed in these market countries would become the dominant global institutions. Therefore, with the onset of transition, former command economies have also entered global markets at a marked disadvantage. The rules of production and international exchange, written by the market economies, do not value the institutions of central planning, so the transition economies must alter their institutions accordingly before they can compete successfully in this environment.

These transformations are particularly acute for the agricultural and food systems in transition economies. Following World War II, the Soviet bloc established a food supply and consumption system completely isolated from outside markets. The limited trade consisted primarily of food from Central European countries and Baltic republics exchanged for energy from the USSR. Food prices were administratively set at low levels, and agricultural production was specified and subsidized, creating a largely self-sufficient system. However, low food prices led to rich country diets with significant over-consumption of livestock products relative to market economies with similar income levels. In the early years, substantial agricultural resources and subsidies allowed production to keep pace with consumption. The infamous "Russian Wheat Deal" in the early 1970s further exacerbated the distortions as the USSR entered world grain markets in a large way to purchase livestock feed necessary to support even higher levels of livestock product consumption.

With the onset of transition in the early 1990s, this "house of cards" came tumbling down as restructuring in countries of the former Soviet bloc brought food prices higher and closer to free market levels while per capita incomes declined. As a result, consumption of livestock products dropped precipitously. Remarkably, production of livestock products declined in line with consumption, partly from the restructuring of agricultural production systems but perhaps as importantly from an inability to meet international market standards for disposition of surplus production (infrastructure asymmetry). In the former USSR, both per capita consumption and production of livestock products fell below 1960 levels, and remain at low levels even today.

Some recovery of consumption and production is evident in the western rim of transition countries where international standards are being imposed by accession rules to the European Union. However, the fact that the base production level for EU agricultural programs is set at the current low level of production (low relative to pre-transition levels) could lead to further consumption–production distortions as incomes and consumption continue to grow in these agricultural countries.

The income–food consumption asymmetry in transition economies

In this study we focus specifically on the paths followed by *consumption* asymmetries. However, as we have noted, a decline in production has accompanied the decline in consumption up to this point, and we raise concerns about meeting food needs as production and consumption are likely to recover at different rates as these economies grow in the future.

It has been shown previously (Rask and Rask, 2004) that there exists a remarkably stable market relationship between per capita income and resource-based food consumption measured in terms of cereal equivalents. Distortions in the centrally planned years created an asymmetry in this relationship between market and non-market economies, reflecting non-market diets unusually rich in livestock products for the given income levels, accompanied by production subsidies and other distortions to enable those diets. Lacking free market prices, free trade and the free expression of comparative advantage, effective participation in economic globalization was precluded for these countries. As distortions are lifted and market institutions arise, the income–consumption relationship for transition economies shifts dramatically and begins to approach the level of market economies, at which point greater participation in global markets becomes possible.

The transition experience of the last decade or so is characterized by widely divergent degrees of success in eliminating the food sector asymmetry. Many transition economies historically enjoyed a strong agricultural sector, but endured significant distortions during the centrally planned years. In particular, low- and medium-income populations in these pre-transition economies were eating high-income diets abundant in livestock products. The higher prices for livestock products and lower incomes characteristic of the early transition years sharply reduced demand for livestock products, bringing consumption patterns closer to those of poorer market economies. Within this general trend, those countries that have experienced income growth during the transition period have reduced this income–consumption asymmetry more quickly, while others still have quite a distance to travel. Once the asymmetry is removed and income improves, we expect significant reverse diet changes as livestock product consumption rises, creating pressure on domestic agricultural resources and perhaps a need for greater imports of livestock products for some countries.

It is significant that livestock production levels have generally fallen commensurately with consumption reductions, reflecting lower demand, internal structural and policy changes, and an inability to access international markets with surplus livestock products. Thus, at later stages of transition and lower levels of per capita food consumption, most countries are still only marginally meeting food requirements. Our analysis indicates that food consumption is now likely to begin increasing significantly as these countries enter a period of economic growth. Increases in production, however, are hampered by a variety of problems, including slow development of the non-agricultural rural economy, slow transformation of the institutional systems of agricultural production (e.g.

consulting, training, research, state administration) and the need to restructure the food industry to accommodate higher quality demands (Csaki, 2000).

This emerging scenario of increased livestock product consumption also poses particular resource use problems for the western rim of transition countries currently entering or about to enter the European Union (EU), since production expansion is discouraged through quotas (milk, sugar) and supply management instruments such as base areas, reference yields and production premiums (EU, 2003), which are set at current, historically low production levels. Other authors have similarly sounded a cautionary note in this respect. Chevassus-Lozza and Unguru (2002) predict a substantial increase in agricultural imports, especially for Poland and Hungary, while the older EU members, particularly Germany, gain export markets. Weber (2001) expects older EU members to export poultry and eggs to acceding members. More fundamentally, Erjavec *et al.* (2003) and Ferto and Hubbard (2003) express concerns that the development of agriculture in acceding countries will be hurt by the distortions embedded in EU agricultural policy. The potential need for imports, therefore, comes from the fact that while consumption is poised to rise, structural adjustments in production agriculture, as noted above, may be more difficult to achieve, and for some countries efficient production will be discouraged by rules of accession to the European Union.

To measure diverse food diets with a common denominator, we use a resource-based per capita cereal equivalent (CE) measure (rather than nutrition, calories or expenditures) that approximates the resource difference in diets experienced at different levels of income. Progress in the transition to non-distortionary market institutions is indicated by proximity to the market-based relationship between real income and CE consumption. Individual transition country as well as group experience is compared to the world market trend, highlighting contrasts, projections for future changes in food consumption and implications of EU membership.

The income–food consumption relationship during economic development and the cereal equivalent factor measure are discussed in the next section. The model and data are presented in the third section, with individual country experience detailed in section four. The fifth section extends the analysis to livestock production changes associated with transition, including policy implications, with a summary presented in the final section.

Income–food consumption relationship using cereal equivalent factor values[2]

The income–food consumption relationship in market-based development

In the early stages of development, food consumption responds dramatically to income changes, due both to the high proportion of income devoted to food consumption and the high marginal propensity to consume food (Rask, 1991; Kydd *et al.*, 1997). These changes are due primarily to the substitution of higher order foods (e.g. livestock products) for cereals and tubers. Growing populations also generate growing demand for food.

At higher levels of income, population growth typically slows, while the percentage of income spent on food consumption plummets, reducing the impact of income growth on food demand. As absolute food consumption levels off at high incomes, changes in demand center around "convenience and quality factors" such as packaging, advance preparation and away from home consumption (Rask, 1991). Therefore, while expenditures on food continue to rise, the demand on raw food production resources eventually stabilizes. In order to portray changes in basic food resource consumption we use the CE measure, which accounts for both quantity and quality diet adjustments but excludes convenience factors.

Development of the cereal equivalent (CE) measure

The CE measure captures the changing resource requirements consistent with changing diets across countries and level of development, especially in regard to consumption of livestock products. Weight, calorie and monetary measures do not reflect resource use since an ounce or a calorie of meat requires many more resources to produce than does an ounce or a calorie of cereals, and the use of monetary values is hindered by exchange rate issues, lack of relevant price data in many countries and the inclusion of service and convenience cost factors not related to basic resource use.

Early work on direct and indirect consumption

Yotopoulos (1985) showed that demand for food cereals as a function of income is comprised of a *direct* demand and an *indirect* demand. *Direct* consumption of cereals initially rises with income (under low elasticity) but then decreases at higher income levels. *Indirect* demand for cereals (animal protein), however, is very elastic to income changes. Using recent data, Figure 7.1 illustrates this point, showing dramatic increases in the portion of food consumption devoted to livestock products as per capita income (real US$) grows. Note that cereal consumption declines marginally at higher incomes, while fruit and vegetable consumption rises slightly.[3] The inefficient conversion of cereals (feed) into animal protein therefore has serious consequences for total resource availability, contributing to the paradox of worsening famines as global incomes rise. For our analysis, we have extended the concept of cereals to cereal equivalents, to include all forms of food.[4]

Cereal equivalent factor values

Recognizing that cereals are consumed directly and indirectly, we use CEs to define diets across all stages of development, expressed in tons of cereal

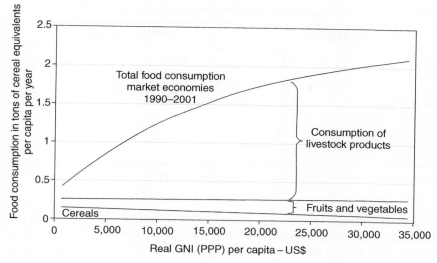

Figure 7.1 Food consumption measured in cereal equivalents: cereals, fruits, vegetables and livestock components.

equivalents per capita per year. CE values for crop products consumed in vegetable form (cereals, root crops, fruits, vegetables) are calculated based on their caloric content relative to the caloric content of an equal weight of cereals.[5] The specific CE coefficients for crops will vary slightly by country. A sample of crop coefficients for world averages for 2001 developed from FAO food balance sheet data is presented in Table 7.1.

CE factor values for animal products are calculated using the CEs of feeds consumed by the animal relative to production of specific consumable livestock products. Grains and cereals are assigned a CE factor value equal to "1". Production livestock and livestock products are then converted to CE factor values based on the feed embedded in their production. This live weight measure includes all forms of feed such as grains, protein supplements, forages (including pasture) and other feeds, and includes feed consumption by breeding herds. The live weight calculation is then adjusted for dressing weight percentage to give a final CE value for consumable product. The principal consumable livestock product CE coefficients are shown in Table 7.1 and their derivation is explained further below.

The livestock product CE coefficients were developed from USDA data on US feed consumption, feed conversion ratios and livestock production for the ten year period 1964–73 (USDA, 1975), chosen for data availability. US feed conversion ratios from this period are probably equal to or somewhat more efficient than in many transition countries today, but less than in many developed economies. The USDA data for all feeds is given in corn equivalents. The caloric content for current (2001) FAO data for the US for the cereal category is exactly equal to the caloric content for corn on a per unit weight basis.

Table 7.1 Sample cereal equivalent coefficients for crop and livestock products

Crop products		Livestock products	
Cereals	1.00	Beef	19.8
Fruits	0.15	Pork	8.5
Pulses	1.09	Chicken	4.7
Starchy roots	0.26	Milk	1.2
Sugar, sweeteners	1.11		
Tree nuts	0.79		
Vegetable oils	2.78		
Vegetables	0.08		

Source: authors' calculations based on FAO (2004a) and Rask (1991).

Thus we feel it is appropriate to use feed corn equivalents for determining CE coefficients for livestock products. For the world average, corn has a slightly lower caloric content than the cereal category. As with livestock production in much of the world, non-concentrate feeds are a substantial part of the US livestock feed supply with forages making up over three-quarters of all beef cattle feed and over 90 percent for non-feeder beef cattle.

The income–food consumption relationship using cereal equivalents

The model and data

We begin with the straightforward model developed in Rask and Rask (2004). Food consumption rises as income increases, but at a decreasing rate.

$$C_{ce} = g(GNI_{PC}), \quad g' > 0, \quad g'' < 0 \tag{1}$$

where C_{ce} is per capita consumption measured in CE factor values and GNI_{PC} is real per capita gross national income. The independent variable proxies the level of economic development, which directly affects consumption in terms of CEs. Recall that this measure of food consumption focuses on *resource use*, eliminating packaging and convenience aspects which dominate food *expenditures* at higher incomes.

Updating previous work (Rask and Rask, 2004), we used data from a broad range of market economies to estimate the income–consumption relationship in equation (1) in which annual per capita CEs of food consumption developed from FAO (2004a; 2004b) data were regressed against annual real GNI per capita in PPP, purchasing power parity (World Bank, 2002), using the following functional form:

$$C_{ce} = A_1 - A_2 e^{-kGNI_{PC}} \tag{2}$$

The criteria for selecting data points for this group of market economies are the following. The time period covers the initial transition decade and more recent data, 1990–2001. Transition economies are excluded from the comparison group, as are countries with low or negative income growth, defined as less than 10 percent aggregate growth in real gross national income per capita for years 1990–2001.[6] Only countries within a broad range of 0.7 to 1.3 agricultural self-sufficiency ratios are included in the comparison group, as countries with very high or low self-sufficiency ratios have a significantly different food resource base and pricing structure, such as Japan and Australia. All transition economies currently fall within this range. Countries at all income levels are included for the purpose of describing a market-based development pattern throughout the development process. Finally, small countries of less than one million population are excluded as outliers. The resulting market economy group represents 56 countries with 672 observations for the 1990–2001 period. Regression results are detailed in Table 7.2, with the market-based relationship shown in Figure 7.1 above.

The market income–food consumption relationship

In the process of market development, per capita consumption measured in tons of CEs per capita per year rises rapidly with income growth at low levels of income, but the growth rate slows at higher income levels, and begins to stabilize above US\$25,000 GNI (PPP) per capita. Over this income range, annual consumption per capita increases about fivefold, from less than 0.4 to over 2.0 tons of cereal equivalents per capita per year. Clearly, people do not eat five times as much food; rather, the diet change incorporating more livestock products reflects more cereal or grain equivalents consumed. As is shown in Figure 7.1, cereal consumption decreases marginally with development, fruit and vegetable consumption increases marginally, and almost all of the fivefold increase in consumption is accounted for by livestock products. Recall that consumers in centrally planned economies consumed a far higher proportion of livestock products, and therefore cereal equivalents, than the market-based curve would predict for their income levels. The transition process is therefore seen in part as a movement from this distorted position toward the market relationship defined here.

Table 7.2 Income–consumption relationship: estimates for market economies, 1990–2001

	Estimate		*Asymptotic standard error*
A_1	2.374		0.0749
A_2	2.036		0.0649
k	$5.89 \cdot 10^{-5}$		$4.471 \cdot 10^{-6}$
		$R^2 = 0.90$, $n = 672$	

Reducing the consumption asymmetry during transition

Throughout the pre-transition era consumers in centrally planned economies consumed as much food in terms of cereal equivalents as consumers in market economies with income levels more than 75 percent higher (Rask and Rask, 2004). As transition to market began, these countries experienced severe declines in consumption, which leveled off for some countries, but continue for others. We begin by dividing the transition countries into three country groups to highlight three very different paths of income–consumption adjustment. These groups are: the former USSR, the Central European countries (Czechoslovakia, Hungary, Poland) and the Balkan countries (Albania, Bulgaria, Romania). The paths followed by the Central European countries highlight the importance of income growth in removing the asymmetry with less consumption loss. Note that China is not included in FAO data for transition economies and is not considered in our analysis here due to its very different transition process and timing. We have, however, shown its income–consumption path in Figure 7.2 as a contrast to that of other transition countries, and indicated its current position relative to the market trend in Figure 7.4. Given the statistical dominance of the Russian Federation and the Ukraine in the former USSR, we then disaggregate the USSR in Figure 7.3 to display the diversity of experience in this region. The current position of all countries is shown in Figure 7.4, with anticipated changes in consumption for selected countries and country groups presented in Table 7.3.

Each group shown in Figure 7.2 follows a significantly different path of adjustment. From 1975 to 1989, both China and the USSR enjoyed increasing real income as well as increasing per capita food consumption, with the USSR showing a greater asymmetry in its relationship compared to the market trend. After 1989, the USSR (and eventually the 15 countries comprising the former USSR) took a sharp turn in the reverse direction, losing both in income and consumption on a per capita basis. There is some income recovery beginning in 1999, while consumption remains at a level 40 percent below its 1989 peak. China, in contrast, began its transition much earlier and had less distortion to begin with, resulting in a continuous positive trend for both income and consumption not exhibited by any other transition economy. In 2001 China was experiencing consumption levels somewhat above that of market economies at similar income levels, reflecting increasing asymmetry. Surprisingly, after starting from very different initial conditions, the USSR and China are converging in terms of their income–food consumption relationship.

The Balkan countries (Figure 7.2) experienced rising income prior to 1989, while consumption remained roughly steady and slightly above the market trend to that point. After 1989, income fell sharply, turning around only recently. Food consumption per capita initially rose, then declined to below its pre-transition level. There is, as yet, no clear trend toward removing the asymmetry in these countries. The Central European countries showed much greater distortion in food consumption relative to market trends initially, but consumption dropped off sharply after 1989. Their rapid return to growing incomes has enabled these

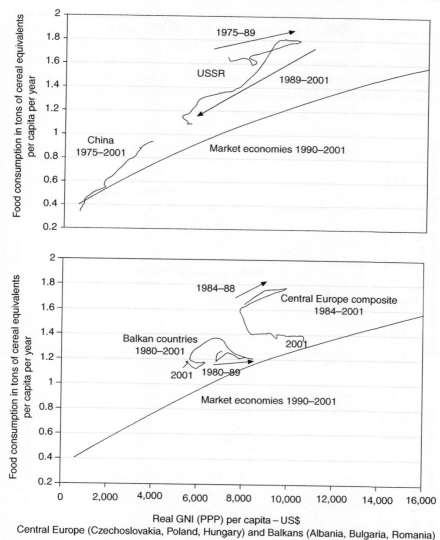

Figure 7.2 Per capita consumption adjustments pre- and during transition for selected countries and regional groups, 1975–2001.

countries to approach the market relationship with less consumption adjustment compared to the former USSR. With little or no income growth, their path would have continued to descend vertically, whereas consumption has in fact steadied at around the 1.4 level. Per capita consumption in these countries as a group now approaches the market trend, indicating the successful elimination of that asymmetry.

On an individual country basis, it is clear that the income changes associated with transition are critical determinants of the degree to which the consumption asymmetry is eliminated. CE consumption levels in most countries (except Romania or some former Soviet republics) prior to transition had nearly reached the level of high-income market economies, but at substantially lower incomes. Czechoslovakia had in fact surpassed the average Western Europe consumption

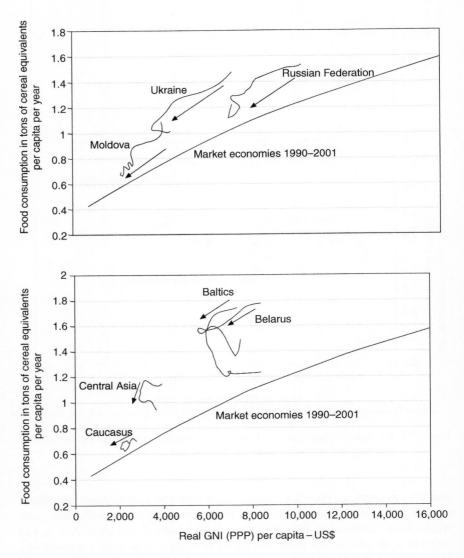

Figure 7.3 Per capita consumption adjustments pre- and during transition in former Soviet republics, 1992–2001.

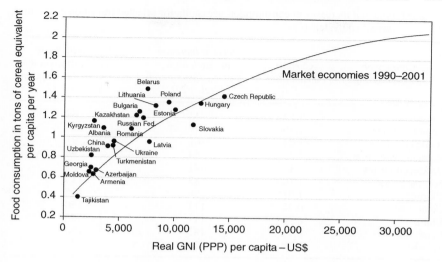

Figure 7.4 Positions in food consumption–income relationship relative to market trend, 2001.

level in 1989. With the onset of transition, consumption dropped dramatically, but the individual approaches to the market economy curve following this early drop have differed due in large part to the income changes accompanying their economic restructuring processes. (The poorer countries of the Caucasus and Central Asia have experienced less dramatic income–consumption adjustments, but consumption continues to remain above market economy levels.) For those countries with fairly constant incomes, the path descends vertically (e.g. Latvia, shown as part of the Baltic countries in Figure 7.3) until consumption eventually stabilizes near the market trend. For countries with income growth, the path angles to the right toward the market curve necessitating less adjustment in consumption (e.g. Poland and Hungary, composite in Figure 7.2, and to a lesser extent Belarus, Lithuania and Estonia). In the case of the Russian Federation, Ukraine and Moldova (Figure 7.3), income fell so dramatically that even greater consumption adjustment was required. Thus, income changes are critical determinants of both the speed and level of consumption adjustment and the attainment of income–consumption equilibrium in a market context.

Each transition country included in this study is identified in Figure 7.4 in terms of its current income–food consumption relationship relative to the market trend. Two implications immediately appear. First, while a few countries have reached (Hungary, Estonia) and even crossed (the Czech Republic, Slovakia, Latvia) the market trend line in recent years, most are still consuming diets higher in CEs than market economies at similar income levels. Further adjustments are required to eliminate this asymmetry. Second, transition countries are clustered in the low to middle income range, resulting in the projection that once the market relationship is achieved, income growth will result in significant

Table 7.3 Potential increases in consumption per capita for selected transition economies (cereal equivalents)

Country or regional group	Current consumption	Percent increase to reach high income consumption level = 2.0	Percent increase to reach estimated maximum consumption level = 2.37
Belarus	1.50	33	58
Central Europe	1.36	47	74
Baltic countries	1.24	61	91
Russian Federation	1.22	64	94
Balkan countries	1.17	71	103
Former USSR	1.10	82	115
Ukraine	1.01	98	135
Central Asia	0.95	111	150
China	0.95	111	150
Caucasus	0.71	182	234
Tajikistan	0.38	426	524

increases in per capita food consumption (especially livestock products) measured in CEs for all transition countries. Based on current per capita consumption levels compared to a high-income consumption level of two tons of CEs per capita per year, future consumption increases could range from 33 percent (Belarus) to over 400 percent (Tajikistan), with a possible doubling of consumption for a number of countries (Table 7.3). The issue now becomes, can production rebound to match these projected consumption increases, and in addition contribute product to world markets, or will transition countries become net importers of food?

The food production conundrum: signs of an emerging problem

Since the pre-transition consumption asymmetry reflected expanded consumption of livestock products, the subsequent decline in food consumption during the transition period has been largely a reversal of that trend, resulting in lower livestock product consumption. Livestock production has followed suit, as evidenced by relatively stable agricultural self-sufficiency ratios (Rask and Rask, 2004). The reasons for these production losses go beyond the reduced demand from consumption adjustment to include restructuring problems in agriculture and the inability of transition countries to market surpluses to the international economy, largely stemming from the quality and institutional asymmetries referred to earlier. For transition economies, these asymmetries are *in addition* to the institutional asymmetries associated with levels of development and noted by other authors (Yotopoulos, Chapter 1; Romano, Chapter 10). The net result is a significant underutilization of agricultural resources when compared to the production levels experienced prior to transition. Now, with consumption of livestock products poised to rise in a number of these countries, can production rebound in a commensurate way?

While production issues are not a central focus of our analysis, research findings from other studies and production limitations embedded in the rules of accession to the EU raise concerns that rapid expansion of agricultural production, particularly for livestock products, is unlikely. These concerns are noted below. First we quantify the level of reduction in livestock output during transition to provide dimension to the current reduced resource use in the livestock production sector.

Reduction in livestock output

The degree of loss in livestock-based food production during transition is here assessed by means of the CE measure to capture underlying resource needs. Recall that a given reduction in beef production idles more resources than does an equal reduction in poultry production (Table 7.1). Comparing total livestock output production levels at the onset of transition (1989 for non-Baltic countries, 1992 for Baltic due to data availability) with levels in 2001, yields the percentage reductions presented in Table 7.4. The eight individual countries shown in Table 7.4 have joined or will soon enter the European Union. Data for all transition countries and the former USSR, as well as selected individual products, are shown for comparison purposes.

Table 7.4 Percentage changes in livestock product output since transition (1992–2001 for Baltic countries; 1989–2001 for other transition countries)

Country or regional group	All livestock	Bovine meat	Milk products	Pigmeat	Poultry meat	Eggs
(percent change 1989–2001)[a]						
All transition	−43	−53	−41	−42	−32	−30
Former USSR	−47	−55	−45	−58	−59	−35
Poland	−18	−50	−32	0	105	1
Czechoslovakia	−43	−64	−45	−39	33	−17
Hungary	−26	−51	−32	−45	8	−28
Bulgaria	−34	−42	−32	−40	−43	−41
Romania	−20	−34	8	−42	−16	−16
(percent change 1992–2001)[a]						
Estonia	−53	−69	−42	−33	−11	−39
Latvia	−66	−84	−52	−69	−58	−24
Lithuania	−38	−72	−36	−41	−2	−16

Source: authors' calculations based on FAO (2004b).

Note

a Percentage changes based on cereal equivalent values, estimated.

The reduction in production of livestock products is common to all transition countries and is most apparent in the former USSR, especially the Baltic countries. For transition countries as a group, livestock production declined 43 percent between 1989 and 2001, while the former USSR suffered a 47 percent loss. Production of bovine meat and dairy, the most resource-intensive products, experienced the greatest decline for most countries. Poultry production, the most efficient in resource use, declined the least and actually increased in Poland, Czechoslovakia and Hungary. This substitution of more resource-efficient livestock products (lower price) is consistent with what we would expect in a market economy, especially during a time of declining income.

For Poland, constant pigmeat production and increased poultry production largely offset significant declines in beef and dairy, resulting in a modest 18 percent reduction in total livestock production. At the other extreme, the Baltic countries have experienced very deep cuts in livestock production, as they have suffered reductions in both internal and external (within the greater USSR) markets that once existed for their former high levels of production. It is probable that if comparable data back to 1989 were available the declines in production noted for the Baltic countries in Table 7.4 would be even larger. In fact, livestock production in the combined countries of the former USSR, of which the Baltics are a part, had already dropped 21 percent by 1992.

Can production rebound?

Several studies indicate continuing production concerns for transition countries. Csaki (2000) predicts that animal husbandry will continue to stagnate in CEECs, while declining in CIS countries.[7] He also concludes that the need to restructure the food industry to accommodate rising quality demands will restrict the growth of output for a long time. (This view is in broad agreement with our earlier assertions concerning asymmetries in agricultural institutions.) While predicting that the region will be able to export pork and poultry, he expects the region to be a net importer of beef, and a net importer of food in general.

Moreover, this current situation of historically low production levels forms the basis for the supply management instruments negotiated for those countries entering the European Union (CEC, 2002; EBRD, 2002). In general, such supply management policies aimed at restricting agricultural production pose fewer problems for the established EU members, since almost all EU countries have reached stable food consumption levels. However, these same policies introduce potential supply difficulties for new members, whose CE consumption is expected to grow from 30 percent to near 100 percent, with these difficulties further compounded by the low, newly established basis levels. Weber (2001) predicts that acceding countries will import poultry and eggs from older EU nations. Balcombe et al. (1999) see Bulgaria as a net importer of food from the EU. Erjavec et al. (2003) and Ferto and Hubbard (2003) express broader concerns about EU agricultural policies hindering healthy market development of the agricultural sector.

Unfortunately, this asymmetry in the current level of livestock production relative to available productive resources (as demonstrated by pre-transition production levels) must still overcome many structural and institutional problems. Furthermore, for some countries, this asymmetry forms the basis for production limitations based on quotas and other supply management measures upon entrance to the European Union. Production resource asymmetries appear set to expand as consumption asymmetries decline.

Summary and conclusions

The process of globalization poses unique challenges for transition economies struggling to overcome consumption asymmetries created by distortions in the centrally planned era. The largest asymmetries were experienced by those countries with relatively high per capita incomes prior to transition, such as the Central European nations of Poland, Hungary and the former Czechoslovakia, as well as the Baltic countries and Belarus. These populations as a group enjoyed diets rich in livestock products, similar to those of market economies with much higher income levels and, in the case of Czechoslovakia, per capita food consumption (measured in CEs per capita) exceeded the Western European average in 1989.

Alleviating the consumption asymmetry has entailed early reductions in livestock food consumption and income for all transition economies. The adjustment paths for these countries after the initial drop have been highly dependent on their ability to stabilize or increase income levels. Those countries experiencing income growth during transition (Central European countries, Belarus, the Baltic countries) have been able to reduce or eliminate the asymmetry with much less reduction in per capita food consumption. Those countries with continued falling incomes (Ukraine, Russian Federation) have suffered larger consumption losses.

As transition economies eliminate the distortions and begin to develop along market lines, per capita CE food consumption is projected to increase according to the identified market trend. Based on the current income range for these countries, we therefore expect per capita CE consumption to rise between 30 percent and 100 percent for most individual countries before stabilizing.

An emerging problem concerns the ability of these once major agricultural producing countries to match the dynamic consumption changes with a rebound in production, principally in livestock products. Food production in the centrally planned economies mirrored the high consumption levels prior to transition, highlighting the enormous agricultural potential in these countries. The sharp drop in production coinciding with the loss of consumption points both to the severe disruptions in production caused by transition and to the inability of these countries to market the surplus globally as consumption plummeted. As other authors have noted, the necessary structural and institutional adjustments within the agricultural sector as well as in the surrounding rural economy will require considerable time to complete.

142   *K.J. Rask and N. Rask*

Moreover, the current low level of food production is particularly troubling for those countries entering or about to enter the European Union (the Baltic countries, Central European countries, Romania and Bulgaria). The terms of accession are based on the current low levels of agricultural output, making more difficult the process of recovering their traditionally high production levels for meeting increasing consumer demand and possible exports in the future. EU agricultural policies designed for stable consumption populations do not translate well for populations whose consumption is poised to rise. On the other hand, to the extent that production is allowed to recover, the discipline forced on these acceding countries in terms of transforming their agricultural institutions to conform to world standards may provide some benefits in terms of participating in global markets outside the EU.

The projected significant increases on the consumption side combined with continued difficulties on the production side set the stage for a growing production asymmetry just as the consumption asymmetry inherited from the command economy years is being resolved for many transition countries. To the asymmetrical impact of globalization on rich and poor countries must be added the specific problems faced by intermediate income, formerly command economies which must now overcome their unique initial conditions. While entering world markets can help spur certain positive changes, the particular legacy of agricultural policy in the pre-transition years has created its own impediments to realizing gains from trade. Thus, after more than ten years of transition, these countries face continuing challenges in adjusting their institutions to integrate their economies into world markets in order to benefit from globalization.

Notes

1 The authors would like to thank the editors for their vision and support, and also the anonymous reviewers for their valuable comments on an earlier draft of this chapter. Any errors that remain are, of course, our own.
2 This section draws heavily on Rask and Rask (2004).
3 The data and regression analysis are discussed in the third section of this chapter.
4 Extensions of this work into the concept of CE factor values can be found in Gilland (1979), Sanderson and Mehra (1988), Rask (1991), Rask and Rask (2004).
5 CE coefficient refers to number of tons of cereals that is equivalent to one ton of crop or livestock product. See below for further explanation.
6 Countries with low or negative growth do not have enough variation in income to provide sufficient additional information for statistical analysis.
7 CEECs are Central and Eastern European countries, and CIS refers to the Commonwealth of Independent States.

References

Balcombe, Kelvin, Sophia Davidova and Jamie A. Morrison (1999), "Consumer Behaviour in a Country in Transition with a Strongly Contracting Economy: The Case of Food Consumption in Bulgaria," *Journal of Agricultural Economics*, 50 (1): 36–47.
CEC (2002), "Enlargement and Agriculture: Successfully Integrating the New Member States into CAP – Issue Paper." Brussels: Commission of the European Communities.

Chevassus-Lozza, Emmanuelle and Manuela Unguru (2002), "Agri-food Exports to the CEECs: Winners and Losers from EU Enlargement," *Euro Choices*, 1 (3): 18–23.

Csaki, Csaba (2000), "Agricultural Reforms in Central and Eastern Europe and the Former Soviet Union: Status and Perspectives," *Agricultural Economics*, 22 (1): 37–54.

EBRD (2002), "Transition Report 2002: Agriculture and Rural Transition." London: European Bank for Reconstruction and Development.

Erjavec, Emil, Miroslav Rednak, Tina Volk and Jernej Turk (2003), "The Transition from 'Socialist' Agriculture to the Common Agricultural Policy: The Case of Slovenia," *Post-Communist Economies*, 15 (4): 557–69.

EU (2003), "The Treaty of Accession 2003 of the Czech Republic, Estonia, Cyprus, Latvia, Lithuania, Hungary, Malta, Poland, and Slovenia to the European Union." Brussels: European Union.

FAO (2004a), *Food Balance Sheet Data*. Rome: Food and Agriculture Organization.

FAO (2004b), *Livestock Production Data*. Rome: Food and Agriculture Organization.

Ferto, Imre and Lionel J. Hubbard, (2003) "Revealed Comparative Advantage and Competitiveness in Hungarian Agri-Food Sectors," *World Economy*, 26 (2): 247–59.

Gilland, Bernard (1979), *The Next Seventy Years: Population, Food and Resource*. Kent, UK: Abacus Press.

Kydd, Jonathan, Allan Buckwell and Jamie A. Morrison (1997), "The Role of the Agricultural Sector in the Transition to a Market Economy in Central and Eastern Europe: An Analytical Framework." In Jonathan Kydd, Sophia Davidova, Miranda Mackay and Thea Mech, eds, *The Role of Agriculture in the Transition Process towards a Market Economy*. New York: United Nations.

Rask, Norman (1991), "Dynamics of Self-Sufficiency and Income Growth." In Fred J. Ruppel and Earl D. Kellogg, eds, *National and Regional Self-sufficiency Goals: Implications for International Agriculture*. Boulder, CO and London: Lynne Rienner Publishers.

Rask, Kolleen J. and Norman Rask (2004), "Reaching Turning Points in Economic Transition: Adjustments to Distortions in Resource-based Consumption of Food," *Comparative Economic Studies*, 20 (4): 542–69.

Sanderson, Fred H. and Rekha Mehra (1988), "Brighter Prospects for Agricultural Trade." In M. Ann Tutwiler, ed., *US Agriculture in a Global Setting*. Washington, DC: National Center for Food and Agricultural Policy, Resources for the Future.

USDA (1975), "Livestock-Feed Relationships, National and State." Washington, DC: United States Department of Agriculture, Economic Research Service.

Weber, Gerald (2001), "The CAP's Impact on Agriculture and Food Demand in Central European Countries after EU Accession: Who Will Lose and Who Will Gain?" In George H. Peters and Prabhu L. Pingali, eds, *Tomorrow's Agriculture: Incentives, Institutions, Infrastructure and Innovations*. Burlington, VT: Ashgate, pp. 498–505.

World Bank (2002), *World Development Indicators 2002*. Washington, DC: World Bank.

Yotopoulos, Pan A. (1985), "Middle-income Classes and Food Crises: The 'New' Food–Feed Competition," *Economic Development and Cultural Change*, 33 (3): 463–83.

Part III

Agricultural poverty and decommodification

8 Genetically modified seeds and decommodification

An analysis based on the Chinese cotton case[1]

Michel A.C. Fok, Weili Liang, Donato Romano and Pan A. Yotopoulos

Introduction

Decommodification of international trade is becoming a pervasive phenomenon even in a sector, like agriculture, where products are primarily traded as commodities. Of course, this is not an entirely novel breakthrough since international trade in high-value differentiated agricultural products, such as wines, cheeses, etc., has been taking place for centuries. What is new is the acceleration of this trade and the expansion of its domain under the current wave of globalization as a result of a complex set of technological and institutional changes that occurred in the last two decades (Yotopoulos, Chapter 1).

One of the driving forces of this process of decommodification is agricultural biotechnology. Indeed, the application of new scientific methods – more precise and more effective than the traditional ones – makes possible a degree of product "customization" that was simply unimaginable a few decades ago. But those changes would not have made much difference if they had not been favored by policy interventions that reshaped the institutional set-up at the national as well as at the international level. The worldwide strengthening of the protection of intellectual property rights (IPR) provided robust incentives for unprecedented private investments in biotechnology. This is good news, because it has brought more private resources into the agricultural research industry. Yet it is also a fundamental cause of systematic asymmetries in globalization (Pagano, Chapter 2). In fact, as artfully written by Michael Pollan in presenting the story of a recent agricultural biotechnology innovation:

> In the case of the NewLeaf [potato] a gene borrowed from one strain of a common bacterium found in the soil – *Bacillus thuringiensis*, or Bt for short – gives the potato plant's cells the information that they need to manufacture a toxin lethal to the Colorado potato beetle. This gene is now Monsanto's intellectual property. With genetic engineering agriculture has entered the information age, and Monsanto's aim, it would appear, is to become its Microsoft, supplying the proprietary "operating systems" – the metaphor is theirs – to run this new generation of plants.
>
> (Pollan, 2001: 191)

As Pollan adds, the Peruvian Incas, whose ancestors domesticated the *Solanum tuberosum* 7,000 years ago, can never claim property rights over the domesticated potato genes since intellectual property can be recognized only to individuals and corporations – not to tribes! Furthermore, the economic rents accruing to the IPR holder seem systematically to favor the developed countries (DCs) vis-à-vis the less developed countries (LDCs) because the former have a stronger institutional setting and a better resource endowment to produce decommodified goods, market them and enforce compliance of the customers with the IPR regulations.

This chapter provides an assessment of the application of genetic engineering to agriculture and its marketing to LDCs in the specific case of a success story, namely the creation of a genetically modified (GM) seed, Bt-cotton (GM cotton from here on), and its adoption in China. Although a thorough and exhaustive assessment of the adoption of GM seeds in LDCs is still far to come, there is quite a widespread disbelief regarding the suitability of GM seeds for LDCs, justified with the claim that GM seeds do not match poor farmers' real needs and, even if suitable, they cannot be accessed because they are too expensive (Myers, 1999; Mazoyer, 2000). On the contrary, the Chinese case seems to contradict the expected adverse impacts on LDCs of decommodification of agricultural inputs:[2] about one-half of the total Chinese cotton acreage is currently in GM cotton and this has led to a decrease in insecticide use, a reduction in the related costs, an increase in cotton yields and a higher profitability due to significant labor savings (Pray *et al.*, 2001; Huang *et al.*, 2002; Huang *et al.*, 2003a; Huang *et al.*, 2003b). But, on balance, we argue that welcome as it is, the counter-example of the Chinese cotton case is unique and as such it represents an exception which confirms the general rule.

This chapter is organized as follows. The next section is devoted to the analysis of the changes of the rules of the game that accompanied the emergence of the GM seed industry and summarizes the debate about the pros and the cons of GM seed adoption in LDCs. The third section analyzes the Chinese GM cotton case using original data from a survey carried out in 2002–3 in Hebei Province that show the positive impact of GM seed adoption by farmers. In the fourth section the institutional and economic conditions that made possible this success are assessed, contrasting them with the conditions existing in most LDCs. The fifth section analyzes the likely future evolution of GM seed diffusion and the interventions required to ensure a reasonably high likelihood of success. The final section summarizes the main findings of this study.

The gene revolution: "pan-positional" IPR protection and product decommodification

The advances in biotechnology, especially genetic engineering, and the contemporary change of IPR regulation at the national as well as the international level marked a profound change in agricultural research and development (R&D) activities that can qualify as a true revolution, the so-called "gene" revolution. We argue that the shift towards stronger plant IPR protection and the contemporary presence of product "decommodification" dramatically changed the rules of the game of competition in the agricultural sector and ultimately determines asymmetric outcomes between DCs and LDCs.

Strengthening of IPR protection

Prior to 1980 patenting was applied only to inanimate things like machines and equipment. The situation changed with the advent of modern biotechnology. The application of genetic engineering to living things represents indeed the fundamental justification for claiming intellectual property protection through "expanded patents," on the grounds that an "inventive" step is involved in creating the GM good, in a process that is not dissimilar to that of standard patents. However, the IPR protection granted with expanded patents, i.e. the ones that apply to genetically engineered plants and animals, is much stronger than that granted in traditional patents, as in the fields of mechanics, electricity or chemistry, for instance.

In the case of expanded patents, the traditional removal-from-secrecy clause that was intended to make public the knowledge associated to the invention no longer applies, so that a researcher or inventor is not free to use it in making a follow-on invention. The IPR owner of expanded patents has the right to exclude their use in breeding programs because the parental components can be identified in the biological progeny, which can be regarded as an IPR-protected component of the invention. This "high-potential" nature of expanded patents is further compounded by the fact that the knowledge of useful genes (genomics) and of engineering transgenic plants is "basic" in the sense that it is located at the upstream extreme of the R&D process and can be used in a variety of downstream innovations. It is this prospect of capturing the huge economic rents accruing to the GM innovator that makes entering the agricultural biotech industry so appealing to private firms.

Beginning with the Bayh-Dole Act of 1980, the institutional arrangements for patenting university research discoveries and protecting plant varieties were substantially strengthened in the United States. Other developed countries followed the US example in strengthening domestic intellectual property rights in this area. Eventually also the European Union, which includes some of the most guarded countries on this issue, adopted the Directive 98/44/EC on the legal protection of biotechnological inventions that explicitly allows patenting of all types of life forms except for the clearly stated exceptions, such as the human body.

At supranational level there were several legal and regulatory breakthroughs in this field. In 1991 the Convention for the Protection of New Varieties of Plants was amended strengthening plant breeders' rights, making them more patent-like, and weakening the "farmer privilege" which allowed farmers to replant saved seeds without reference to the breeder (see the next part of this section). More important, in 1994 an agreement was reached at WTO level in

Marrakesh giving the WTO powerful dispute-settlement jurisdiction. This was followed by enacting in 1995 the Trade Related Aspects of Intellectual Property Rights (TRIPS) agreement, which extended US-like patentability of living forms to the global level.

As emphasized by Pagano (Chapter 2), all those regulatory shifts changed the relative position of different individuals, in the sense of who will enjoy the right and who will bear the symmetrical obligation. More specifically, the worldwide extension of IPR protection warranted under the TRIPS agreement, is a proto-typical example of what Pagano calls a "pan-positional good," that is the case where the exclusive right of an individual or a firm implicitly assigns obligations to all other individuals in the world. Paradoxically, it is the non-rival nature of knowledge that determines such a strong asymmetric outcome once knowledge is privatized and its protection is extended to the whole world as within the TRIPS framework.

This has major implications for the international standings of the different countries. In such a context it is easy to anticipate asymmetric outcomes deriving from the different endowment of resources, skills and infrastructures between DCs and LDCs. In fact, for many developed countries the compliance with international regulations often means no more than the application of already implemented domestic regulations. This is not the case with developing, let alone poor countries for which the cost of compliance with international regulations like IPR protection and biosafety risk assessment (food safety and environmental protection) is much higher. On top of the cost of enforcement of the domestically sanctioned standards, the additional obligation to enforce also the internationally sanctioned standards entails an extra cost. This is not a trivial cost for many LDCs, especially if we take into account their meager budgets and if we consider their real opportunity cost in terms of foregone development alternatives (Romano, Chapter 10). This is also a vivid example of what Pagano calls a "legal disequilibrium" because the international regulations, e.g. the TRIPS agreement, while clearly making the "right" of inventors "pan-positional" in protecting their IPR in all WTO member countries, do not explicitly assign the corresponding "obligation" of enforcement, nor do they provide for the cost of such enforcement. Implicitly the obligation of that protection is left to the member-country governments, which may find the cost prohibitive and may not be able to deliver.

GM seeds: decommodification and the ingredients of customization

The rules that form the marketing framework of introducing the Bt-gene into cotton varieties to create the GM cotton were initially drawn up by Monsanto for the USA in the mid 1990s and were subsequently extended to apply to all countries.[3] The commercialization of the GM seeds is illustrative of the approach of customizing a "new" good, the GM cotton in this case, with the objective of embodying in it economic rents that the "producer" can claim. From the point of view of the economic characteristics, the price of the seed remains the same as the price of conventional seeds, but this price is no longer the only cost users have to incur. Indeed, the economic rents accruing to the biotechnology manufacturer are created and captured in a triple customization intervention. First, a surcharge is applied on the price of the conventional seeds in the form of (an annual) "technology fee" for the production of the genetically modified seed for GM cotton.[4] Second, the buyer of the GM cotton seeds assumes a formal contractual commitment not to hold back seeds from one season to another (in any vegetative form). Third, the buyer is also contractually obligated to implement techniques that prevent the development of resistance to the traits incorporated in the GM cotton, in this case of the resistance to Bt-toxins.[5]

The purpose of all three customization features embedded in the GM cotton is to create and protect economic rents, fully exploiting the market power guaranteed by the extension and deepening of IPR.[6] The more conventional means of extorting economic rents are also widely employed. The levels of technology fees seem in fact quite arbitrary. Fees for GM cotton, for example, were first set at US$90/ha, before being reduced to around US$60/ha with some variation between countries, or even between provinces within the same country (Mexico). In South Africa, the technology fees applied differ according to agricultural irrigation features: fees are higher for farmers who produce cotton under irrigation and have higher expected yields.[7] Clearly, the biotechnology service is not being provided at the marginal cost of production but on what the market would bear (Romano, Chapter 10).

More important seem to be the other two institutional innovations devised to extract rents. In fact, the technology fee is a familiar feature of intellectual property rights in various information-technology applications. The fact that it is annualized through the total prohibition of holding back seeds, is a rather blatant and unusual innovation.[8] Software companies, for example, attempt to achieve the same result through creating "upgrades" of their products, but the choice is with the customer whether to buy the upgrade or to continue using the older version of the program. The obligation of the customer to protect the GM cotton from new strains of pests that are resistant to Bt-toxins is an even more creative method of extracting economic rents. It is akin to obliging the passengers of a cruise ship to buy insurance remunerating the ship owners in case the vessel proved not sea-worthy in the event of a storm or, even worse, to contribute to prevent the rising storm!

The essence of decommodification is to remove a commodity from the domain of cost-of-production competition and to launch it into the domain of positional goods, where the ordinal ranking of decommodified goods applies (as opposed to the cardinal measurement of the cost of production), based on "reputation," which is a general term for the ability to extract economic rents (Yotopoulos, Chapter 1). The discussion above on the decommodification in the seed industry makes clear why the diffusion of GM crops in LDCs is questioned and challenged by international environmental groups and by NGOs, although seldom explicitly from the perspective of the decommodification process: there is a risk of exploitation of farmers through the strong market power that has been vested to GM seed companies (McDonald, 2003; Pschorn-Strauss, 2004).[9]

However, decommodification of GM cotton seems to have its limits. In China, for instance, the farmers seem to be those who benefit the most from the adoption of GM cotton.[10] The success of the Chinese experience seems to undermine the argument that LDCs usually lie on the short end of trade asymmetries when decommodification is involved. In order to assess this apparent contradiction, we have first to analyze whether the Chinese case is a success story or not and, if so, what are the conditions that made such success possible and, finally, whether those conditions can be replicated in other LDC contexts.

A success story of GM seed adoption: cotton in Hebei Province

At first glance, the experience with the Chinese adoption of GM cotton looks like a counter-example of the decommodification process which is taking place in the GM seed industry and trade. Indeed, the economic impact of the adoption of GM cotton is beneficial to farmers and no monopolistic exploitation is apparent, as reported by the results from a survey conducted in 2002–3 in Hebei Province.[11] Historically, this province has contributed significantly to Chinese cotton production, but the development of strong resistance in the cotton bollworm (*Helicoverpa armigera* Hübner) in the early 1990s stalled the cotton cultivation. The long legacy of cotton in the province was threatened and the challenge was to find an effective technical solution. Therefore, Hebei Province was the first province where the dissemination of the GM cotton varieties began in 1998 and soon thereafter the entire cotton area of the province was converted to GM cotton, which eventually led to a remarkable rebirth of cotton production in this region (Table 8.1).

Growing GM cotton is very profitable for the farmers, by far exceeding the profits from the main alternative available to the farmers in the province, the cultivation of wheat and maize that are grown in sequence (Table 8.2).

Table 8.1 Cotton Production in Hebei Province (10^3 tons of lint)

Year	1986	1987	1988	1989	1990	1991	1992	1993	1994
Hebei province	511	626	577	536	571	634	306	192	390
China	3,541	4,245	4,149	3,788	4,507	5,673	4,510	3,739	4,342
Hebei/China (%)	14.4	14.8	13.9	14.2	12.7	11.2	6.8	5.1	9.0

Year	1995	1996	1997	1998	1999	2000	2001	2002	2003
Hebei province	370	258	249	270	223	298	419	402	522
China	4,768	4,202	4,603	4,501	3,828	4,417	5,320	4,920	4,870
Hebei/China (%)	7.8	6.1	5.4	6.0	5.8	6.7	7.9	8.2	10.7

Source: Fok *et al.* (2004b: Table 1, p. 48).

Table 8.2 Comparison of profitability of cotton, wheat and maize cultivation (US$/ha)

	Gross revenue		Income net of input costs	
	2002	*2003*	*2002*	*2003*
Cotton	1,716	2,377	1,425	2,064
Wheat	781	819	461	554
Maize	814	880	578	707

Source: Fok *et al.* (2004b: Table 8, p. 52).

At the international level also, and in comparison with other LDCs, Chinese farmers dominate in terms of profitability. The financial profitability of growing GM cotton depends on the level of yields achieved and on the favorable output–input price ratios. In fact, the price of cotton is quite high due to the continuing protection of the domestic market from imports and despite China's entry into the WTO. The cotton lint farm gate prices found in the survey were US$0.57/lb and US$0.89/lb in 2002 and 2003, respectively, whereas the world market parity prices (c.i.f. Northern Europe) were US$0.41/lb and US$0.63/lb.

On the input side, the average cost of production inputs (fertilizers, pesticides, seeds, plastic film, growth regulators, irrigation water) is only 15–20 percent of the output value, while for instance in West African cotton countries it is roughly twice as much (Béroud, 2001; Fok *et al.*, 2004a).[12] More specifically, the cost to Hebei farmers for accessing GM cotton seeds is far less than in other countries. This is the outcome of an effective competition between several GM seed suppliers, foreign as well as domestic, with the result that the farmers can choose from a large portfolio of distinct GM cotton varieties.[13] The access to GM cotton seeds by Hebei farmers seems quite easy as shown by the fact that many of them grow more than one variety and by the mode of GM seed acquisition: more than half of farmers use either partly or totally the seeds they held back from the previous season, at virtually zero cost (Table 8.3).

Even when farmers access the GM cotton seeds through market purchases, the cost they have to pay is lower than in other countries. In fact, no supplier has been able to maintain a monopolistic position in the province. In particular, despite the fact that Monsanto had a virtual monopoly in marketing GM cotton seeds when the government first gave permission for GM cotton cultivation, its market share has been gradually decreasing as a result of the competition from an increasing number of domestic GM varieties which are commercialized at a lower price (Table 8.4).

Although the profitability of cotton seems to rest on the technological features of GM cotton (e.g. higher yields, fewer pesticide sprays, etc.), it should be stressed that institutional factors played a crucial role in encouraging the adoption of GM cotton and in gaining from it higher profits with little risk. Indeed, China succeeded in designing and enforcing quite particular rules of GM seed commercialization that can hardly be found in other countries.

Table 8.3 Distribution of farmers adopting GM cotton, according to their seed acquisition mode and the number of adopted GM cotton varieties (percent)

Seed acquisition mode	Farmers adopting[a]			All farmers adopting GM seeds[b]
	One variety	Two varieties	Three varieties	
By exchange	1	0	0	1
Partly bought	26	29	75	30
Totally bought	53	33	0	44
Totally held back	20	38	25	25
Total	100	100	100	100

Source: adapted from Fok *et al.* (2004b: Table 14, p. 58).

Notes
a The percentages reported in these three columns are the shares to totals after partitioning the farmer sample according to the number of GM cotton varieties they adopted.
b The percentages reported in this column are the shares to the whole sample of farmers adopting GM cotton varieties.

China launched a very ambitious biotechnology research program from the mid 1980s. This enabled Chinese scientists to identify many genes, to build new specific gene constructions of their own and to master an original method for gene transfer through the pollen tube.[14] With this head start in the field of research and development of GM varieties, Chinese institutions had been networking successfully. The Chinese government endorsed a joint venture between Monsanto and the local Hebei Seed Company. At the same time, a "private" Chinese biotech firm that held the rights of Chinese Bt-genes, the Bio-century Transgene Company Limited (BTCC), started a collaboration with the Chinese Academy of Agricultural Sciences and its local branches to develop GM cotton seed varieties adapted to the different ecological conditions of China. In parallel, the government-sponsored field experiments to determine the

Table 8.4 Market share and cost of GM cotton seeds in Hebei Province

Origin of varieties	Type of varieties[a]	2002			2003		
		Seed cost (US$/kg)	% users	% surface	Seed cost (US$/kg)	% users	% surface
China	Population	3.3	29	39[b]	4.5	43	49[b]
	Hybrids	4.8	4		5.4	6	
USA	Population	5.0	67	61	6.1	51	51

Source: adapted from Fok *et al.* (2005: Table 8, p. 21).

Note
a Populations are varieties composed of plants which are not completely identical from the genetic point of view, but whose genetic composition is stable; vice versa hybrids are made from the crossing of two parents which are pure lines, that is varieties composed of plants which are completely identical from the genetic point of view.
b Sum for China of population and hybrids.

suitability of GM cotton cultivation in the region led to approval of GM cotton. As a result, when Monsanto started marketing its own GM cotton varieties in 1998, China had already put in place the local institutions that would eventually contain the voracious appetite of the multinational.

The success of the Chinese plan was immediate, as shown by the willingness of Monsanto to adjust its standard "rental" seed contract, giving favourable treatment for China. As a result the GM cotton varieties were supplied right from the beginning under the same conditions that usually prevail for conventional seeds. Farmers were not required to sign a contract that prevented the possibility of holding back seeds or commited them to special cultivation techniques (e.g. refuge plots to prevent the emergence of resistance by the targeted pest to the Bt-toxin).[15] The prices farmers paid were all inclusive, with no distinction or mention of any technology fee.[16] Finally, as the local GM cotton varieties were being released into the market, the farmers had more seed choices. By the time of the survey, farmers could choose from 20 local GM cotton varieties that compete with the two varieties of Monsanto. Moreover, the ample varietal offerings of local GM cotton not only are better matched to the ecological adoption conditions than the alternative two varieties, but they are also cheaper than the foreign GM cotton seeds (Table 8.4). All these conditions contribute to make cotton production very attractive and profitable and reduce the financial risk in adopting GM cotton.

Replicability: is the Chinese success with commodified GM seeds a unique case?

As mentioned already in the previous section, the Chinese case cannot be regarded as a general counter-example of the decommodification process because China basically is not representative of LDCs. Referring to the economic results of GM cotton adoption, it should be noted that China ranks as one of the top three countries in terms of yield among the countries with substantial cotton production in the world. This means that an attractive price impacts greatly on farmers' revenues. Moreover, such a high level of yield is the outcome of a high degree of intensification in using production inputs (fertilizers, pesticides, etc.). The direct implication is that the additional cost deriving from using GM seeds appears to be relatively more acceptable, compared to countries where agricultural intensification is low.[17]

In terms of technological abilities, China was able to decrease further the cost of adopting GM cotton. As mentioned earlier, the country has its own endogenous, and flexible, GM technology that is adaptable to producing many GM cotton varieties characterized by a great genetic diversity and being adaptable to various micro-environmental conditions. This home-grown technology can be managed independently of the strategy of any multinational firm.

In terms of the rules under which the GM cotton is being diffused, the government played a crucial role that is multifaceted. The Chinese success was not due so much to Adam Smith's invisible hand on market operation as it was to the strong arm of the government's intervention. It was the suasive power of the state that changed the extortionary terms of the standard contract of the multinational. This power became even more persuasive as a result of China's general policy for managing foreign investment through joint ventures, in this case that by Monsanto and the Hebei Seed Company that was mentioned earlier. In summary, there was a comprehensive package of technical and institutional factors that worked synergistically in recommodifying the GM cotton seeds for sale to the farmers at minimum production cost, thus thwarting the decommodification regime of globalized IPRs and of multinational corporations.

Can this pattern be replicated in the developing countries? Considering different categories of countries according to their ability to carry out biotech R&D, India and Brazil can be ranked at the same stage of technological sophistication as China and as a result they may achieve substantial GM seed diffusion soon. On the other hand, most developing countries lack the technological and institutional infrastructure that makes the diffusion of GM agriculture possible. For the purpose of making an assessment of the replicability of the Chinese experience, we examine the case of India and Brazil, along with the Sub-Saharan African (SSA) countries, that have featured on the international radar screen as promising for the adoption of GM varietal agriculture.

The objective of Table 8.5 is to compare the three cases in terms of various factors that can be considered as proxies for the requisite infrastructural endowments, both technological and institutional, that would be favorable to GM agriculture, more specifically, GM cotton. Of the 13 indicators appearing in the table, India and Brazil have a modest command in the first eight factors that relate to agricultural and technological preconditions. They have solid "No"s on the last five institutional factors, weighing the balance between free markets and regulation. These indicators are eclipsed in India and Brazil by the tendency to consider the free market approach to globalization as an "up-by-the-bootstraps" universal prescription for development. This may, or may not be the case. But it is certainly different from the Chinese approach to GM agriculture. As for the SSA countries, the favorable factors are the existence of a pool of cotton varieties and the number of research institutions, plus an ambivalent approach to state involvement in reaching the pro-farmer GM goals. The conclusion is that the Chinese pragmatic approach that yielded the pro-farmer outcomes of GM cotton introduction, is not easy to replicate in the three cases examined in the table. In other words, there is no guarantee whatsoever that other LDCs could easily copy China's achievements.

There are, however, some promising signs that the competition in the biotech sector is being further opened up. Multinationals are no longer the unique providers of commercial biotech outputs. Due to the high price of GM cotton seeds in India (as a consequence of the Monsanto monopolistic position in providing the Bt-genes), some Indian companies are establishing partnership with the Chinese biotech firm BTTC to contest the Monsanto supremacy (Jishnu, 2006). This is made possible because the Chinese biotech firm gained a reputation by successfully challenging the US multinational at home. And it also

Table 8.5 Factors affecting GM cotton diffusion in selected LDCs

Factors	India	Brazil	SSA[a]
High pest resistance to insecticide	Yes	No	No
High yield	No	Yes[b]	No
High intensification in input use	No	Yes[b]	No
Availability of own Bt-gene technology	No?	No	No
Good command of biotechnology	Yes	Yes	No
Availability of a gene portfolio from national research	Yes?	No	No
Existence of a great pool of cotton varieties	Yes	Yes	Yes
Existence of many research institutions	Yes	Yes	Yes
Willingness for the state to get involved	No	No	Yes
Sufficient bargaining power	No	No	No
Foreign direct investment policy favoring domestic firms	No	No	No
Capacity to adjust diffusion rules to the interest of the smallholders	No	No	No
Capacity to ensure favorable price for cotton produced by smallholders	No	No	No

Source: Fok *et al.* (2004b: Table 15, p. 63).

Notes
a Sub-Saharan Africa.
b Valid for commercial farms, not necessarily for smallholders.

shows that in positional competition the reputation ranking of the contestants is fluid and changes with each outcome of gain or loss. This means that once defeated in China, the biotech multinationals do not look convincingly invincible anymore.

Counter-balancing the decommodification process in the agriculture biotech industry

The view expressed above might be too pessimistic. The future may be better than expected if some institutional reforms aimed at making agricultural biotech R&D work for the poor were implemented and if some promising emerging trends materialized. Addressing the current issues of IPR protection means essentially focusing on: (i) the asymmetric and costly burden that LDCs bear of enforcing the IPR protection on account of owners in DCs who are the holders of these "pan-positional" rights and (ii) the lack of incentives for private companies to invest in LDC-oriented agricultural biotechnology research. The difficulty lies in balancing patent protection to induce private sector investment in research, with offering access to cheap GM products for the poor of this world.

Some ideas that have been recently proposed to solve similar problems in the pharmaceutical sector can provide inspiration for the reform in the agricultural biotech sector as well (Lanjouw, 2002). For instance, considering that the worldwide markets for GM products of interest for LDCs are very different from the markets for the same products in DCs, the IPR protection system would be improved by being tailored to the differences in these markets. In the case of "global" crops, those that can be raised both in LDCs and DCs, the domain of application of IPR can be restricted by making them weaker in LDCs.[18] The patentee would be required to choose enforcement of his IPR protection either in rich or in poor countries, but not in both.[19] For GM crops that are LDC-specific (mainly subsistence crops) the problem is that there is no market because the prospective adopters cannot afford them. In such a case, IPR protection alone is ineffective in stimulating the biotech company to invest in such crops. Therefore, other mechanisms should be devised, like investing public grants or private benevolent donations to research on LDC-specific GM crops.[20] Alternatively, investments should be channeled to make biotechnology R&D available as a free-share (public) good, as it has been recently made by the CAMBIA consortium or the BIOS initiative, under an "open-source" license scheme (*Nature*, 2004; *The Economist*, 2005).[21]

IPR compliance might become less constraining in the near future even if IPR rules remain unchanged, because many patents covering biotechnology outputs are about to expire with the outputs falling into the public domain (Kowalski *et al.*, 2002). If this materializes, it may be possible to establish a clearing-house of those most suitable for LDCs' biotechnology techniques and outputs, making them thus more accessible for public research (Graff and Zilberman, 2001).

Another potentially positive factor is that some countries like China and India own genes of agronomic interest through their public research institutions. Private and multinational companies are no longer having the monopoly on genes of agronomic interest. This new context might offer some room to negotiate more affordable conditions of technology transfer to LDCs, provided that international organizations are invested with some leading role in these negotiations.

Finally, the effective adoption of GM seeds depends also on the economic conditions of crop intensification. In most developing countries the cost of crop intensification has increased as a consequence of the implementation of structural adjustment interventions that canceled all extraneous support for input use. Hopefully, this situation may positively unwind as acknowledged in the WTO Doha Round, where in earlier discussions the principle of supporting poor farmers to get into crop intensification has been rehabilitated (Fok, 2002).

Conclusions

There are various controversies raging about agricultural biotechnology in general, and genetic modification in specific, that this chapter has totally overlooked. Instead, building on the theme of this volume, *The Asymmetries of Globalization,* it focuses on a specific characteristic of agricultural biotechnology that on an a priori basis is expected to tip the balance of the benefits of biotechnological agriculture in favor of the developed countries, while rendering trivial residual profits to the farmers in the LDCs. The spring that releases this asymmetry is decommodification, more specifically the decommodification of the seeds that farmers used to carry forward from one season to the other in order to plant the next year's crop.

The profits from decommodification are, generally, slanted in favor of the DCs, where the new technologies originate and where the reputation that creates and captures the economic rents resides, being normally an attribute of wealth and power. In the case of agriculture this asymmetry is especially pronounced since the IPRs the producers of biotechnology have been granted claim global applicability. These rights not only create an obligation for all countries to protect them for the benefit of their right holders, in this case multinational corporations, but the beneficiaries themselves have creatively exploited the protective fence of international legislation built around their product to construct a most generous rent-generating "operating system that runs the biotechnological agriculture." This "high-tech envy" does not constitute an idle boast. It has materialized in "renting" for one year's use the GM seeds that the farmers purchased, with the obligation to "re-rent" them for the next year! After a multinational has squeezed dry all possible economic rents out of agricultural biotechnology, one would have expected that there is precious little left in terms of profits for the farmer in an LDC.

The case of GM cotton in China is unique in that it has turned the tables on the patent holders, thus making GM cotton cultivation one of the most profitable crops growing in China and among the top profit earners of cotton cultivation in the world. The bottom line of this success rests with the ability of the local biotechnology industry to compete on equal grounds with imported GM cotton seeds. For this to happen, a certain institutional flexibility is required along with the determination of the government. The resultant success consisted of re-commodifying the GM cotton seeds, so that the economic rents of the new technology are captured in loco and go to the farmers, as opposed to corporate profits that flee abroad.

The analysis of the replicability of the Chinese experience in other LDCs comes to the conclusion that China should be considered as the exception that confirms the general rule of biotechnological agriculture having little to offer in alleviating rural poverty in LDCs. At present the adoption of GM seeds in developing countries is not gaining much traction, nor is it likely soon to become sufficiently rewarding for the local farmers. This pessimistic outlook could be moderated if the bar of the IPR barrier protecting the use of GM seeds could be lowered. But this outcome would not materialize automatically. Initiatives are needed to reform the current institutionalization of the WTO–TRIPS agreement. This is a necessary condition. Beyond that, LDCs need to create an environment that is conducive to implementing crop intensification, since this is the essence of GM agriculture. In the meanwhile, a more definitive prospect is that various GM genes and some biotechnology methods will be maturing beyond their statutory patent protection and will be falling in the public domain. At that stage, public research initiatives at the international level could play an active intermediation role in identifying such opportunities and help the LDCs take advantage of these "second hand technologies" to create a remunerative biotechnological agriculture.

Notes

1 The authors acknowledge the contribution of Guiyan Wang and Yuhong Wu in the conduct of the survey in Hebei Province.

2 Another apparently success story of GM cotton adoption is South Africa, where a higher profitability is reported by smallholder growers in the Makhatini Flats, Kwazulu Natal Province (Ismaël *et al.*, 2002; Gouse *et al.*, 2002; Thirtle and Jenkins Beyers, 2003). However, the dramatic reduction in cotton production in the Makhatini Flats during the 2002–3 crop season, due both to institutional and climatic reasons, as well as the rising cost of GM seeds due to an increasing market concentration in the seed industry, show that the alleged success of the South African case must be more balanced (Fok *et al.*, 2004a).

3 Monsanto (and its seed subsidiary Delta and Pineland Co., hereafter just Monsanto), were the first to market GM cotton, and they have enjoyed so far nearly a monopoly power in this area.

4 The effective price the farmer pays for the GM seeds is higher than the price of conventional seeds by the amount of the "technology fee." The latter represents the economic rents accruing through decommodification to the producer and claimed on the grounds that the GM seed is a totally new product which required a substantial investment and which must be used according to particular specifications. This procedure of distinguishing between seed price and technology fee is legally devolved into the partnership between the biotech firm (Monsanto) which owns the IPR on the Bt-gene and its subsidiary seed company (Delta and Pineland) that produces (with the Bt-gene) and markets the GM cotton seeds.

5 This contractual clause in the case of GM cotton is honored by forcing the farmers to set up in adjacent fields "refuge plots" to be sown with conventional varieties that are not to be controlled chemically. The purpose of this intervention is to prevent the emergence of new strains of pests resistant to the Bt-toxin that might be metabolized within GM cotton.

6 Another feature signaling the market power enjoyed by the agro-biotech companies is the promotion of a very limited number of GM cotton varieties, a feature which is more or less hidden through the use of distinct varietal trade names: in the USA and Australia, the same GM cotton variety is commercialized with two different varietal names (Bollgard and Ingard), in South Africa only two varieties (NuCotton and NuOpal) were successively launched, and in China and also Mexico the same two US GM cotton varieties (named 33B and 99B) are commercialized. The strategy of disseminating a very limited number of varieties makes sense for Monsanto that probably holds the patents only on 33B and 99B varieties, but it is quite suboptimal and certainly unusual from an agronomic standpoint. Objectively, one can hardly expect that the same varieties could be adapted to growing conditions which vary greatly from one country to another, if not from one region to another within the same country.

7 For example, in the Makhatini Flats, where rain-fed production still dominates, smallholders paid fees of about US$50/ha during the 2002–3 crop season.

8 In contrast, in the case of conventional seeds the notion of "farmers' seeds" is retained so as to enable their producers to reuse them to their convenience although they can no longer pass them to other farmers, either donating or selling them. In Europe, the transmission to third parties of farmers' seeds has been seriously curtailed by Directive 98/95/CE after the appearance of GM seeds.

9 On the distribution of costs and benefits of adopting GM seeds over the traditional seeds some studies for DCs show that biotech companies actually capture a big share of the additional gains generated (cf. Falck-Zepeda *et al.*, 1999; McBride and Books, 2000). For instance, in the USA the trend of the share of Monsanto in the gains generated by using GM cotton in 1996, 1997 and 1999 were 26 percent, 44 percent and 47 percent, respectively, while the farmer shares decreased accordingly. In South Africa, the share of the GM cotton gains accruing to smallholders is more favorable (Gouse *et al.* 2004).

10 In 1999, it was estimated that the Chinese farmers' share in the gains from adopting GM cotton varied between 82.5 and 87.0 percent, depending on the use of either a Chinese or an American GM cotton variety, respectively (Pray *et al.*, 2001).

11 The Hebei Province is situated in northern China, along the Yellow River. The survey covered 218 farms across seven counties in the five most important cotton producing districts of the province (Cangzhou, Handan, Hengshui, Shijiazhuang, and Xingtai). The average family size in the survey was four people, cultivating about 0.7 ha, 40 percent of which was devoted to growing cotton. These figures are consistent with earlier studies (Pray *et al.*, 2001; Huang *et al.*, 2003b).

12 Chinese farmers benefit from easy access to production inputs. One-half of surveyed farmers could access their farm inputs from quite a few input providers located within one kilometer from their farms. Therefore, the problem of monopoly in supply of inputs does not exist. Farms in general have a certain degree of motorization, while mechanization is very common. All farmers are equipped with tractors and chemical sprayers, and they can also easily call for other mechanized field operations on a service basis.

13 In fact, at least 22 distinct cotton GM varieties are grown in the survey area. Only two of these varieties are supplied by a foreign company (Monsanto), while there are ten varieties provided by research institutes operating at the national level, five at the provincial level and five at the district level.

14 A Chinese research company, the Biocentury Transgene Co. Ltd (BTCC), is the owner of a new Bt-gene construction technology, based upon sequences controlling Cry 1B and Cry 1C toxins: those are the genes used in all Chinese GM cotton varieties. China also launched, more or less at the same time as Monsanto, a new variety with dual-gene resistance to bollworms (SGK 321) by combining a Bt-gene and a protein inhibition gene. The combination of two distinct pest control mechanisms could potentially be more sustainable than just combining two Bt-genes as Monsanto did.

15 It is worth noting that this contractual clause can be hardly justified on pure technical grounds in many LDCs. In fact, while the obligation to keep refuge plots can be justified in countries where farmers grow the crop extensively, as in the US, its application becomes disputable in the Chinese environment featuring a multi-cropping pattern based on smallholder farms that already serve as refuges for cotton pests (Wu *et al.*, 2004).

16 It is noteworthy that BTCC initially tried to act as any private biotech company by claiming a high technology fee. This was considered excessive by the Chinese breeders and the central government intervened to support the breeders' position by forcing a revision of the commercialization conditions.

17 For example, the adoption of GM seeds in Mali, with the same degree of intensification of other inputs as in China, would have doubled the total input costs the farmers are facing (Fok *et al.*, 2004a).

18 This is based on the premise that the profit derived from having a patent-based monopoly in poor countries makes a very limited contribution to the worldwide profits realized by the biotech company (cf. Taylor and Cayford, 2003).

19 There are several advantages in a proposal like this, but the most relevant for our case is that the mechanism relies on the quality and reliability of the DCs' institutions and

will not impose any extra-burden on LDCs' institutions. Moreover, it does not contravene existing treaties.

20 This mechanism mimics in the agricultural sector what, for instance, the Melinda and Bill Gates foundation is doing in the drug sector to induce research on combating malaria and AIDS in LDCs.

21 CAMBIA is the Australian Center for the Application of Molecular Biology to International Agriculture based in Canberra. BIOS is the Biological Information for Open Society initiative that attempts to extend the achievements originating with CAMBIA. Both try to foster collaborative open-source development of sets of key enabling technologies that intend to develop licensing strategies inspired by the open-source movement in software.

References

Béroud, François (2001), "Sans dopage, le coton africain reste en course," *Marchés Tropicaux*, 27 July 2001: 1538–41.

Falck-Zepeda, José B., Greg Traxler and Robert G. Nelson (1999), "Rent Creation and Distribution from the First Three Years of Planting Bt-Cotton," *ISAAA Briefs*, no. 13. Ithaca, NY: International Service for the Acquisition of Agri-biotech Applications.

Fok, Michel A.C. (2002), "Intégration de l'agriculture dans les négociations internationales de l'OMC: comment saisir les opportunités offertes pour les filières cotonnières." Online, available www.cmaoc.org (accessed 2 August 2002).

Fok, Michel A.C., Hamady Djouara and Carlos Tomas (2004a), "Progress and Challenges in Making Productivity Gains Cotton Production by Smallholders in Sub-Saharan Africa." In Anna Swanepoel, ed., *Proceedings of the 3rd World Cotton Research Conference, Cape Town, South Africa, 9–12 March 2003*. Pretoria: Agricultural Research Council, Institute for Industrial Crops, pp. 1515–30.

Fok, Michel A.C., Weili Liang, Guiyan Wang and Yuhong Wu (2004b), "I risultati positivi della diffusione del cotone Bt in Cina: limiti al trasferimento dell'esperienza cinese in altri paesi in via di sviluppo," *Nuovo Diritto Agrario*, 3/2004: 45–67.

Fok, Michel A.C., Weili Liang, Guiyan Wang and Yuhong Wu (2005), "Diffusion du coton génétiquement modifié en Chine: leçons sur les facteurs et limites d'un succès," *Economie Rurale*, 285: 5–32.

Gouse Marnus, Johann Kirsten and Lindie Jenkins Beyers (2002), "Bt-Cotton in South Africa: Adoption and the Impact on Farm Incomes Amongst Small-Scale and Large-Scale Farmers." Working Paper no. 2002–15, Department of Agricultural Economics, Extension and Rural Development, University of Pretoria, Pretoria.

Gouse, Marnus, Carl E. Pray and David E. Schimmelpfennig (2004), "The Distribution of Benefits from Bt-Cotton Adoption in South Africa," *AgBioForum*, 7 (4): 187–94.

Graff, Gregory and David Zilberman (2001), "An Intellectual Property Clearinghouse for Agricultural Biotechnology," *Nature Biotechnology*, 19: 1179–80.

Huang, Jikun, Ruifa Hu, Scott Rozelle, Fangbin Qiao and Carl E. Pray (2002), "Transgenic Varieties and Productivity of Smallholder Cotton Farmers in China," *Australian Journal of Agricultural and Resource Economics*, 46 (3): 367–87.

Huang, Jikun, Ruifa Hu, Hans van Meijl and Franck van Tongeren (2003a), "Economic Impacts of Genetically Modified Crops in China." Proceedings of the XXV Conference of International Association of Agricultural Economists, Durban, South Africa, 16–22 August 2003. IAAE, pp. 1075–83.

Huang, Jikun, Ruifa Hu, Carl E. Pray, Fangbin Qiao and Scott Rozelle (2003b),

"Biotechnology as an Alternative to Chemical Pesticides: A Case Study of Bt-Cotton in China," *Agricultural Economics*, 29 (1): 55–67.

Ismaël, Yousouf, Lindie Jenkins Beyers, Colin Thirtle and Jennifer Piesse (2002), "Efficiency Effects of Bt-Cotton. Smallholder Adoption and Economic Impacts of Bt-Cotton in Makhathini Flats, KwaZulu Natal, South Africa." In Evenson, Robert E., Vittorio Santaniello and David Zilberman, eds, *Economic and Social Issues in Agricultural Biotechnology*. Wallingford, UK, and New York: CABI Publishing, pp. 325–49.

Jishnu, Latha (2006). "Bt-cotton: The Chinese Are Here Almost." Online, available www.businessworldindia.com/sep0803/indepth_btchinese.asp (accessed 24 February 2006).

Kowalski, Stanley P., Reynaldo V. Ebora, David R. Kryder and Robert H. Potter (2002), "Transgenic Crops, Biotechnology and Ownership Rights: What Scientists Need to Know," *Plant Journal*, 31 (4): 407–21.

Lanjouw, Jean O. (2002), "A Patent Proposal for Global Diseases." In Boris Pleskovic and Nicholas Stern, eds, *Annual World Bank Conference on Development Economics, 2001/2002*. Washington, DC: World Bank, pp. 189–219.

McBride, William D. and Nora Books (2000), "Survey Evidence on Producer Use and Costs of Genetically Modified Seed," *Agribusiness*, 16 (1): 6–20.

McDonald, Nick (2003), "Genetically Modified Organisms – The Last Thing the Developing World Needs." Online, available globalvision.org/library/6/561 (accessed 16 November 2003).

Mazoyer, Marcel (2000), "La moitié de la paysannerie mondiale n'est pas solvable pour les grands laboratoires," *Le Monde*, édition électronique, Paris, 16/10/2000. Online, available www.lemonde.fr (accessed 16 October 2000).

Myers, Dorothy (1999), "GM Cotton Fails to Impress," *Pesticides News* (*The Pesticide Trust*), 44 (June): 6.

Nature, (2004), "Open-Source Biology," *Nature*, 431 (30 September): 491.

Pollan, Michael (2001), *The Botany of Desire: A Plant's-Eye View of the World*. New York: Random House.

Pray, Carl E., Danmeng Ma, Jikun Huang and Fangbin Qiao (2001), "Impact of Bt-Cotton in China," *World Development*, 29 (5): 813–25.

Pschorn-Strauss, Elfrieda (2004), "Bt-Cotton and Small-scale Farmers in Makhatini. A Story of Debt, Dependency, and Dicey Economics." Online, available www.grain.org/research/btcotton.cfm?id=100 (accessed 23 September 2004).

Taylor, Michael R. and Jerry Cayford (2003), "American Patent Policy, Biotechnology, and African Agriculture. The Case for Policy Change," RFF Report, November 2003. Washington DC: Resource for the Future.

The Economist (2005), "The Triumph of the Commons: Can Open Source Revolutionise Biotech?" 12 February: pp. 61–2.

Thirtle, Colin and Lindie Jenkins Beyers (2003), "Can GM-technologies Help African Smallholders? The Impact of Bt-Cotton in the Makhatini Flats of Kwazulu-Natal," *World Development*, 31 (4): 717–32.

Wu, Kongming, Hongqiang Feng and Yuyuan Guo (2004), "Evaluation of Maize as a Refuge for Management of Resistance to Bt-Cotton by *Helicoverpa armigera* (Hübner) in the Yellow River Cotton-farming Region of China," *Crop Protection*, 23 (6): 523–30.

9 Globalization and small-scale farmers

Customizing "fair-trade coffee"[1]

*Marijke D'Haese, Jan Vannoppen and
Guido Van Huylenbroeck*

Introduction

Globalization, either directly or indirectly, has brought about profound changes in the previously existing institutional order. Specifically, in the agricultural sector, structural adjustment reforms called for the disappearance of governmental regulatory institutions (e.g. marketing boards) and lowering, if not totally removing, of various trade protection barriers in many developing countries. However, the long overdue changes in the previously extant institutional order that globalization entails surely cannot be reduced to no institutions at all. In fact, the changes in the institutional environment have had dramatic impacts on the production and market environment of many producers in less developed countries (LDCs), especially for small, non-organized farmers because of, for example, the resulting more risky environment.

At the same time, a new international institutional order is being created by organizations and world agencies like the WTO. For example, the institutionalization of a worldwide intellectual property rights (IPR) protection under the so-called Trade Related Aspects of Intellectual Property Rights (TRIPS) agreement dramatically changed the room for maneuver of economic agents under globalization. As emphasized by Yotopoulos (Chapter 1) these changes entail systematically asymmetric outcomes that usually work against the LDCs because the preconditions of success (i.e. the existence of physical infrastructures and appropriate economic institutions) are more likely to exist and are easier to satisfy among the rich countries than among the poor countries.

This is especially true under globalization where the trade composition changes towards "decommodified trade," that is, trade of products that have moved up the value-added scale by incorporating a greater degree of customization, or a significant reputation component in the spirit of this volume. In such a situation, international trade is not anymore the Ricardian least-cost trade based on comparative advantage and becomes, instead, trade in "positional goods" that is based on the reputation of the product. The TRIPS framework reinforces this trend imposing what Pagano (Chapter 2) calls a "pan-positional" legal order, which grants an exclusive "right" to the IPR holder, while involving "obligations" (duties) for all other individuals. Therefore, in order to prevent outcomes that may be systematically distorted against the poor (countries and/or people), globalization needs to be enhanced by incorporating also pro-poor institutions. This chapter provides an application of such an institutional enhancement in the case of "fair-trade coffee."

Until 1989 the international coffee market was regulated by the International Coffee Agreement, which warranted a stable economic environment. Agreements were made on predetermining the overall coffee supply levels through export quotas for producing countries and enforcing a price band to keep the price of coffee relatively stable. In 1989 the regulations on supply and price stability were dismantled (Oxfam, 2002). The orthodox mechanism of coping with increased price risk, i.e. futures markets, is non-existent and is also unaffordable to producers in most LDCs. "Fair-trade coffee" represents an alternative institutional arrangement that guarantees fairly stable prices to the producers by filling in for the erstwhile marketing boards that operated in the rural setting of LDCs and have by now fallen victims of globalization. Fair-trade coffee organizes the environment-friendly production of coffee and helps in strengthening the bargaining power of small producers vis-à-vis the intermediaries.

Furthermore, the branding of fair-trade coffee is an institutional innovation that mimics the formal protection of intellectual property rights, that is available for (mostly developed country) services and manufactures, in order to ensure some economic rents also to small farmers in the form of higher prices at the farm gate. More specifically, fair trade is an example of how the same strategy adopted by developed countries' producers/processors (i.e. the sequence of product differentiation, institutional certification and advertising) can be used by LDC producers to increase the reputation content of the good they produce. Fair-trade labeling is viewed as a form of "decommodification" (Yotopoulos, Chapter 1) that differentiates the decommodified (i.e. customized and more reputed) good from its standard counterparts on "ethical grounds." The good news is that under globalization it is much easier to find a market for such highly-reputed goods because there will be consumers with preference for this "(ethically) customized" coffee that can be reached at relatively affordable costs. On the other side, it should be stressed that this outcome cannot be taken for granted since investments are needed to produce high quality coffee for marketing, plus an institutional arrangement which safeguards the identity of the differentiated product.

This chapter is organized as follows. The next section provides an overview of the problems faced by small-scale coffee producers in view of the novel globalized economic and institutional environment in which they operate. The third section discusses the effects of fair-trade labeling in mitigating market failures and shows the features of the decommodification process in the specific case of fair-trade coffee. The fourth section analyzes the institutional changes required for the marketing of fair-trade coffee and assesses the pros and cons of the process of coffee decommodification through fair-trade labeling. The final section summarizes the main findings of the study.

Small-scale coffee producers under globalization

Smallholder coffee producers have been experiencing very harsh times since the early 1990s. Decreasing prices and reduced market opportunities have severely affected producers' livelihoods (Ponte, 2002; Taylor, 2005). This is mainly due to the changes induced by globalization, such as the dismantling of pre-existing market institutions (e.g. the International Coffee Agreement) and the entry of new suppliers in the world market, that compounded the already existing weaknesses of the coffee supply chain. The final outcome was that coffee production became less profitable which in turn increased the vulnerability of coffee producers, especially those who are small scale and are not organized.

The coffee supply chain is structured in an articulated and complex cobweb of relationships that links production and consumption, where information asymmetries and market power are pervasive problems (Figure 9.1). For instance, on the consumption side the information on the origin of the beans and on the cultivation methods is merely anecdotal, while on the production side the information on prices and market opportunities is hardly accessible to the farmers, especially to the small-scale producers.[2] In the pre-globalization years, many operators (including marketing boards, domestic traders, exporters, international traders, brokers, retailers and restaurateurs) used to transact along the supply chain. Under globalization, the market liberalization induced a reorganization of the worldwide coffee supply chain, which implied the disappearance of the marketing channel that used to pass through coffee marketing boards (cf. the dotted-arrow links in Figure 9.1) and nowadays the supply chain is dominated by five multinationals that control almost 70 percent of the product transformation and marketing (Ponte, 2002).

Overall, the international coffee trade is characterized by the increase in market power at the marketing and processing stages that, along with excess supply, contributed to a dramatic decrease of the green coffee price at farm gate. Although since 1989 the world consumption of coffee has been growing at an average rate of about 1.5 percent per annum, the price at farm gate has been decreasing in real terms and in 2003 it barely reached a quarter of what it had been in 1960.[3] At the same time, the prices at consumption level have been increasing or not decreasing in real terms (Figure 9.2).

In more recent years the situation has become even more critical for producers because of the structural oversupply of coffee at world level. In fact, world coffee production increased from 5.9 million metric tons in 1989 to 7.8 million metric tons in 2004 (FAO, 2005). We can identify three main factors that contributed to the oversupply and therefore to the constant decline of prices for green beans on the world market. First, coffee production techniques drastically improved in Brazil, as consequence of the cultivation of less frost-prone areas and of a more extensive use of irrigation and mechanical harvesting.[4] Second, the entry of Vietnam into the world coffee market, in the last decade, caused a dramatic increase in supply of low cost coffee.[5] Third, the increasing production

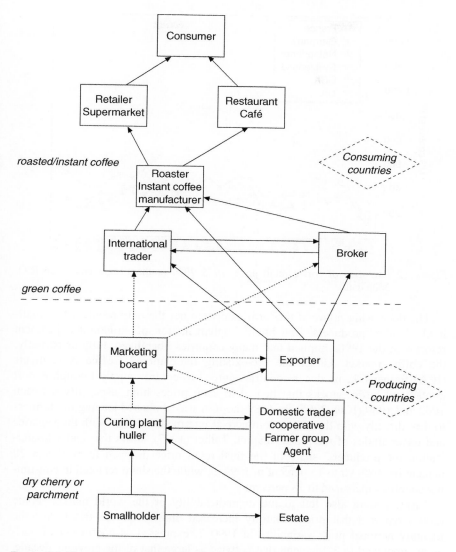

Figure 9.1 The supply chain of coffee (source: Ponte, 2002).

and use of *robusta* variety coffee contributed further to softening the coffee market. On the production side *robusta* is much more resistant to adverse environmental conditions than *arabica*.[6] On the consumption side, innovations introduced at the processing stage reduced the acid taste of *robusta*, thus making it usable in blends, especially in popular flavored coffees sold in price-sensitive countries.

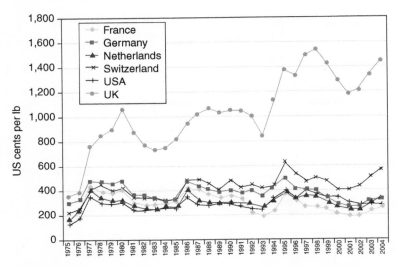

Figure 9.2 Evolution of coffee retail price, 1975–2004 (authors' calculations on ICO, 2006 data).

The decreasing prices at the farm gate were not the only problem for small-holder coffee producers. The broad implementation of structural adjustment reforms in the 1990s implied that many countries liberalized, fully or partially, the coffee market. Under the pre-existing International Coffee Agreements (ICA) framework, producer countries agreed to control supply through export quotas and buffer stocks that helped to keep prices high, especially between 1962 and 1989 (ICO, 2006). In 1989 the ICA was abolished leaving the farmers to deal directly with the strong commercial intermediaries and with the vagaries and uncertainties of the global market. Talbot (1997) shows that under liberalization the producers' share of the final retail price dropped from almost 20 percent in 1989–90 to 13 percent in 1994–5, while the share retained in consuming countries increased to 78 percent.

Farmers were also left to the unpredictability of the world market. Ponte (2002) reported that price volatility increased dramatically in the 1990s: the monthly nominal price variability in 1990–7, expressed as coefficient of variation, amounted to 37 percent, that is twice as large that of the previous decade, and it has further increased to 43 percent by 1998–2000. But farmers have only limited mechanisms of coping with increased risk. Coffee is a perennial crop, hence production is not adaptable to price shocks in the short run. Diversification to other crops and/or income-generating activities is too expensive and risky in itself. The standard institution for hedging against price risks, i.e. future markets, is not available for the smallholder producers. Moreover, the reduction in subsidies for coffee production and agricultural services, such as credit for input procurement, left the producers, and especially the small-scale and non-organized farmers, especially vulnerable to the vagaries of a receding coffee market.[7]

In response to the problems of smallholder farmers, a new international coffee agreement was signed in 2001. Its aim was to promote coffee consumption, to provide a forum for the private sector and to promote farmer training and information programs in member countries (ICO, 2006). However, the lack of economic coordination and the opportunism of producers and intermediaries in the marketing chain undermined its effectiveness. There have been numerous cases reported of traders taking advantage of the lack of price information to cheat farmers and of farmers who breached their contracts with traders when they could obtain a higher price elsewhere (Vannoppen, 2003).

In conclusion, the old institutional order disappeared with globalization and has not been adequately replaced. Fair-trade labeling can be viewed as an alternative institutional arrangement that provides the farmers with an opportunity to organize production as well as to strengthen their bargaining power vis-à-vis the intermediaries.

Fair-trade coffee: a case of product decommodification

The origin of fair-trade can be traced back as far as the early 1950s, when it was promoted to support farmers in war-hit regions. Trade of fairly priced products from developing countries increased since the 1968 UNCTAD conference that launched the so-called "Trade not Aid" initiative. This was an incentive for NGOs, like SOS Wereldhandel in the Netherlands and Oxfam in UK, to develop a fair-trade campaign (Solagral, 2002). The first fair-trade label for coffee was launched in 1988 and fair-trade coffee is currently available in some 20 countries worldwide (Rice and McLean, 1999).

Fair-trade initiatives intend to provide farmers with a more favorable position in the market and to solve the problem of information asymmetries between producers and consumers (Renard, 1999). A firm can choose to disclose information on a given product through labels that provide missing information on the production process and/or through product attributes, like minimum requirements for social, economic and environmental development (Bougherara and Grolleau, 2002). This information is disclosed and advertised because consumers are willing to pay a premium for these extra attributes (Golan *et al.*, 2000).

Voluntary labels, i.e. the ones developed by an individual or a group of firms, can be viewed as a marketing tool and in this case it is imperative that the benefits from increased sales of a labeled product outweigh its costs. On the other hand, mandatory labels, i.e. those issued by the government, pursue instead a social goal and can be seen as providing a public good (e.g. information on food safety). Yet both voluntary and mandatory labels try to target the consumers' behavior by attracting attention to certain product attributes, that usually are either "experience" or "credence" attributes.[8] A third-party assessment is commonly required in order to add credibility and ensure a trustful relationship between consumers and producers.

Therefore, the fair-trade label signals the commitment of fair-trade organizations that the premium paid by consumers represents a fair value of additional attributes of coffee and also contributes to a more remunerative price for the farmer (Browne *et al.*, 2000; Leclair, 2002).[9] The direct welfare effect of fair-trade on individual farmers is difficult to assess because of the very different operational environments where fair-trade initiatives are implemented (e.g. the cooperative costs and the distribution of the social premium indeed differs for each cooperative) but it has been reported by many studies as significantly positive.[10]

Fair-trade labeling is a genuine example of "decommodification" (Yotopou-los, Chapter 1): fair-trade coffee is differentiated from the bulk of coffee, and the fair-trade label signals to the consumers the higher ethical reputation of the former vis-à-vis the latter. This process of product differentiation required some institutional innovations in order to succeed. The most important institutional development was the establishment in 1997 of the Fair-trade Labelling Organizations International (FLO), an umbrella organization for 17 national initiatives, that has built up partnerships with 197 coffee producer partners in Africa, Asia and Latin America (Table 9.1), 33 export partners, 105 importers, manufacturers, roasters and distributors, and 402 license holders who market the coffee. Simultaneously a single fair-trade label was created and an agreement was made on fair-trade standards.[11] The FLO and national initiatives certify the compliance to the standards throughout the supply chain (Figure 9.3).

Until now farmers have not been charged any certification fee. However, the investment required to comply with the knowledge and the quality standards of the fair-trade organizations is substantial. Small-scale producers, in particular, have to struggle with developing the required technical knowledge as well as building up the organizational structures and trust relationships in the chain. The process is long and requires intensive training and follow-up activities. Farmers' organizations may provide support to their members by covering inspection fees after the first harvest, pre-financing investments and at times providing a subsidy in lieu of wage, even in the period before the first harvest.

FLO and national initiatives are financed through the contribution of the licensees. The control procedures are issued by the FLO, and include quarterly administrative controls, reports to auditors and visits of local consultants trained by the FLO. The controls are performed throughout the supply chain in collaboration between the national initiatives and the FLO (Max Havelaar, 2002). Recently, however, FLO has drafted a Producer Fee System that anticipates the introduction of a producer certification fee to all producers applying for a fair-trade FLO certification (FLO, 2005).[12]

Although the consumption of fair-trade coffee is increasing, it remains a niche-market segment that reaches only 0.03 percent of the overall world coffee trade amounting to slightly more than 24,000 metric tons in 2004 (FLO, 2004). Yet its sales are steadily increasing (Table 9.2) at an average annual growth of 9.3 percent over the past ten years. This is remarkable because the increase of fair-trade coffee took place in an environment where traditional

Table 9.1 Number of fair-trade cooperatives by regions (total) and partner countries (indicative)

Regions/Countries	Number
Regions	
Central America	93
Caribbean	9
South America	63
Africa	27
Asia	5
Countries	
Bolivia	17
Brazil	5
Cameroon	1
Colombia	19
Congo	2
Costa Rica	1
Dominican Republic	2
East Timor	1
Ecuador	2
El Salvador	3
Ethiopia	3
Guatemala	16
Haiti	7
Honduras	19
Indonesia	1
Mexico	40
Nicaragua	14
Papua New Guinea	2
Peru	17
Rwanda	2
Tanzania	6
Thailand	1
Uganda	13
Venezuela	3

Source: FLO (2004).

and larger brands are struggling to keep their market shares. Major markets for fair-trade coffee include France, Germany, the Netherlands, UK and the USA (Table 9.3).

Giovannucci and Koekoek (2003) estimate that consumers in 11 major European coffee markets consumed more than 15.4 million kilograms of certified fair-trade and 11.2 million kilograms of certified organic coffees in 2001.[13] Out of these, 5.3 million kilograms were double certified as both fair-trade and organic. Sustainable coffees (grouping fair-trade, organic and eco-friendly coffees) represent on average less than 2 percent of the consumption in developed markets, even though with large variations across these markets, ranging from 0.3 percent to 3.4 percent.

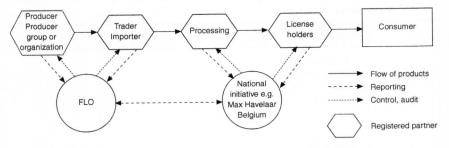

Figure 9.3 Product flow, reports and controls in the fair-trade coffee supply chain (source: Max Havelaar, 2002).

Institutional innovation through fair-trade labeling

Customizing coffee through fair-trade labeling is an institutional innovation that makes possible a fairer distribution of value added along the supply chain and the empowerment of the weakest agents (i.e. small-scale producers) vis-à-vis the strongest ones (i.e. commercial intermediaries). However, this institutional innovation brings about far reaching consequences that go well beyond the distribution to poor producers of a share of the price premium paid by consumers in purchasing fair-trade coffee. It guarantees, in fact, a stable access to global markets, the access to otherwise inaccessable production assets and the development of safety nets to increase risk-coping capacity. In short, it creates the required preconditions in terms of institutional infrastructure and capacity building that may help poor farmers to fend off the adverse effects of globalization (Romano, Chapter 10).

The access to fair-trade marketing channels is more than just the physical possibility of selling the product. It is also about finding traders and creating a trust relationship while negotiating prices. The business of poor farmers is

Table 9.2 Trade volume of fair-trade coffee, 1995–2004 (metric tons)

Year	Sales volume	Annual change (%)
1995	9,971	
1996	10,883	9.1
1997	11,370	4.5
1998	11,663	2.6
1999	11,819	1.3
2000	12,818	8.5
2001	14,387	12.2
2002	15,780	9.7
2003	19,872	25.9
2004	24,223	21.9

Source: Max Havelaar, the Netherlands for data prior to 1998; otherwise, FLO (2005).

Table 9.3 Major consumers of fair-trade coffee, 1995–2004 (metric tons)

Countries	1995[a]	2004[b]	1995–2004 change (%)
USA	Not yet started	6,577	NA
The Netherlands	3,100	2,982	−3.8
United Kingdom	427	3,339	681.9
Germany	3,984	2,981	−25.2
France	Not yet started	2,784	NA
Switzerland	1,389	1,462	5.3
Belgium	472	865	83.3

Sources: a: Max Havelaar, the Netherlands; b: FLO (2005).

indeed too small and often too remote to make possible the development of a complete set of markets that can span space, time and uncertainty. This is the main reason why farmers generally sell on a spot market, whereas private traders can hedge on private commodity markets, thus reducing price risks significantly (Tollens, 2003).

Therefore, fair-trade initiatives can be seen as triggers for farmers to self-organize in new networks that increase their bargaining power in price and contract negotiations, enhance their access to credit and their creditworthiness and create more room for the exploitation of economies of scale in using indivisible physical infrastructures (Dankers and Liu, 2003). The institutional innovations can operate at different levels in the coffee supply chain, both horizontally, as farmers associate collectively to market coffee, and vertically, as the farmers' association engages in new trade arrangements with private traders. An example is the creation of small-scale coffee producer cooperatives.[14] In this case, the advantage derives from the possibility of collective grading and sorting of coffee beans, thus providing the trader with properly packaged cherries of different qualities. In this sense the fair-trade new institutional arrangement, guaranteeing a higher price, provides also incentives to farmers to improve quality. Moreover, transaction costs will be lower because of the economies of scale in the use of indivisible inputs like managerial abilities (e.g. information gathering, contract negotiation) and physical infrastructure (e.g. storage facilities, transport equipment). Furthermore, it also increases the credibility of suppliers, because social control among the group members could increase the reliability of compliance to the codes of practices. In short, collective action and better access to information help lower the transaction costs and stimulate farmers to invest time, knowledge and assets in the production.

New institutional arrangements (e.g. contracts and management tools) need to be developed not only between the farmers, but also vertically along the supply chain up to the consumers. In this case, the trader who is part of the fair-trade initiative is contractually obliged to pay the farmers a "fair" price. The fair-trade experiment can even go further and provide a market access to those farmers who want to add extra attributes to their product, for example the production of organic coffee, the identification of special characteristics of the production area or traditional processing techniques (Dankers and Liu, 2003). Considering the credence nature of fair-trade labeling attributes, those institutional arrangements need to be based on a trust relationship. Trust can arise either from interpersonal contacts or from general knowledge about the population (Fafchamps, 2004). Strong networks and dense social ties reinforce the interpersonal contacts and thereby personalize trust, while trading experience creates generalized trust between the trader and the farmer cooperative (Lazzarini *et al.*, 2001; Hayami, Chapter 5). This trust is reinforced by the operation of a third-party organization, FLO, that adequately monitors and controls the compliance with the codes of production along the whole supply chain.

In conclusion, the fair-trade initiatives create value in two ways, namely through capacity building and collective action in the cooperatives (Dankers and Liu, 2003), and by increasing the market efficiency along the supply chain.[15] The institutional arrangements provided under fair-trade initiatives are therefore close to what Kydd (2002a, 2002b) describes as an ideal institutional arrangement for smallholder farmers, that should be deliberative, working horizontally inside a sector and vertically along the supply chain and need to be based on a consensus of what may constitute a just and fair outcome.

Conclusion

The impact of globalization on the operational environment of many small-scale farmers has been dramatic. The old institutional order disappeared and there is a clear need for a new institutional order that can help small-scale farmers to deal with the adverse effects of globalization. Fair-trade coffee represents a case study that shows how this can be done.

Fair-trade labeling involves the use of rather common marketing tools such as product differentiation, certification and advertising for the purpose of breeding reputation, and thereby value, to a traditional product such as coffee. The label itself helps to overcome pervasive information asymmetries between the producers and the consumers.

Large coffee roasting companies are reluctant to develop or join a fair-trade label, as they consider it not to be a solution to the crisis in the coffee market. They argue that providing an incentive for farmers to continue producing coffee can restrain them from thinking about available economic alternatives, and therefore prolonging their economic dependence. On the other hand, it can be argued that fair-trade coffee can help to offset the negative effects of the crisis of the coffee market on small-scale producers, that derive from the oversupply of low quality coffee cherries. Therefore, fair-trading initiatives, especially those focusing on quality and on the marketing of high reputation coffee, should be able to mitigate the effects of the crisis.

Whether fair-trade labeling can make a difference on world production and provide an incentive towards the production of more quality and less quantity is still under debate. However, considering the structural change in international trade from a commodity-based trade to a reputation-based trade, this can be viewed as an example of the strategy LDC farmers can adopt to exploit the opportunities offered by globalization. "Decommodifying" coffee through fair-trade labeling can in principle help small-scale coffee producers to enter the globalized markets and to increase their own revenues. However, this outcome cannot be taken for granted since non-trivial investments are needed to promote the required institutional innovations.

Notes

1 The authors gratefully acknowledge the comments of the editors of this volume and of anonymous reviewers of earlier drafts. We also thank Max Havelaar Belgium, Max Havelaar the Netherlands and the Fair-trade Labelling Organizations International for their help. The usual disclaimer applies.
2 The lack of information for small-scale producers is compounded by the structural rigidity in coffee bean supply due to the fact that it takes three years before new trees start to produce fruit, and to the requirement of picking coffee cherries yearly for maintaining healthy trees, regardless of the market price.
3 Lewin *et al.* (2004) report that since 1970 prices have declined on average 3 percent and 5 percent per year for *arabica* coffees and *robusta* coffees, respectively. Occasional price rebounds have been reported in 1995 and 1997 (Chalmin, 2003) and 2005 (Muradian and Pelupessy, 2005).
4 Moreover, the Brazilian government improved the operational environment of Brazilian producers by providing price forecasting and risk management services and favoring the enhancement of productivity, coordination and market responsiveness throughout the supply chain (Technoserve, 2003).
5 Coffee production in Vietnam increased from virtually nil in early 1980s to 41,000 metric tons around the end of 1980s, to more than 830,000 metric tons in 2003–4 (FAO, 2005). The average growth rate of Vietnamese production in the 1990s was an astonishing 25.2 percent per annum and Vietnam became the second largest producer in the world at the end of the decade, with a share of 9.9 percent in world production (Ponte, 2002). The share of Brazil, Vietnam and Colombia in global production has increased from about 30 percent in 1970 to 52 percent in 2004 (Lewin *et al.*, 2004).
6 Most commercial green coffee is either the *Coffea arabica* or *Coffea canephora* species, which are referred to commercially as *arabica* and *robusta*, respectively. *Arabica* beans are generally considered of higher quality and fetch slightly higher prices than *robusta* beans. Historically, *arabica* coffee was cultivated in Latin America, Ethiopia and Kenya, while Brazil, Vietnam and Uganda were the major producers of *robusta* coffee (Bacon, 2005).
7 Subsidized production inputs, such as fertilizers, pesticides and credit for input purchase, were provided through state or parastatal organizations. Yet both the credit services and subsidies were removed with the economic structural adjustment in many countries (Hillocks, 2001).
8 Product attributes can be classified into three groups: "search" attributes provide information on the product quality that can be perceived before purchase through product inspection; "experience" attributes can be assessed after purchase through product consumption; while "credence" attributes cannot be accurately assessed even after consumption (Darby and Karny, 1973). The latter are better known by the producers than by the consumers, as is the case for environmental or ethical attributes.
9 Certified producer organizations are paid a price that covers the production costs. "Buyers shall pay producer organizations at least the fair-trade minimum price as set by FLO (Fair-trade Labeling Organizations International)" (FLO, 2004). The

fair-trade minimum prices vary according to the type and origin of the coffee. In addition to the fair-trade minimum price the buyers pay a fair-trade premium as set by FLO at US$0.05/lb. For certified organic coffee an additional premium of US$0.15/lb of green coffee is charged on top of the fair-trade minimum price or market-reference price respectively. The market price referred to above is based on the New York "C" contract for *arabica,* and on the London "LCE" contract for *robusta* and it becomes relevant any time the fair-trade minimum price, enhanced by the relevant premiums, is lower than the market price (FLO, 2002).

10 Taylor *et al.* (2005) report that in the case of Majomut cooperative (Chiapas, Mexico), by entering the fair-trade scheme, the cooperative members increased their earnings from US$550 of the conventional trade to US$1,700. Furthermore, indirect effects of fair-trade initiatives should not be underestimated. Building on the experience of seven case studies in Latin America, Taylor *et al.* (2005) conclude that fair label initiatives are conducive to a greater economic and social stability by (i) improving the organizational capacity of the farmers' association; (ii) developing the farmers' ability to handle administration; (iii) enhancing farmers' capacity to negotiate; (iv) developing greater social and trade networks; and (v) improving the access to credit. Moreover, diverse community projects are financed through the social premiums.

11 Generic fair-trade standards are issued for small farmers' organizations and for hired labor on plantations with the aim to ensure that (i) fair-trade benefits reach the small farmers and/or workers; (ii) the small farmers' organizations and/or the workers have potential for development; and (iii) fair-trade instruments can take effect and lead to a development which cannot be achieved otherwise (cf. FLO, 2001a, 2001b, 2002).

12 FLO certification fees include an application fee and initial certification fee as well as yearly renewal certification fees and follow-up inspection fees. The amount of such a fee depends, among others, on the nature of the organization, number of products to be certified, number of members, products and processing installations (FLO, 2005).

13 The relevant countries are: Belgium, Denmark, Germany, Italy, Finland, France, the Netherlands, Norway, Sweden, Switzerland and the United Kingdom.

14 The focus of such cooperatives is on post-harvest activities, not on production itself: this avoids the adverse incentive problems usually reported in the case of production cooperatives (Hayami, Chapter 5).

15 It should be recalled, however, that critics against fair trade (cf. among others, Zehner, 2002) have stressed that: (i) fair trade is a poor vehicle to transfer wealth from consumers to producers, and (ii) eliminating middlemen is unlikely to resolve problems in the traditional supply chain.

References

Bacon, Christopher (2005), "Confronting the Coffee Crisis: Can Fair Trade, Organic, and Specialty Coffees Reduce Small-scale Farmer Vulnerability in Northern Nicaragua?" *World Development*, 33 (3): 497–511.

Bougherara, Douadia and Gilles Grolleau (2002), "Can Ecolabelling Mitigate Market Failure? An Analysis Applied to Agro-Food Products." In Willie Lockeretz, ed., *Ecolabels and the Greening of the Food Market. Proceedings of a Conference.* Boston, MA: Tufts University, pp. 111–20.

Browne, Angela W., Phil J.C. Harris, Anna H. Hofny-Collins, Nick Pasiecznik and R.R. Wallace (2000), "Organic Production and Ethical Trade: Definition, Practice and Links," *Food Policy*, 25 (1): 69–89.

Chalmin, Philippe (2003), *Le marches mondiaux. Cyclope 2003.* Paris: Economica.

Dankers, Cora and Pascal Liu (2003), "Environmental and Social Standards, Certification and Labelling for Cash Crops." Report prepared for the Commodity and Trade Division of the Food and Agriculture Organization of the United Nations. Rome: FAO.

Darby, Michael R. and Edi Karny (1973), "Free Competition and the Optimal Amount of Fraud," *Journal of Law and Economics*, 16 (1): 67–88.

Fafchamps, Marcel (2004), *Market Institutions in Sub-Saharan Africa. Theory and Evidence*. Cambridge, MA: The MIT Press.

FAO (2005), "Statistical Database." Online, available www.fao.org (accessed 15 December 2005).

FLO (2001a), "Generic Fair-trade Standards for Hired Labour." Version November 2001. Online, available www.fairtrade.net/pdf/hl/english/Generic%20Fairtrade%20Standard %20Hired%20Labour%20Dec%202005%20EN.pdf (accessed 23 February 2004).

FLO (2001b), "Generic Fair-trade Standards for Small Farmers' Organisations." Version November 2001. Online, available www.fairtrade.net/pdf/sp/english/Generic%20Fair-trade%20Standard%20SF%20Dec%202005%20EN.pdf (accessed 23 February 2004).

FLO (2002), "Fair-trade Standards for Coffee." Version April 2002. Online, available www.fairtrade.net/sites/standards/standards.html (accessed 15 February 2004).

FLO (2004), "FLO Coffee Sales." Online, available www.fairtrade.net/sites/products/ coffee/sales.html (accessed 10 December 2004).

FLO (2005), "Draft FLO-Cert Producer Certification Fees." Online, available www.fair-trade.net/sites/certification/fee_2006.html (accessed 27 December 2005).

Giovannucci, Daniele and Freek Jan Koekoek (2003), *The State of Sustainable Coffee: A Study of Twelve Major Markets*. An IISD–UNCTAD–ICO Book. Cali: Feriva.

Golan, Elise, Fred Kuchler and Lorraine Mitchell (2000), "Economics of Food Labelling." Agricultural Economic Report no. 793, Economic Research Services, US Department of Agriculture, Washington, DC.

Hillocks, Rory (2001), "Coffee: Is It Still a Viable Cash Crop for Smallholders in Africa?" *Outlook on Agriculture*, 30 (3): 205–12.

ICO (2006), "International Coffee Organization." Online, available www.ico.org (accessed 4 April 2006).

Kydd, Jonathan (2002a), "Agriculture and Rural Livelihoods: Is Globalisation Opening or Blocking Paths Out of Rural Poverty?" Agricultural Research and Extension Network, Agren, Network Paper no. 121. London: Overseas Development Institute.

Kydd, Jonathan (2002b), "Trade Liberalisation, Institutions and Agriculture." Centre for Development and Poverty, Imperial College at Wye, Wye.

Lazzarini, Sergio C., Fabio R. Chaddad and Michael L. Cook (2001), "Integrating Supply Chain and Network Analysis: The Study of Netchains," *Chain and Network Science*, 1 (1): 7–22.

Leclair, Mark S. (2002), "Fighting the Tide: Alternative Trade Organizations in the Era of Global Free Trade," *World Development*, 30 (6): 949–58.

Lewin, Bryan, Daniele Giovannucci and Panos Varangis (2004), "Coffee Markets: New Paradigms in Global Supply and Demand." Agricultural and Rural Development Discussion Paper no. 3. Washington, DC: World Bank.

Max Havelaar, (2002), "Max Havelaar: Het keurmerk voor eerlijke handel. Criteria, certificering en controle." September 2002. Online, available www.maxhavelaar.be (accessed 31 March 2004).

Muradian, Roldan and Wim Pelupessy (2005), "Governing the Coffee Chain: The Role of Voluntary Regulatory Systems," *World Development*, 33 (12): 2029–44.

Oxfam (2002), "Mugged. Poverty In Your Coffee Cup." Oxfam International. Online, available www.maketrade.fair.com (accessed 13 December 2005).

Ponte, Stefano (2002), "The 'Latte Revolution'? Regulation, Markets and Consumption in the Global Coffee Chain," *World Development*, 30 (7): 1099–122.

Renard, Marie-Christine (1999), "The Interstices of Globalization: The Example of Fair Coffee," *Sociologia Ruralis*, 39 (4): 484–500.

Rice, Paul D. and Jennifer McLean (1999), "Sustainable Coffee at the Crossroads." A Report for the Consumer's Choice Council. Washington, DC. Online, available www.consumercouncil.org (accessed 28 February 2004).

Solagral (2002), "Etat des lieux et changement d'échelle du commerce équitable. Solidarité agricole et alimentaire." Online, available www.solagral.org (accessed 13 March 2004).

Talbot, John M. (1997), "Where Does Your Coffee Dollar Go? The Division of Income and Surplus Along the Coffee Commodity Chain," *Studies in Comparative International Development*, 32 (1): 56–91.

Taylor, Peter L. (2005), "In the Market But Not of It: Fair Trade Coffee and Forest Stewardship Council Certification as Market-based Social Change," *World Development*, 33 (1): 129–47.

Taylor, Peter L., Douglas L. Murray and Laura T. Raynolds (2005), "Keeping Trade Fair: Governance Challenges in the Fair Trade Coffee Initiative," *Sustainable Development*, 13 (3): 199–208.

Technoserve (2003), "Business Solutions to the Coffee Crisis." 2 December 2003. Online, available www.technoserve.org (accessed 2 February 2004).

Tollens, Eric (2003), "Fair Trade: An Illusion?" Working paper 2003/84, Department of Agricultural and Environmental Economics, KU Leuven, Leuven.

Vannoppen, Jan (2003), "A Coordinated Market Economy to Benefit the Poor," *Tijdschrift Economie en Management*, 48 (4): 641–52.

Zehner, David C. (2002), "An Economic Assessment of 'Fair Trade' in Coffee," *Chazen Web Journal of International Business*, (autumn). Online, available www.gsb.columbia.edu/chazenjournal (accessed 31 March 2004).

Part IV

Conclusions

10 What have we learned about globalization?[1]

Donato Romano

Introduction

No recent economic phenomenon has received more attention than globalization in scholarly circles as well as in the policy arena and even among laypeople. And no other phenomenon has so polarized the discussion around two contrasting views which ultimately reflect alternative assessments of the benefits and costs of globalization. The critics have argued that globalization has exploited people in developing countries, caused massive disruptions to their lives and produced few benefits in return. Its supporters point to the significant reductions in poverty achieved by countries which have embraced integration with the world economy, with China and India being the current poster-countries of such success.

Irrespective of which side of globalization people stand on, both critics and supporters would agree that the pace of globalization is uneven across the world and that its outcomes are differentiated. Where people disagree is on the explanation of the differentiated impacts of globalization and, indeed, there is scant literature that attempts to provide a causal and systematic framework for the uneven outcomes of globalization. This is the general objective of this volume, which through theoretical and empirical contributions goes even farther arguing that the effects of globalization are not only differentiated, but also fundamentally asymmetric and generally detrimental to poor countries unless specific pro-poor policy reforms are implemented. The purpose of this concluding chapter is to add emphasis to the analytical component of the chapters collected in this volume and to organize them around the various sources of the asymmetries of globalization that have been identified.

In pursuing this objective, the chapter is organized as follows. The next section focuses on the systematic asymmetries that weigh against the developing countries by having their origin in inherent characteristics of poverty, such as lack of basic infrastructure. The novel contribution of this volume comes in the third section which focuses on the asymmetries that arise when international exchange transcends the traditional trade in commodities and extends to trade in services, which includes trade in "pure" services but also a broad range of more-or-less "decommodified" goods. This is the signature trade of the modern era of globalization and constitutes the second cause of systematic asymmetries of globalization. It incorporates "reputational payoffs" that accrue in the form of economic rents which the developed countries are best positioned in capturing. In the same section a third source of asymmetry is presented, that is trade in currency that is used as an asset, primarily the reserve currency. This third source of systematic asymmetries is also rooted in reputational asymmetries and materializes in munificent payoffs in the form of economic rents to the reserve/hard currency countries and to the rich in the developed and the developing world. The fourth section argues that a unifying feature of international trade under the current wave of globalization is that services, decommodified goods and currencies are all "positional goods" and briefly discusses the consequences of this in terms of development perspectives for poor countries. In this case, the specialization of the First World in reputational and intellectual goods, which are often protected by "pan-positional" global rights, can be a cause of asymmetric development. This is associated with serious disadvantages for the countries producing standard commodities and implies de facto trade restrictions and unequal exchanges that favor the richest countries.

The fifth section highlights some policy implications that arise from the endogeneity of the asymmetries of globalization. The final section draws the conclusion that structural differences among developing countries matter but only some of them are the inevitable offspring of poverty. As a result, poverty alleviation alone is not sufficient for restarting growth in poor countries. Some structural characteristics of the international trade system that yield presumptively unfair outcomes also need to be addressed.

Asymmetric infrastructural endowments

Globalization is predicated on the extension and deepening of the market as a result of the reduction of the transaction costs of trading internationally. The most striking feature of modern globalization is the increase in trade[2] and in financial integration[3] as a percent of GDP across the world, an observation that stands true both over time and across countries. Not unlike the experience of the nineteenth century globalization, the trade outcome can be attributed largely to the innovations in transport and communication technologies, and it was enhanced and complemented with the extension of international finance in the post-WTO years, due to the parallel liberalization of trade and capital flows (Baier and Bergstrand, 2001; WTO, 2003, 2004).

One would have expected that an increase in international competition would normally benefit the less developed countries (LDCs) by strengthening their comparative advantage in operating with low wage costs vis-à-vis the developed countries (DCs). This expectation does not seem to be warranted by aggregate data on LDC shares of trade in world totals.[4] Although the aggregate data are rough-strewn and hide dramatic differences among LDCs, they serve to highlight that trade in general, and international trade specifically, is founded on infrastructural and institutional prerequisites that may be wanting in LDCs to various degrees. The benefits of trade can be reaped only if the necessary physical infrastructures (e.g. road, storage facilities and distribution networks) as well as "immaterial" infrastructures (e.g. telecommunication networks, good educational systems) are already in place. To the extent that LDCs are infrastructure-poor they are also handicapped in taking full advantage of the trade opportunities that might arise.

Strictly related to infrastructures is another prerequisite, the existence of appropriate legal and economic institutions. It is a trite proposition that a state where there is no security ensured by a police force, where the legal system is weak and where the courts are not impartial is unlikely to see economic activities flourishing. This precondition for growth was first emphasized by Adam Smith and played a crucial role in Myrdal's "soft state" (Myrdal, 1968). It has been tested more recently by statistical analyses that proved the importance of security, stability and accountability as factors conducive for growth,[5] and it has become by now a staple in all good-governance packages that are targeted to LDCs (World Bank, 2004). While the existence of the requisite economic and legal institutions is taken for granted in DCs, it is the lack of the same that is the norm in many LDCs. The main reason that most political, economic and legal institutions do not exist is that poor countries cannot afford their cost. And even where they exist they often end up being captured by special interests and by the local elites that may pay lip service to growth but they scarcely contribute to promoting development.

The core argument regarding institutions is that they do not come for free and, consequently, a necessary condition for having them in place is their affordability. This condition is not successfully met in many LDCs. For instance, recent data show that globalization has caused a sustained increase in commodity price uncertainty (Dehn, 2000). This calls for interventions to cope with price volatility. Derivative markets represent one of the more effective and non-distorting instruments for intervention in such cases (World Bank, 1999; UNCTAD, 2002). While such markets routinely exist in the DCs, they have first to be set up and regulated in LDCs, which becomes an expensive exercise that poor counties usually cannot afford. In the same vein, the spanning of space is not possible unless a road network and storage facilities are already in place, while spanning space and uncertainty requires a stock exchange plus a network of contingent markets. Lacking these, there is not an Arrow-Debreu world, and the failure of the dynamic version of the fundamental theorems of welfare economics means that free markets and free trade do not elicit Pareto-optimal outcomes. In other words, the mutual benefits of free trade are no longer automatic and regulation becomes necessary because of market incompleteness.

Related to the existence (or the lack) of institutions is the access to social capital. In fact, many routine market exchanges involve matters of trust because of the pervasiveness of information asymmetries. Social capital is an important ingredient in generating the trust that is necessary for transactions. Trust is channeled either formally, through an extant institutional infrastructure as is the case in mature market economies, or by means of informal institutions, as is common in many LDCs. The positive role played by social capital as contract enforcer has been emphasized by many authors in this volume. For instance, Hayami (Chapter 5) stresses how trust implicit in long-term repetitive transactions, as is the case in communities like tribes and villages,[6] can play a crucial role in the enforcement of trade contracts and how this can be conducive to the transition from a traditional informal economy to a modern market economy that could be subsequently integrated into the globalized world.

Serious problems arise when the existing social capital gets squandered without leaving a working substitute in its stead.[7] The economic history of Eastern Europe over the last two decades provides a vivid example of institutional derangement that resulted from the disruption of the old economic order as a result of the abrupt introduction of unbridled market forces, without the buffer of time or resources for building a new formal institutional setting which could guarantee a certain level of social capital that would provide the benefit of continuity. The Russian story is paradigmatic of the perils of institutional derailment that abrupt change entails. Its "big-bang" transition to capitalism broke the social contract which bound citizens together with their government and created an anomous and kleptocratic environment that was inimical to investment, slowed down the process of restructuring and, ultimately, undermined macroeconomic stabilization (Stiglitz, 2000).

A unique example of the backlash created by the combination of big-bang capitalism and the sudden undermining of the social contract is provided by Rask and Rask (Chapter 7) in connection to the transition of the centrally planned economies into the market-oriented regimes of the current globalization era. The three groups of countries that the authors distinguish – the former USSR, the Central European countries, and the Balkan countries – benefited before the collapse of the Soviet bloc by enjoying better nutritional conditions, especially in terms of high indirect consumption of cereals (in the form of meat) as compared to market economies in the West with comparable per capita income. This benefit was the outcome of two factors: most of the planned economies had fertile and productive agricultural lands, the output of which was shielded from international trade and was reserved for "domestic" consumption within the former Soviet bloc; and second, and most important, good nutrition was considered an entitlement in the social contract of the Soviet era.

With the collapse of the Soviet empire and the abrupt advent of the shock-treatment transition to the free market system, the insularity of the agricultural sector was removed, the pre-existing structure of agriculture collapsed and so did the per capita incomes of the countries in transition. The dissonance between the Soviet era institutions and the free market institutions that were suddenly introduced when the former collapsed is responsible for the current "dislocation" between income and cereal consumption. Even worse, graduating to the income levels that could support the current level of consumption is bound to be a lengthy and difficult process.

Asymmetries arising from reputation differentials

Change in the composition of international trade: trade in services and in decommodified goods

The institutional and infrastructural poverty of developing countries becomes even more binding for growth and development if we look beyond the trade aggregates and focus on the composition of trade with respect to goods and services. In the 20 years since the mid 1980s the share of exports of commercial services to total world exports rose drastically.[8] What are the implications of this change in the composition of trade that may relate to the theme of this volume?

In the classical model of international trade the DCs have an absolute advantage in producing the high-productivity good (services) while the LDCs have a relative advantage in the production of the low-productivity good (commodities). All the same, the trade is of mutual advantage and services and commodities are supposed to trade at their marginal cost of production. Yotopoulos (Chapter 1) introduces a slight modification in this model, by recognizing as a component of the price of services the economic rents that originate in monopolistic elements (certification, copyrights, etc.) or in "brand" name recognition, in one word the economic rents that accrue to reputation. In this formulation, services do not trade anymore at their marginal cost of production, but on the basis of "what the market will bear;" nor is trade mutual advantage trade, but it is biased to favor the producer of services.

In this specification DCs are better positioned to hold an absolute advantage in the production of services as long as services are goods that trade on a reputational basis. DCs, as a result, are better qualified as exporters of "decommodified" trade, and in capturing the economic rents that the production of services entails. But there exists an additional advantage that drives the DCs to specialize in the production of services, and it comes from the demand side. Specialization in production is predicated on the existence of a corresponding demand for the output, whether this is domestic or foreign demand. Linder (1961) is credited for having rounded the classical supply-side oriented theory of comparative advantage by elaborating on the impact of an increase in incomes that induces the creation of "more sophisticated" commodities to fill what otherwise would have been merely a "basic needs" consumer basket. The DCs have by definition a head start in the production of services since they have a captive domestic demand from their middle income classes that have an income elasticity of demand for services greater than one.

Bergstrand (1991) tested for the Linder effect of a shift in tastes in an international cross-section of countries with the conventional PPP data. The findings suggest that the "creation" of demand for more "sophisticated," decommodified trade in the above formulation of Yotopoulos is no longer the exogenous result of advertising. It becomes the result of increasing real incomes, whether this increase is spread across socioeconomic classes (in the DCs?) or it reflects the ballooning incomes of the middle class and the elites (in the LDCs?). This formulation of the increasingly important trade in services is a novel contribution of *The Asymmetries of Globalization* and it has grave political-economy implications.

Miniesy and Nugent (Chapter 4) address precisely this wrinkle in a Linder-type hypothesis, by pursuing the asymmetries when the commodities and services to be traded are subject to reputational effects and the trading partners have an unequal infrastructural and institutional playing field between them. The hypothesis they formulate and test for, in an otherwise standard gravity-type model of international trade, attempts to answer the following question: "If you want to trade in such a way as to avoid being on the short end of asymmetries in trade and to trade more, thereby supporting economic development, with whom should you trade?" The answer is that countries tend to share more equally the benefits of trade when they trade broadly with their (income) counterparts – and more selectively with their income peers.

The crucial role played by reputation in determining asymmetric outcomes in international trade has been emphasized also in other contributions that add empirical content to the present volume by discussing the cases of the adoption of genetically modified seeds in China, the production and trade of "fair-trade" coffee in Latin America, and the double outsourcing in Taiwan.

The first two case studies (Fok *et al.*, Chapter 8; D'Haese *et al.*, Chapter 9) build on the same hypotheses, namely there are fundamentally two non-mutually exclusive mechanisms that allow firms to capture the rents generated from reputational advantages by moving along the continuum from pure commodities to pure services: first, by building an institutional "fence" around their product that guarantees differentiation, whether it is branding, certification, protected denomination of origin and so on; second, by using advertising and marketing to create and secure consumer loyalty.

Fok *et al.* (Chapter 8) discuss the operation of these two mechanisms in the case of the agricultural biotech sector that, in recent years, went through a dramatic change in the locus of agricultural research that shifted from public institutions, where it was located during the period of the "green revolution," to private multinationals, as is the case with the biotechnology advances of the "gene revolution." The driving forces of this change are both technical innovations (e.g. genetic engineering) and institutional innovations (strengthening of intellectual property rights) which create a completely new environment where the prospect of extracting substantial economic rents becomes highly attractive to private investors.

The application of biotechnology makes possible a degree of product customization that enables the "decommodification" of otherwise standard agricultural commodities, the planting seeds for next year's crops. In fact, the application of recombinant-DNA techniques constitutes the fundamental justification for claiming that the creation of transgenic varieties involves a genuine inventive step and therefore the "new" good, the genetically modified (GM) seed, is eligible for intellectual property right (IPR) protection through "expanded patents."[9] The immediate consequence from the economic point of view is that the producer of this new good can claim the economic rents that come along with the production and commercialization of the GM seeds under the new proprietary regime. The authors show that only under the very peculiar Chinese conditions the adverse impacts of decommodification of GM seeds can be balanced through a process of "re-commodification" which can be hardly replicated outside China.

D'Haese *et al.* (Chapter 9) present another case study of decommodification, which this time applies for the benefit of poor countries and people. It is an example of how the same strategy adopted by DC producers/processors (i.e. the sequence product differentiation – institutional certification – advertisement) can be used by LDC producers to increase the reputation content of their outputs by transforming them from mere commodities into "decommodified" (i.e. customized and more reputed) goods. More specifically, they report how the "fair-trade" labeling for coffee in Latin America made possible the customization of a bulk commodity, coffee, so as to match the preferences of "ethical" consumers in DCs. The branding of fair-trade coffee is an institutional innovation which mimics the IPR protection available for services and manufactures, thus making possible the transfer to small farmers of a share of the accruing economic rents in the form of higher prices.

Globalization makes easier the process of decommodification, because the reduction of transportation and information costs makes more affordable the purchase of such highly-reputed goods by consumers with preference for this ethically customized coffee. Fair-trade coffee was thus able to penetrate the markets of developed countries and increase by 140 percent its sales in the last decade, despite the price differential that it bore relative to the standard coffee. On the other hand, it should be stressed that this outcome cannot be taken for granted because moving up the reputational ladder requires some sensible institutional changes, which safeguard the identity of the differentiated product, and considerable investments to produce high-quality coffee for marketing. Still, this is a story that inspires and can conceivably be transplanted elsewhere.

Traditional trade in goods can also include a component of decommodified trade when it becomes subject to the "double outsourcing" that Liu *et al.* (Chapter 6) present. During the industrialization period of Taiwan's development, from the early 1960s to the early 1990s, the country developed a thriving export trade, especially in domestic appliances and manufactures. The tight resource endowment of the island, as opposed to the cheap sources of supply that were available in other Asian countries, made the continuation of this type of Taiwanese export trade doubtful in more recent years. The solution was found in a new type of export outsourcing that is based on the interplay between production costs and reputation differentials. It involves a Taiwanese outsourcee (sub)contracting out some of its export orders to manufacturers in lower-wage countries, thus playing the dual role of a middleman and a manufacturer and capturing their respective economic rents.

As the title of the Liu *et al.* chapter indicates, this double outsourcing is the result of exploiting the Taiwanese reputational advantage in the export trade.

The fundamental reason that leads to this intermediation opportunity lies in the information asymmetry between the buyer (a DC firm) and the producer (a candidate LDC firm). Necessary conditions for the intermediation are that the middleman knows what the buyer wants, what the producer is capable of, and how to coordinate the two parties. The long-term partnership experienced in the past by the Taiwanese export outsourcing firms with industrial country buyers eventually developed into a trusted relationship, so that the latter would prefer not to change partners even though their orders would have cost less should they have been placed directly with the supplier in the low-wage country. Here, the cost advantage of the low-wage country is more than offset by the reputation advantage of the Taiwanese firms as credible suppliers of stable quality with timely delivery – a reputation that is costly to establish for an upstart poor-country supplier.

Asymmetric reputation in currencies

The reputational ladder of decommodified trade underlies the treatment by Yotopoulos (1996 and Chapter 1) of currency as the prototypical case of positional good. When currency is held as an asset, instead of being used for transaction purposes alone, reputation becomes a discriminant factor for ranking currencies in a continuum that goes from the reserve currency, at the top, to the hard, the soft and the worthless currency. In a free currency market with free flows of financial capital, the reputation differential that favors accumulation of financial assets in the reserve/hard currency, translates operationally, into a process of currency substitution of the more reputed (i.e. reserve/hard) currency for the less reputed (i.e. soft) currency.

This type of currency substitution is analyzed as a parallel metathesis of the standard theory of incomplete markets, but on grounds of asymmetric *reputation*. It otherwise parallels the incomplete market of credit. In the case of credit, a higher interest rate will induce adverse selection of risk. Similarly in the case of foreign exchange, the local currency is the certain loser when the devaluation is not in response to the current account fundamentals of the economy but to the reputation contest with the reserve currency for preserving the value of liquid assets. Thus the currency substitution-induced devaluation constitutes a confirmation of the ability of the reserve currency to protect the liquid assets invested in it, and the next devaluation becomes a self-fulfilling prophecy. This is a paradigmatic case of "bad" competition and a "race for the bottom" (Yotopoulos, Chapter 1).

Positional goods as determinants of the globalization asymmetries

The discussion in the previous sections highlighted some stylized facts about globalization that feature in this volume. The purpose of this section is to weave these facts into a tapestry using the thread of a (relatively) novel economic concept, that of positional goods.

Standard economics acknowledges the existence of two types of goods, private and public. According to Samuelson's classical analysis, pure private goods are characterized by rivalry in consumption and by excludability while the opposite holds true for pure public goods (Samuelson, 1954). The operational consequences of these features are that for private goods the consumption choices of each individual are independent of the choices of others, while for public goods (and "bads") the individual consumption choices must move in the same direction. More recently a third category of goods has been proposed, that of "positional" goods (Hirsch, 1976; Frank, 1985). One can think of positional goods in terms of a reputation ladder, with the ranking ranging from the best to the worst. In this context, a pure positional good is a good such that, given the consumption choice of one agent, another agent must consume a corresponding negative amount of what the first chooses to consume (Pagano, Chapter 2). For one individual to be more reputable, another one has to be less reputable. In the positional ladder the measurement is ordinal which implies that, for example, the second-ranked positional good can advance to first rank by the first-ranked good losing (in reputation) to anyone in the ladder or by the second-ranked winning in competition with the first-ranked. Positional goods are the classic case of the "tennis ladder."

The link between positional goods and globalization asymmetries is a novel contribution of this volume. It is based on the reputation differentials that exist among "decommodified" goods and also services, and among various currencies (Yotopoulos, Chapter 1). The implication of the increasing decommodification of trade is that international competition is also shifting from a comparative advantage-based trade that rewards the least-cost producer to a reputation-based trade that conveys economic rents for reputational advantage. In this latter case, the customization of reputation in the transaction of services and of decommodified goods turns this dominant component of international transactions into trade in positional goods. Moreover, due to the advantage in reputation that the DCs enjoy, decommodified trade between rich and poor countries is likely to become one-way trade from the DCs to LDCs.[10] Furthermore, the economic rents that accrue to reputation can be compounded by the existence of network effects thus distorting even further the mutuality of benefits between developed and developing-country trade partners (Yotopoulos, Chapter 1).

The various gradations of trade under globalization that have been treated in the previous sections fit in well with the embellishment that Pagano (2006) makes on the asymmetric outcomes of standard competition, the one that features trade in pure commodities, vis-à-vis positional competition, the one that features trade in services and in decommodified goods. Trade in commodities is an example of mutually beneficial exchange between the trading partners. The picture is completely different when we consider trade in services and in decommodified goods in a context where the intellectual property right (IPR) protection is extended worldwide as is the case under the WTO–Trade Related Aspects of Intellectual Property Rights (TRIPS) agreement. This qualifies the current international order of IPR protection as a "pan-positional" legal right (Pagano, Chapter 2) that benefits the right holder, while imposing the costs of the obligation of protecting the economic rents attached to the decommodified good on all economic agents through third-party governments, whether these costs are affordable for them or not. The pan-positional nature of worldwide IPR protection extends the reputational ladder beyond the limits of the community and beyond the borders of the nation state, to cover the world, developed and developing countries alike. This is a heavy burden, especially so for LDCs that have neither the legal infrastructure, nor the policing capability to deliver.[11] The "legal disequilibrium" of pan-positional goods in assigning explicit rights but only implicit obligations to third parties is the source of additional inefficiencies in an economic system (Pagano, Chapter 2).

As shown by Fok *et al.* (Chapter 8) in their discussion of the GM seeds case, the joint result of the decommodification of GM products and their mandated expansionist international IPR protection, implies a change in the mutuality of the benefits of international trade. The economic rents accruing from the decommodification of GM seeds are more easily captured by global multinationals from DCs than by the farmers in LDCs. In fact, the international enforcement of IPR, as well as the dissemination of global advertising, is generally uni-directional, from the DCs to LDCs, for reasons relating to the stronger institutional setting and to the richer resource endowment of the former as compared to the latter.

Balancing the asymmetric effects of this positional competition is very hard. In the case of the Chinese GM cotton seeds this was achieved through a process of "recommodification" of the GM seeds. Unfortunately, this success case rests on very unique conditions that cannot be easily replicated in other LDCs. In fact, the Chinese scientists had already developed their own technology for incorporating new genetic traits into cotton and subsequently Chinese GM cotton varieties were available to farmers along with the GM cotton varieties that Monsanto was exporting. Moreover, the Chinese government was able to negotiate with the biotech companies and succeeded in having the Chinese farmers absolved from the obligation of signing the standard contract that included payment of annual "technology fees" and the prohibition of "holding back" of seeds between seasons for replanting. As a result it was the competition between the local GM cotton varieties with the imported GM varieties that worked to the benefit of the Chinese farmers. In general, positional competition has adverse impacts on LDCs.

Both Yotopoulos (Chapter 1) and Pagano (Chapter 2) emphasize that positional competition has more asymmetric and damaging effects in the case of currency, which is indeed the prototypical case of positional good (cf. also Yotopoulos, 1996). As emphasized in the previous section, the differential reputation of currencies as store of value determines a ranking from the reserve to the worthless currencies and eventually, in a context of liberalized financial markets, their very positional nature triggers a process of currency substitution which is generally detrimental for LDCs.

Sawada and Yotopoulos (Chapter 3) test precisely for this proposition in the sample of the poor countries that have been targeted in the Millennium Development Goals (MDGs) initiative. The objective of MDGs is to help the target countries in order to lift out of abject poverty one-half of their "poor" populations by year 2015. The question asked is how many of these countries could reach their MDGs target by following their "historical record of growth" (that includes at least ten years of the globalization era). The answer is that at least one-half of all the targeted countries, and the totality of countries in the poorest group, will not reach the set target of graduating from poverty if they were to continue on the trajectory of their growth experience.

In the same chapter, the authors provide an indirect test of some causal factors that relate to globalization and may explain the poor growth record of many LDCs, especially the poorest of them. Their target is the equilibrium exchange rate ("a non-misaligned" exchange rate) and it is confirmed that it is important for achieving economic growth. But totally unexpectedly for the orthodox view, the results indicate, in general, that the more open the economy is the greater is the misalignment of the exchange rate towards excessive devaluation of the domestic currency. This result is interpreted as an indirect confirmation that currency substitution in the capital account, as opposed to deficits in the current account, is the likely cause of this undervaluation-tripped exchange rate misalignment that works to the detriment of economic growth. This finding highlights the importance of the proper combination of trade and exchange rate policies in fostering growth in developing countries in the current environment of globalization.

This evidence, along with the experience from the Asian crises of 1997, suggests that currency substitution is an economic infectious disease that has reached epidemic proportions in a globalization environment where the principle of "free-market, free-trade, laissez-faire" has been extended to cover free exchange rates and free movements of portfolio ("speculative") capital (Yotopoulos and Sawada, 1999; Yotopoulos, Chapter 1; Sawada and Yotopoulos, Chapter 3).[12]

Having acknowledged the existence of positional differences in trade relationships between LDCs and DCs we can ask ourselves why should those differences matter? The obvious answer that has been already anecdotally anticipated above is that positional competition is much harder than competition for pure private goods (Pagano, Chapter 2). In standard competition if people work harder they may consume more private and public goods, thus improving their own welfare position. But the same is not true for positional goods where if *all* worked harder none could consume more of the positional goods. In other words, climbing up the reputational ladder of decommodified goods or currencies is much harder as compared to operating in (and profiting from) trade competition for pure commodities.

Policy implications

The central theme that links together the chapters in this volume is that the current wave of globalization, as it impacts different countries, yields differentiated outcomes that are systematically referenced to the level of development of a given country. These outcomes depend on the asymmetric endowments of DCs and LDCs in terms of physical and social infrastructures as well as in human and social capital. The interaction of such differential endowments with the ongoing change in the rules of the game of international trade – that is, from comparative advantage-based trade to reputation-based trade – reinforces the asymmetric impacts of the current wave of globalization.

The dominant hue in the tapestry of the differentiated outcomes of globalization that was woven in the previous sections is gray. It adumbrates the Panglossian outcomes for growth in poor countries that the selling of globalization in the last two decades has energetically postulated. Moreover, the findings in this volume strengthen the motivation for further searches for modifying the standard recipe of "free-market, free-trade and laissez-faire" that has been cooking up now for more than two decades. It is, indeed, well known that the lack of an appropriate physical infrastructure in most LDCs is one of the basic determinants of coordination failures and is bound to lead to missing markets. By the same token, the lack of some economic institutions like derivative markets implies market incompleteness because it prevents the spanning of time, space and uncertainty. On the other side, reputation differentials represent formidable barriers to entry in both the domestic and the international markets and become a determinant of increasing returns to scale and of network effects. All those features represent exceptions to the fundamental theorems of welfare economics – either in their static or dynamic version – and are legitimate causes that may lock the LDCs in a low equilibrium trap.

The acknowledgement of the existence of systematic asymmetries between DCs and LDCs in globalization trade calls for a different approach that goes beyond simple and uniform recipes, and requires differentiated and cautious interventions. Intervention, in turn, opens Pandora's box of good governance – which is another commodity that is expensive and in short supply in poor countries.[13] Therefore, improving governance both at the international and at the national level is crucial for designing a successful development strategy. The policy interventions that are designed for such a pro-development strategy need to take into account the institutional differences between DCs and LDCs and especially the positional nature of trade in services, in decommodified goods and in currencies. A few examples can help to clarify this statement.

The prevailing view of WTO and other multilateral lending institutions, articulated since the early 1980s, has been that integration of the LDCs into the global economy is an essential determinant of their economic growth and it is good for the poor (Dollar and Kraay, 2001). However, opening up the economy is hardly ever a key factor at the outset of the development process (Rodrik, 2001). A critical assessment of the modern economic growth experience shows that market incentives, macroeconomic stability and sound institutions are instrumental for economic development, but these requirements can be generated in a number of different ways.[14] A gradual and sequenced approach is needed in opening-up to imports and to foreign investment, and this should be part of a broader strategy based on the combination of the opportunities offered by world markets. In the meantime resources need be shifted into building institutions and providing incentives for investment and for domestic entrepreneurship. This is a tall order, but historically development never came on the cheap. For instance, Miniesy and Nugent (Chapter 4) refer to the European type of globalization that was based on quite a long and expensive period of pre-accession to the European Union that was aimed at leveling the playing field. The success in integrating the latecomers came at great expense of the initial partners. Their empirical tests also emphasize that a selective integration in the world markets, so that the competition can take place among countries that belong to the same level on the development ranking, has a tremendous impact in determining the long-term effect on trade.[15]

As long as the various currencies by definition stand on different steps of the reputational ladder the control of the flows of financial capital becomes an important precondition for preventing currency substitution. Whether hot money is or is not controlled, the remedy for the market ailment of currency substitution is foreign exchange controls. This means maintaining exchange rates at mildly repressed levels through rationing out of the market the component of the demand for foreign exchange that emanates from people hoarding foreign currency (or spiriting it out of the country) as a hedge against the potential devaluation of the local currency. The financial crises experienced in the last 20 years are consistent with the hypothesis that views free currency markets and free movement of portfolio capital as enabling currency substitution which is particularly harmful for LDCs (Yotopoulos, Chapter 1; Sawada and Yotopoulos, 2005).

Last, but not least, in a world where a multilateral system of international trade deregulation is becoming more important by the day, there is a need to rebalance the institutional asymmetry that works against poor countries, starting with the ruling institution of international trade – the WTO. It is important to recognize that accepting all the WTO clauses is not cheap for developing countries. For most DCs whose systems are compatible with international conventions, admission to the WTO implies no more than an obligation to apply their domestic regulations fairly at the border. Vice versa, an LDC that currently applies its own standards has the additional, and far larger, obligation to apply the internationally sanctioned standards in its domestic economy. This trade-related reform comes with the opportunity costs of crowding out alternatives that may be more development friendly.[16] Acknowledging this at WTO level means condoning institutional diversity, rather than seeking to eliminate it, and tolerating a nuanced freedom of trade for LDCs and temporary suspension of their existing WTO obligations when their development priorities are in the balance (Rodrik, 1997). In the example of the European Union, the WTO may also find room for membership with subsidiarity rights, especially for the LDCs.

Conclusion

The theme of this volume is that globalization is a process characterized by fundamental asymmetries that eventually result in differentiated economic outcomes. There is no simple explanation for this. However, a common feature that emerged from the analyses carried out in this volume is that trade in positional goods – that is goods to whom a different reputational rank ordering can be attached, notably trade in services, in decommodified goods and in currencies – is becoming increasingly more important under globalization. Reputation is the key competitive factor in the current wave of globalization and narrowly frames the room of maneuver of economic agents, whether those are individuals, firms or countries. Unfortunately for LDCs, the relative position of a given country on the reputational ladder, as well as the likely economic impacts induced by reputation asymmetries, seem to be *systematically* related to the level of the country's development.

Here the emphasis is on the adverb, in the sense that the asymmetries of globalization are likely to work *systematically* against the poorer countries. In fact, the preconditions for the success of globalization are more likely to exist and are easier to satisfy among the rich, whether countries or (social and economic) strata within a country, than they are among the poor. The same can be said considering the different endowments between DCs and LDCs in terms of human (i.e. competence, skills) as well as social (i.e. trust) capital that is required in order to produce high-reputation goods. In other words, the poorer the country the less likely it becomes that it can afford the entry costs necessary to claim benefits from globalization. Moreover, globalization also affects adversely some macro-fundamentals of LDC economies and the basic reason for this has to be sought in reputation effects operating both in the real and in the monetary economy. In summary, it seems there is a new poverty trap in the modern globalization that compounds the traditional negative effects of the lack of physical capital and infrastructure, as noted first by Nurkse (1953), with the lack of appropriate institutions, of human and social capital, of governance skills and with the adverse change of some macroeconomic fundamentals.

The contributions collected in this volume have emphasized various conduit mechanisms that can lead to asymmetric outcomes under globalization. Notwithstanding, the attempt made in this volume to find out the common "whys" to explain the "whats" and "hows" of globalization sheds light on a unifying source of asymmetric outcomes. It is the combination of some structural changes in world trade and the simultaneous enforcement of a new international institutional order that is transforming global competition into a "positional" competition. In fact, trade in services and in decommodified goods is gaining momentum in global transactions, while the movement of financial capital, especially hot money, has literally exploded in the last two decades. The common feature that trade in services and decommodified goods share with trade in hard currencies for asset-holding purposes is that both relate to positional global competition.

The structural change in trade is compounded with a legal architecture of world trade that reinforces the positional nature of global competition. The predicament of free capital movements in an environment characterized by the positional nature of currencies is bound to cause systematic devaluations of LDCs' softer currencies. For the same reasons, the simultaneous enforcement of open markets and the worldwide protection of intellectual property rights – as is the case under the WTO–TRIPS framework – translates into institutionalizing of positional competition in open (but protected) markets for decommodified trade, while leaving the (standard) commodities trading in open and free (contestable) markets that are found preponderantly in LDCs (Yotopoulos, Chapter 1). These global legal positions create and reinforce the conditions for an increasing asymmetry in the process of development (Pagano, Chapter 2).

Is therefore globalization bound to be detrimental for LDCs? Not necessarily. Globalization proved to be very successful for some LDCs, particularly in East Asia (e.g. China, India, South Korea). What makes the difference between these success stories and the numerous dismal LDC failures is that the former played the globalization game being willing and able to define it in their own terms: they were invariably more elastic in interpreting and applying the standard "free-market, free-trade, laissez faire" recipe predicated by international organizations in the last two decades.

The fundamental lesson learned from these experiences is that differences matter and, consequently, better-articulated policy responses are required. The "one-size-fits-all" approach pursued by the Washington Consensus failed because its recipe is a standard package of reforms while policies need be country specific, and need be flexible enough so that their mix can evolve along with the evolution of the economic system at hand. The assessment carried out in *The Asymmetries of Globalization* concurs and calls for a profound rethinking of the development practice.

Notes

1 I am grateful to Samar Datta, Jeff Nugent and especially to Pan A. Yotopoulos for helpful comments on earlier versions of this chapter. Of course, any remaining errors are my own.

2 The change of the share of trade in GDP between 1981–5 and 1997–2001 was 3.9 percent for developed countries and 15.4 percent for developing countries (IMF, 2002). The estimate is based on measuring trade flows and it is consistent with more robust price-dispersion measures of trade integration (cf. among others, Parsley and Wei, 2001; Hufbauer *et al.*, 2002).

3 The change in the ratio of external finance (that is the sum of external assets and liabilities of FDI and portfolio investments) to GDP between 1981–5 and 1997–2001 was 77.3 percent for developed countries and 19.9 percent for developing countries (IMF, 2002).

4 In fact, in the period 1981–5 to 1999–2003 the share of LDC exports in world totals rose only from 35.6 percent to 37.0 percent (+4.0 percent) and their share of exports in world commercial services exports increased even less, from 27.2 percent to 27.8 percent (+2.1 percent) (WTO, 2004).

5 This hypothesis has been tested in different contexts, for example with reference to

trade liberalization (Dollar and Kraay, 2001) and aid (cf. among others, Burnside and Dollar, 2000; Easterly *et al.*, 2004).

6 This is well known in the anthropological literature (cf. Geertz, 1978 on "clienteliza-tion") as well as in game theory (the Folk theorem), both emphasizing the role of reputational mechanisms.

7 The same dislocation occurs when a new institutional order is superimposed onto the old one, as was the case with private property rights which substituted for common property rights in Sub-Saharan Africa under colonization, causing an "institutional dissonance" between what was felt and accepted by the society and what was written in the law.

8 In percentage terms the share of services in total world trade rose from 16 percent to 20 percent while in absolute terms the increase was more than fourfold since the early 1980s (WTO, 2004). Moreover, this is most likely an underestimate since WTO takes an extremely limited view of "services," totally disregarding the intermediate degrees of "decommodification" that intervene between pure goods and pure services (Yotopoulos, Chapter 1).

9 The three basic requirements for obtaining patent protection are novelty, usefulness and invention. While the first two requirements apply both to the breeders' rights (i.e. the IPR that can be claimed using traditional breeding techniques, already in force before the gene revolution) and to expanded patents (i.e. the IPR that can be claimed in the case of GM innovations), the third feature, invention, is non-existent or very weak in the breeders' rights, but very strong in the expanded patents.

10 The success of globalized logos in a developing or a transition country – e.g. McDon-ald's in Moscow – is largely due to this reputation effect, as opposed to the superior-ity of McDonald's in terms of comparative advantages. The difficulty of reputation-based competition is stressed also by the reported example of the Tai-wanese outsourcing firms which are able to capitalize on the economic rent embodied in their implicit reputational assets (Liu *et al.*, Chapter 6).

11 For an assessment of those costs in the case of IPR protection under the TRIPS framework see Louwaars *et al.* (2005); for the costs of compliance to the Biosafety Protocol under the Convention on Biological Diversity see Cohen (2005).

12 For modeling and directly testing the case of currency substitution, see Sawada and Yotopoulos (2005).

13 Good governance requires the government's competence and integrity and represents a necessary precondition of successful economic development. Competence is neces-sary to guarantee that the policy maker knows in which cases he should intervene – i.e. only in cases of market failures or market incompleteness – and how to intervene, in other words what to do, and when and where to do it. On the other hand, integrity is necessary also because in a less than perfect world, the economic rents of interven-tions are pervasive and can be misapplied to private gain (Yotopoulos, 1996: 150–2, 290–2).

14 This is valid for many countries that developed under different growth strategies ranging from import-substitution industrialization (e.g. Brazil, Ecuador, Iran, Morocco, Cote d'Ivoire and Kenya before 1973), to outward orientation (e.g. Taiwan and South Korea, among others), and the so-called "dual-track" approach (e.g. China). For a detailed account of these historical records, cf. Yotopoulos (1996) and Rodrik (1999).

15 Some proposals aimed at favoring more south–south trade, rather north–south trade seem to acknowledge this need.

16 It has been estimated that the implementation of just three WTO agreements (customs valuation, sanitary and phytosanitary standards, and intellectual property rights) costs a typical LDC an amount which in many cases is in the same order of magnitude with a year's development budget (Finger and Schuler, 1999; Lengyel, 2004).

References

Baier, Scott L. and Jeffrey H. Bergstrand (2001), "The Growth of World Trade: Tariffs, Transport Costs, and Income Similarity," *Journal of International Economics*, 53 (February): 1–27.

Bergstrand, Jeffrey H. (1991), "Structural Determinants of Real Exchange Rates and National Price Levels: Some Empirical Evidence," American Economic Review, 81 (1): 325–34.

Burnside, Craig and David Dollar (2000), "Aid, Policies, and Growth," *American Economic Review*, 90 (4): 847–68.

Cohen, Joel I. (2005), "Poorer Nations Turn to Publicly Developed GM Crops," *Nature Biotechnology*, 23 (1): 27–33.

Dehn, Jan (2000), "Commodity Price Uncertainty in Developing Countries." Working Paper no. 2426, Rural Development, Development Research Group. Washington, DC: World Bank (August).

Dollar, David and Aart Kraay (2001), "Growth Is Good for the Poor," World Bank Development Research Group. Washington, DC: World Bank.

Easterly, William, Ross Levine and David Roodman (2004), "Aid, Policies, and Growth: Comment," *American Economic Review,* 94 (3): 774–80.

Finger, J. Michael and Philip Schuler (1999), "Implementation of Uruguay Round Commitments: The Development Challenge," Policy Research Working Paper Series no. 2215. Washington, DC: World Bank (October).

Frank, Robert H. (1985), "The Demand for Unobservable and Other Non-Positional Goods," *American Economic Review*, 75 (1): 101–16.

Geertz, Clifford (1978), "The Bazaar Economy: Information and Search in Peasant Marketing," *American Economic Review*, 68 (2): 28–32.

Hirsch, Fred (1976), *Social Limits to Growth.* Cambridge, MA: Harvard University Press.

Hufbauer, Gary C., Erika Wada and Tony Warren (2002), "The Benefits of Price Convergence: Speculative Calculations," Policy Analyses in International Economics no. 65. Washington, DC: Institute for International Economics.

IMF (2002), *World Economic Outlook*, September 2002. Washington, DC: International Monetary Fund.

Lengyel, Miguel (2004), "The Implementation of WTO Agreements: The Case of Argentina," Latin America Trade Network working paper. Online, available at www.latn.org.ar (accessed 17 January 2006).

Linder, Steffan (1961), *An Essay on Trade and Transformation.* Stockholm: Almqvist and Wicksell.

Louwaars, Niels P., Robert Tripp, Derek Eaton, Victoria Henson-Apollonio, Ruifa Hu, Maria Mendoza, Fred Muhhuku, Suresh Pal and Joseph Wekundah (2005), "Impacts of Strengthened Intellectual Property Rights Regimes on the Plant Breeding Industry in Developing Countries: A Synthesis of Five Case Studies." Wageningen: Center for Genetic Resources, Wageningen UR (February). Online, available at www.cgn.wur.nl (accessed 31 March 2006).

Myrdal, Gunnar (1968), *Asian Drama: An Inquiry into the Poverty of Nations and the Challenge of World Poverty.* New York: The Twentieth Century Fund.

Nurkse, Ragnar (1953), *Problems of Capital Formation in Underdeveloped Countries.* Oxford: Clarendon.

Pagano, Ugo (2006), "Legal Positions and Institutional Complementarities." In Fabrizio Cafaggi, Antonio Nicita and Ugo Pagano, eds, *Legal Orderings and Economic Institutions.* London: Routledge, pp. 54–83.

Parsley, David C. and Shang-Jin Wei (2001), "Limiting Currency Volatility to Stimulate Goods Market Integration: A Price-Based Approach," NBER Working Paper no. 8468. Cambridge, MA: National Bureau of Economic Research.

Rodrik, Dani (1997), *Has Globalization Gone Too Far?* Washington, DC: Institute for International Economics.

Rodrik, Dani (1999), *The New Global Economy and the Developing Countries: Making Openness Work.* Washington, DC: Overseas Development Council.

Rodrik, Dani (2001), "The Global Governance of Trade as if Development Really Mattered," paper prepared for United Nations Development Programme, New York. Online, available at www.servicesforall.org (accessed 12 August 2005).

Samuelson, Paul A. (1954), "The Pure Theory of Public Expenditure," *Review of Economics and Statistics*, 36 (4): 387–9.

Sawada, Yasuyuki and Pan A. Yotopoulos (2005), "Corner Solutions, Crises, and Capital Controls: Theory and Empirical Analysis on the Optimal Exchange Rate Regime in Emerging Economies." Stanford Institute for Economic Policy Research, Paper no. 04–037 (September 2005). Online, available at siepr.stanford.edu/papers/pdf/04-37.html (accessed 13 September 2005).

Stiglitz, Joseph E. (2000), "Whither Reform? Ten Years of the Transition." In Joseph E. Stiglitz and Boris Pleskovic, eds, *Annual World Bank Conference on Development Economics 2000.* Washington, DC: World Bank, pp. 27–56.

UNCTAD (2002), "Farmers and Farmers' Associations in Developing Countries and Their Use of Modern Financial Instruments," Study prepared by the UNCTAD Secretariat, UNCTAD/ITCD/COM/35. Geneva: UNCTAD.

World Bank (1999), *Dealing with Commodity Price Volatility in Developing Countries: A Proposal for a Market-Based Approach.* Washington, DC: World Bank.

World Bank (2004), *World Development Report 2005: A Better Investment Climate for Everyone.* New York: Oxford University Press.

WTO (2003), *World Trade Report 2003.* Geneva: World Trade Organization.

WTO (2004), *World Trade Report 2004.* Geneva: World Trade Organization.

Yotopoulos, Pan A. (1996), *Exchange Rate Parity for Trade and Development: Theory, Tests, and Case Studies.* Cambridge and New York: Cambridge University Press.

Yotopoulos, Pan A. and Yasuyuki Sawada (1999), "Free Currency Markets, Financial Crises and the Growth Debacle: Is There a Causal Relationship?" *Seoul Journal of Economics*, 12 (Winter): 419–56. (Available also online siepr.stanford.edu/papers/pdf/99–04.html.)

Subject index

References to tables and figures are presented in italics.

absorptive capacity 49
accountability 84n8
adverse selection *see* asymmetric
  information: adverse selection
advertising 14, 22, 24n9, 105, 165, 174,
  185, 186, 190
Arrow-Debreu world *see* globalization and
  requisite institutions: Arrow-Debreu
  world
ASEAN (Association of Southeast Asian
  Nations) 80, *81*
asymmetric information 9, 19, 22–3, 61,
  89–91, 109, 111, 117, 118–22, 188;
  adverse selection 9, 104, 188; credence
  goods and experience goods vs. search
  goods 169, 174, 175n8; moral hazard
  92, 95, 100, 103, 104
asymmetric trade *see* international trade:
  reputation-based trade
asymmetries of globalization: definition 1,
  48; causalities of 1; consumption
  asymmetries 23, 30–3, 41, 128–33, 184;
  currency substitution as source of 1–2,
  8, 18–21, 35–6, 59–61, 62, 188;
  decommodification as source of 1–2, 8,
  10–15; infrastructure and institutions as
  source of 1, 8–10, 15–16, 67, 70, 182–4;
  positional goods and asymmetries of 2,
  13–15, 44–5, 61, 62, 63–4; production
  asymmetries 138–41; systematic
  asymmetries against LDCs 1–2, 15, 148,
  159, 192–3

Balkan countries 134–8, *135, 137, 138,
  139*; *see also* transition economies
biotechnology 147–52, 157–8, 186, 190;
  gene revolution vs. green revolution
  186; institutional innovations 148–52;
  technical innovations 147–8

black market premium 49, 58, 61
brain drain 24n11
branding *see* economic rent: branding;
  reputation: branding
Brazil 155–7, *157*, 166, 175n4, 175n5,
  196n14
buffer stocks 168

CACM (Central American Common
  Market) 80, *81*
capital controls 24n17, 25n18, 25n19, 49,
  64n8, 182
capital movements 8, 19–20, 35, 49,
  59–62, 182, 191, 193, 195; *see also*
  financial crises
CARICOM (Caribbean Community) 80,
  81
CEEC (Central and Eastern European
  Countries) 134–8, *135, 136, 137, 138,
  139*; *see also* transition economies
cereal equivalent 129–32, *131, 132*
certification 12, 165, 170, 176n12, 185,
  187
China 25n24, 116–17, 118, 122n11,
  123n25, *135, 137, 138*, 152–7, *152, 153,
  154*
clientelization 92, 196n6
coffee: consumption 166–7, 170–1, *173*,
  175n8; fair-trade 165, 169–74, *171, 172,
  173*, 187; ICA 166, 168, 169; price
  166–7, 168, *168*, 169–70, 175n3, 175n9;
  production 166–7, 168, 169, 172, 174,
  175n5, 175n9; supply chain 166–7, *167*,
  172–4
collective action 90, 173–4
commodities: commodification/
  decommodification 2, 13–15, 19, 24n7,
  36, 45, 102–5, 147, 157–8, 164–5, 169–70,
  185–8; trade in commodities vs. trade in

13–14, 24n16, 31, 36–40, 45, 157, 189–91, 194–5; positional goods vs. private goods and public goods 29–31, *31*, 189; positional goods in agrarian and capitalist societies 33–5; public-positional good paradox 41; reputation and positional goods 2, 35, 36, 64n6, 183–91; status and power as positional goods 33–5, 45n2, 45n3, 64n6; welfare maximization conditions 31–3; *see also* asymmetries of globalization: positional goods and asymmetries of
poverty: exit time 50–1, *52*; MDG 48–9; poverty and exchange rate misalignment 62; poverty reduction through growth 49–50, 52–3; poverty trap 18, 24n16, 35, 36, 61, 194; *see also* asymmetries of globalization: systematic asymmetries against LDCs
poverty trap *see* poverty: poverty trap
power *see* positional goods: status and power as positional goods
private goods 29–31, *31*, 39, 90, 189
product differentiation 69, 81, 165, 170, 174, 186–7; *see also* decommodification
product life cycle 69
property rights 39–40; *see also* intellectual property rights
protectionism *see* international trade: trade openness; economic growth: market liberalization and economic growth
psychological laws (of Keynes) 68
public goods 29–31, *31*, 39, 41–4, 90, 189
purchasing power parity 55, 56, 62, 132

rationing 19, 61, 193; *see also* credit
reciprocity 90
regional blocks *see* integration: trade agreements
rent-seeking activities 10, 104
repeated games 92, 184, 196n6
reputation 14, 18, 60: as a source of positional competition 2, 35, 36, 64n6, 183–91; asymmetric reputation and market incompleteness 18, 24n4, 61, 62, 68, 188; branding 2, 11–15, 17, 22–3, 24n5, 165, 186, 187; decommodification 2, 11–15, 18–21, 35–6, 5–62, 64n6, 105, 109–12, 122n10, 118–22, 150–2, 157–8, 165, 170, 185–91; economic rent 2, 11–15, 17, 22–3, 24n5, 105, 118–22, 122n10, 148, 150–1, 172–4, 185–91; labeling 165, 169–70, 172, 174–5, 176n10, 187; reputation differentials vs.

cost differentials 109, 111–12, 118–22, 187–8; reputational ladder 18, 59, 64n6; trust 12, 22, 89–96, 100, 103, 104–5, 111, 170, 172–4, 184, 194
reputation-based trade *see* international trade: reputation-based trade
reserve currency *see* currency: currency as a store of value
resource allocation 20, 49, 60
Ricardian trade *see* international trade: comparative advantage trade
Ricardo principle 51, 61
rule of law 84n8
Russia 134–8, *135*, *136*, *137*, *138*, *139*, 184; *see also* transition economies

safety nets 90, 172
seignorage 18
self-fulfilling prophecy *see* devaluation: self-fulfilling prophecy
services: services and commodity customization 2, 10–14, 165, 170, 185; trade in services vs. trade in commodities 10–17, *11*, 185–8, 196n8
social capital 183–4, 192, 194
social limits to growth 13, 29; *see also* positional goods: natural scarcity vs. social scarcity
social opprobrium 91, 100, 103
social scarcity *see* positional goods: natural scarcity vs. social scarcity
soft state 183
spanning *see* globalization and requisite institutions: Arrow-Debreu world; market: contingent markets
state 90, 154–6
status *see* positional goods: status and power as positional goods
Sub-Saharan Africa *54*, 155–7, *157*, 196n7

Taiwan 113–18, *114*, *115*, *116*, 122n5, 122n11
technology fee 151, 155, 160n4, 160n7, 161n16, 190; *see also* decommodification: economic rents
terms of trade 16, 21, 56, 69
Thailand 15, 97
three-party game *see* outsourcing: export outsourcing
tradables 55, 56, 57, 79, 60; *see also* Ricardo principle
trade agreements *see* international trade: trade agreements
trade diversion 73

Author index

For Product Safety Concerns and Information please contact our EU
representative GPSR@taylorandfrancis.com Taylor & Francis Verlag GmbH,
Kaufingerstraße 24, 80331 München, Germany

Printed and bound by CPI Group (UK) Ltd, Croydon, CR0 4YY
08/06/2025
01896982-0004